FAKHRADDIN VEYSALLI

PHONETICS AND PHONOLOGY PROBLEMS

Cambridge International Press
London 2016

Published in United Kingdom
Cambridge International Press

Imprint of: Hertfordshire Press Ltd © 2015
9 Cherry Bank, Chapel Street
Hemel Hempstead, Herts.
HP2 5DE, United Kingdom

e-mail: publisher@hertfordshirepress.com
www.hertfordshirepress.com

PHONETICS AND PHONOLOGY PROBLEMS
by FAKHRADDIN VEYSALLI ©

English

Edited by David Parry
Cover design by Aleksandra Vlasova
Translated by an Associate Professor in the Department of Stylistics and Art of Speech in the Azerbaijan University of Languages (AUL)
Vahid Salman oghlu Arabov (Turksoy)

British Library Catalogue in Publication Data
A catalogue record for this book is available from the British Library
Library of Congress in Publication Data
A catalogue record for this book has been requested

ISBN 978-1-910886-18-2

CONTENTS

A PREFACE REMEMBERING WITTGENSTEIN'S GHOST

As a British poet, my own acquaintance with linguistics and phonology tends to be through philosophical routes. Indeed, I have a minor obsession with the investigative work of Ludwig Wittgenstein (1889-1951), along with the deconstructive word-games of Jacques Derrida (1930-2004), both equal masters of text and narrative. And each of whom, of course, would have agreed with Shakespeare (1564-1616) – to slightly paraphrase the Bard - that a "rose by any other name would smell as sweet". A statement challenging the very bases of received language theory, as well as being surprisingly subversive with regard to fundamental physiological assumptions surrounding sound, intercourse, and music.

So noted, in Wittgenstein's case, most scholars agree his writings may be effortlessly divided into two broad categories. Marking, as these classifications do, very distinct ways of engaging with the philosophical enterprise. Undoubtedly, Wittgenstein's initial "brass tacks" approach to language (as expounded in his Tractatus Logico-Philosophicus), influenced the development of logical positivism and the frequently bewildering antics of the Vienna Circle. Each claiming, along with Wittgenstein at this period, our world is composed of elementary "facts", "bodies", "objects" and so on. An allegedly "common-sense" attitude, outlining why they are the natural subject matter of the empirical sciences alone. This viewpoint also implies the principle purpose of language is to state what these "facts" are in themselves. A task it accomplishes by picturing and consequently describing them as a facet of general discourse. Moreover, it claimed when a "fact" is pictured, there is a structural similarity between the lexical items used and what is depicted. Initially reminiscent of Saint Augustine (345-430), young Wittgenstein then goes on to contend an essential ancillary undertaking for language is to formulate tautologies: if a tautology is understood as a necessary figure of speech, whereby information is repeated; or is a term used in logic. Stated otherwise, it expresses the same formulation twice over in different words, and is true only by virtue of its logical form. For instance, the phrase "close proximity", or the sentence "They decided to return again for a second time to that old ancient house" is no doubt correct, but largely empty of meaning. Unquestionably, these vocabulary choices tell us next to nothing extra, although their usage is vital for overall communication. At this stage of his thinking, therefore, Wittgenstein envisages the operations of logic and mathematics as a series of requisite, tautological, prescriptions. Additionally, any claim failing to illustrate a "fact", or for that matter specify a tautology, is incomprehensible. Even young Wittgenstein, this agreed, seems to have felt slightly uncomfortable with the stark implication that ethics, not just metaphysics, fall into this category. Besides, if one aims to be consistent, the Tractatus itself is balderdash in as far as its lessons, once learned, make it completely unnecessary for the learner to be further concerned with "classic philosophy", since he or she will have risen above the temptation to entertain gibberish. Be that as it may, in **Phonetics and Phonology Problems**, the Azerbaijani author Fakhraddin Veysalli defends this somewhat traditionalist stance as (at the very least), a good point of departure.

This book is the famous Azerbaijani linguist Fakhraddin Yadigar oglu Veysalli was first published in the 1993's Baku.V 2008 it was translated into Turkish and published in Ankara Prof. M.Musaogly. Ona used in the Turkish Republic in the universities and other educational institutions... F.Ya.Veysyalli book consists of four chapters and a list of references. Hence, compiled as a textbook with the avowed aim of introducing these heavily intertwined fields for a wide variety of (potential) readerships, one can only feel that his text has clearly reached its goal. Certainly, the sciences informing any backdrop to phonetics, not to mention theoretical debates establishing links between noise, measurement, melody, and method - are equally explored in depth and conveyed with the eloquence of a panegyric. Allied, as each of these topics are, to the fact that a genuine concern to explain the dynamics of every issue involved permeates this book. Assuredly, technical advances in research are fully embraced, while the sheer joy of poetry and musicology are extolled as tantalizing adjuncts to these fascinatingly arcane endeavours. All in all, an intriguing volume to read as well as a thoroughly exhaustive guide to an often neglected branch of academic excellence. As such, I wholeheartedly recommend this book to English speaking readers.

David Parry
London 2016

FOREWORD

The XX century within which we live has in recent decades (from the viewpoint of scientific progress), been characterized by increasingly rapid developments. Indeed, our century - once compared with previous ones - embodies a special stage of creation in scientific endeavour. All meaning, the linguistic sciences have come into a greater maturity than ever before. Therefore, new theoretical insights into language have emerged at this period. Yet, phonology - which occupies an important role in the establishment of linguistic science - still leads the humanities by its testing of conceived objects and general considerations. So, at the beginning of this new millennium, fresh disputes have arisen that seem to sharpen the separation between phonetics and phonology. Certain critics contending an increased distinction between these fields is vital for a genuine advance in linguistic literature.

In this book, nevertheless, the author speaks about the "essence" of language and the creation of language – along with its functions – in order to evolve linguistic science from its prevously established roots. Stated so, the ideas put forth have been thoroughly researched by the writer. Especially when he relies on outstanding scholars to outline his insights into the actual "core" of communication. Interestingly, receved explanations arising from different sources (occasionally obscured in the sophisticated, as well as diverse, strata of historical scrutiny) gives one ground to say the exploration of language is now speedily reaching a much more incisive scholarly foothold than ever before. Each new discovery complimenting age-old language investigations from the East, whilst building upon Western systematic researches: especially those by representatives of the German linguistic schools. Undoubtedly, this mainly happened following XVII century scholarship – an era refocusing on hard data in the linguistic sciences. Thusly, books among Germanic scientists by W.von Humboldt and L.Weisgerber contain codified similarities - and differences - between the German and Russian languages through tables and carefully defined principles. Methodologies manifestly outlining the objective behind the science of phonetics, along with its subjects, aims, duties and characterizations in terms of the phonetic units explained. Nowadays, of course, any consideration of writing and speech tends to take the form of quantifiable linguistic mapping in conformity with present day expectations. Each technique itself giving rise to terse abstractions based on careful, triple language, identifications.

Contrarily, the least investigated issues in scientific papers, let alone textbooks (regarding the ties of phonetics to other fields of science), will be dealt with in this chapter of the book. Notably, the implications of mathematical calculations, as well as the functional load falling on various portions of phonemes, has been analysed and presented for the attention of readers.

In addition, the third chapter of this book is devoted to explanations of those models of communicative intercourse under current construction. Hence, in this clearly interpretive section, every assumption relies on the findings of language scientists themselves. Especially when regarding insights into their own mother tongues, along with the thoughts of those highly suggestive scholars who founded Neoromantism. Using these assertions as a bridge, the argument then turns to the Azerbaijani language itself as a primary source of pure information. Assuredly, one of the most significant languages under examination, since it sheds linguistic light throughout this book - beginning with *"Kitabi Dede Korkut" ("The Book of Father Korkut")* up to nowadays. So confessed, attempts have been made to establish the stages of language development through concrete examples. Perhaps particularly in the case of Azerbaijani. In which case, one supposes the start of this book will be interesting to native readers, even though unexpectedly. Due in large measure to their revealtions of (arguably) rarified features within the Azerbaijani language itself. A regional communication system having a surprisingly long formation process. Once this is conceded, phonetic structures inside the Azerbaijani language - not to mention its phonological shape - are more or less transparently characterized by lagopeds, acousticians, physiologists and specialists in automatic translation. In this fashion, the first and the second chapters are useful for all those interested in languages, irrespective of their specialties.

The author

I CHAPTER

LANGUAGE, ITS CREATION, ESSENCE, FUNCTIONS AND ITS USAGE

I. WHAT IS LANGUAGE?

1. The entire conscious activity of a human being percolates through language. A person thinks through a language, writes in a language, says something to other people, receives information from them, explains thoughts different from them, outlines perceptions on the most difficult pieces of work and expresses pure feelings when speaking of love or hatred. Certainly, human beings use language as an instrument. They write in it, narrate in its sounds, ask something, make an exchange of concepts, deliver speeches, compose books, peep into dark layers of the past by turning each page of an historical text, at the asame time as dispatching information to people in a given period, or to future generation. Unarguably, all the above-mentioned enterprises show that language is a complex phenomenon. This may be why thinkers from the most ancient of times up to the present day

have made concerted attempts to discover the “essence” of a language. In this way, a special field of science has been established called **linguistics**. In other words, every question formulated across human history has been strung into a tapestry, which occasionally supplies an answer before another question emerges that demands a further solution. Thenceforth, investigations to answer each fresh question sometimes took one direction, but sometimes another as a diaeltic of contradictions was generated by this continual flood of information. From here, the idea of inherited ways and methods have emerged. Eventually leading to a practice of science considering all such ways and considerations named **methodology** (i.e.theory on methods)

Now, documenting the nature of language, its essence, mechanics of intercourse, means of expression, attitude to atterance, links with thought, and so on, depends to an extent on this absorptive discipline. In a manner of speaking, it relies on these features in the history of language as they are described through different trends and by various schools. Obviously, as an linguist, I created experiments (carried out for many years) of applying such techniques: which is why in writing this chapter I have used numerous pictures, tables, and other illustrative materials. When contemplating this chapter, therefore, one witnesses that the more complex phonetic structures are portrayed with far greater ease than usual. Their prominent features elucidating language phenomenon in a manner not seen in other sources.

In the fourth and last chapter of this book, an exegesis of practical phonetics - nourished by these modern methods of interpretation - would otherwise be overly difficult to understand. That’s why, before talking on the aims, duties, and places of the experiment undertaken, this text will pay due attention to the position of phonetics, as well as phonology, within the sphere of linguistic history itself. Furthermore, consideration is given to the ideas existing in this field prior to the present, while afterwards an exposition of the main issue –a calculation of acustic parameters occurs. Overall, I think this approach the most effective.

Frankly, long before I had any idea in my head of writing a book in which the phonetic structure of our native Azerbaijani language could be explained, notions regarding this type of textual clarity were already within me.

Only in this way, only if things go on like this, can linguistics as a science win supporters. But in our era, when asked if one wants to be a phonetician, one will tangentially notice advantage given to other branches of linguistics, while potential scholars in this field are sidelined. After all, the general view seems to be that phonetics can be kicked into touch as an unnecessary branch of study. Possibly, this is connected with the errant belief there is not enough scientific literature on phonetics? Either way, while preparing this book for publication both the drawbacks and limitations of such literature have been examined in order that anyone reading this book will discover an accurate reflection of the materials available. Looking back, how this aim was achieved would demand a second text. Moreover, any perceived imbalance in this work will equally be addressed in a future publication.

Beyod doubt, this book will interest all those who have chosen philology as their profession. In addition, it will interest students, interpreters, and translators, whereas people in other professions may find profit in its scrutiny. For instance, workers in communication, or people who learn language by mathematical means, along with radio and television professionals.

Relatedly, the outstanding French scholar Antoine Meillet (1866-

1936) wrote that a language is undoubtedly a social phenomenon. His colleague, Joseph Vendryes, developed this idea by claiming: "Language is established in the society and has appeared since the day when people felt the need of keeping intercourse with one-another…. When a human brain developed well enough and had the power to use language then language was created as a social phenomenon."

It goes without saying, some of the issues mentioned above beg deeper exploration[1].

2. Pertinently, perhaps, initial delvings into language were recorded in the East. To be precise, scholars in India attempted to define religious songs (vedas) in order to to show the distinction betwixt these compositions and spoken prose (prakrit). In itself, Sanskrit, being one of the most ancient languages, became sophisticated in learning and

---

1 In the Christian religious, within a book called the Bible, there is such a story. In Mesopotomia (the cradle of all human Culture), it is said people once had the same language, religion and convictions: that they lived rich and happy lives. One day, however, these people agreed with one- another to erect a tower from the ground to the heights of the sky. By this action, they wanted to reach God and communicate with Him. Yet, secretly, they wanted to compete with His power, so they speedily constructed their building. Getting angry, God mixed up the language of this people. Suddenly, each person spoke with a different tongue. All meaning, one didn't understand the other - forcing them to stop the construction of the tower. From that day onwards, the foundation for different languages was created. Moreover, this event took place in Babilia, which is why this tower enters history as a Babil tower (in the Accad language Babil comes of an ancient word meaning "the door of God"). Later on, when scientists were trying to explain the appearance of different languages, they often recalled this story and entered it into their books. Certainly, those written documents that have reached us speak of numerous ancient languages, not to mention the death of some of them. For example, the Accad language, the Celtic language, ancient Turkic languages, and the language of the Etruscans - who lived in the north part of present day Italy - easily demonstrate this point.

In modern times, there are more than 6 thousand languages - not every one of which has written documents. Survivlas from past languages, nonetheless, were mainly written down: like Sanskrit, ancient Turkic languages, the languages of Greece, Roman Latin, Chinese and Arabic. Interestingly, some scholars have tried to remove linguistic diversity by creating artificial languages. In Europe 100 years ago, some of them manufactured a language called Esperanto to this effect. Ironically, Esperanto has its roots in Indio-European languages, although its suffixes were from Finno –ugric communication systems.

literature. In the IV century before our era, the grammarian Panini created such accomplished grammar books that some of them are still used today. Consisting, as they do, of 3996 rules (in the form of surets), he even managed to reveal the phonetic and morphological features of the Sanskritic system. Thereby, starting to uncover a "phenomenology of language" and answer the question "what is language" centuries before the inner mechanisms of language were debated in Europe. In all probability, this is equally why the old written sources pay special attention to parts of speech (they identified 4 parts of speech: including verbs, prepositions and particles), individual vocabulary items, as well as sentences. Each of which was thoroughly investigated regarding its role in a sentence. In the works of that time, classification of the roots of words, cases, and their morphological characteristics very clearly illustrated.

When all said and done, ancient Indians greatly advanced the field of phonetics. Particularly, the articulatory moments of sound, their interplay and syllabic unions, along with the grammatical purpose of vowels and consonants. So remembered, this Asian science of linguistics ascended into heights it would take Europeans centuries to reach (namely the XIX century, according to W. Thomsen)

3. For their part, ancient Greek philosophers (who took the existence of things, as well as the connections amongst them) as definitive were themselves divided into two camps. Some claimed there a direct connection existed between a phenomenon and its name. Put in another way, from the very day a thing is created, it exists together with its name. As such, the name emerged from the nature of this thing. Contrarily, the second group of philosophers supposed things were named by people alone, and this happened only after mutual agreement.

The Greek philosophers who tried to evaluate language from a philosophical standpoint concentrated on communication in every sense. Thus, the discourses of Hermocrates and Plato were the first serious Western investigations into these subjects. For his part, Plato pointed out in his book Critias there were things more powerful than humanity - and these things were named reflexively. At the same time, he mentioned there existed either a common agreement, or a civic ceremony, when naming such things occured. As we may read, the great philosopher does not directly resolve this question while it is generally felt he is inclined to both of these assumptions in turn.

Curiously, Plato vociferously separates the names in a language from its verbs. The former are valued as the words being talked of (in other words they were said to play the role of subjects), even though the aforementioned secondary terms were said to act in the role of a predicate, i.e. they disclosed what was said about the names.

4. But Plato, who was one of the founders of systematic thinking, excludes any notion of the supernatural in his theory. A fact causing some critics to suggest a sympathy with the materialist Democritas when he contended naming things to be the main role played by linquistic mutual agreement and conditionality. To prove all this, Democritas took as his basis the notion of policemy (multiple meanings of a given word) and synonymy (different words with similar meanings). His third proof declared that names are not constant: especially human names. Yet, the great philosopher had himself put the fundaments of conditionality into linguistics. As for other ground rules, there is no direct connection between the expresser (form - the systematization of voice (sound), or plan of expression) and the expressed (meaning - semantic insights). Besides, words created by way of imitation regarding additional prime lexical items usually agree with this principle. Only in this way it is

possible to explain why Azerbaijanians, Germans, Russians, etcetera name one and the same objects differently (öküz, ox, bık).

5. Another Greek philosopher, Aristotle, in his work Poetics gives a breadth of information on language, while showing that in living speech some linguistic units take their place as basic elements. Be it within a syllable, a conjunction, a name, a member, a case, or a sentence.

For Aristotle, an element is a sound inseparable from the word it establishes. Although, in modern linguistics, an element is part of a **phoneme**. What is more, once elements unite together, an otherwise meaningless ensamble of sounds – evolves into a **syllable**. Furthermore, as a member, each element allows otherwise meaningless particles to frame the beginning, completion and division in a sentence. All causing contemporary linguists to say elements are indicators of borders. Indeed, in the German language, the fact that words, as well as morphemes begin with vowels (knacklaut), sheds an explanatory light on Turkic languages due to linguistic stress falling on the final syllable - thus providing possibilities to determine word borders. But, as far as elements pointing to the division of a sentence is concerned, one may prefer to connote the activities of a pause: syntagm stress, or a falling of the voices tone, because all these serve to indicate the borders of utterance in speech.

As to Aristotel, separately taken conjunctions haven't got meaning either, since they are voices taking part in the unification of meaningful linguistic units. In fact, they are sounds that cannot prevent the establishment of such combinations.

So, Plato, and Aristotle too, looked upon verbs and names as units partially extrapolating linguistic synergies. Names then, are sounds with meaning even if separately taken, whereas verbs do not always indicate time and nouns can be divided into constituent limbs. Differening from them, certain verb-expressions suggest time. For instance, a /tree/, /green/, but; /to come/, /to study/ etcetera. However, none of these units necessarily express features belonging to nouns, while Aristotle simply mentions that names and verbs do indeed have cases. This, of course, includes all the forms, along with plural forms. Examples being /aghaj, aghaci, aghaclar, gelir, geldi, gelirler/ etcetera in the Azerbaijani language.

Additionally, names indicate male and female gender. In German, Russian, and in other languages, this idea can justify itself. Yet, in the Turkic languages (as it is well known), names do not illustrate gender and such information indicates itself as a feature derived from the semantic meaning of the verbs denoting persons.

The determination of a sentence, according to Aristotle, provokes serious interest, because a sentence (being compounded sounds), expresses an independent meaning. Even its ingredients have independent meanings. Its very features are distinguished through the composition of other compound units.

Aristotle continued these thoughts by stating that alongside sentences consisting of names and verbs, there are equally sentences, which can be established from separately taken names. In present day grammar books, those chapters describing "nominal sentences" prove his position has lasted the test of time.

Contrarily, in his book "Rhetric" Aristotle speaks of three parts of speech: the name, verb and conjunction. While the first one has an independent meaning, the others have no independent meaning, even though they bear a certain grammar function.

6. At this juncture, one should mention that the followers of Aristotle - in developing his ideas on language - have proceeded to

increase the parts of speech to 5: verbs, conjunctions, names, adjectives, and elements. However, they differ from Aristotle by contending that each of these parts of speech, if taken separately, has got a meaning.

As such, Aristotle's followers specify the cases, afterwards naming them as they were called in Greek and latin, before dividing them into two-main and (secondary) subsidery parts of speech.

7. In the II – III centuries before our era in the capital of Ptolomey, cosmopolitan Alexandria, the learning of language was preserved and safeguarded by the traditions of ancient Greek literature. For this reason, special systems of notion were worked out and united under the title of "general grammar". Relatedly, it is interesting that the scientists - having joined the arguments of philosophers – were similarly divided into two groups: "analogists" (those linguists who accepted systematic similarities as a basis) and "abnormalists" (who considered exceptions in language as more important). Each clash in this period leading to a new field of science, which studied attitudes between things and names – **etymology. A pursuit** eventually gaining a firm grounding. Nevertheless, the early conceptual schemes of etymology were still simple.

As to the decisions of those scientists, tellingly, the rich heritage of their work has not remained of lasting value. All making one thing abundantly clear. In pioneering language studies, the Greeks could never equal Indian linguists.

In connection with this, one must recall in their latter descriptioms of language, Greek linguists have radically advanced. Correctly characterizing, as they did, consonant and vowel sounds. They then divided vowels into two (as to their length or shortness), gefore turning their attention to semi- vowels as separate entities. It is worth mentioning, no doubt, in the present day French language, it is still possible to come across semi-vowels.

Fascinatingly, the determination of word and sentence by the scholars of Alexsandria was securly enshrined in grammar books up to recent times. A word was valued as the smallest part of speech, whilst a sentence was prized as a word combination expressing a complete thought. Tellingly, the grammarians of Alexsandria determined 8 parts of speech: names, verbs, conjunctions, members, pronouns, prepositions, adverbs and conjunctions. Ancient linguists in Rome adding "interjections", to this list, since they did not exist in Latin. Perhaps it also needs to be mentioned that the founder of the Alexandrian school (a disciple of Aristotle) Dionis Frankiyski, was said to have determined these of parts of speech himself. A determination not having lost its influence to this day. Partially explaining why the linguists of Rome looked upon Latin as international: considering it as the sole language of Catholic religion worldwide.

8. In the Middle Ages, the centre of linguistic study passed to the Caliphate. Clearly, in the VII – XII centuries, the Caliphate strengthened, and for this reason the linguistic sciences entered a special stage of development in the cities of Basra and Kufe - situated between the rivers Dajla and Farat. Henceforth, Arabic linguistics (understanding the necessity of transferring the Koranic tongue into a language easily grapsed by everyone, quickly superceded the achievements of their Indian and Greek colleagues. And as such, a new period of linguistics flourished. In Bagdad, for example, though the personality of Sibaveykh, linguistic sciences reached previously unknown peaks. Resulting in "Al kitab" (a book) wherein great scientist revealed the meanings of 1000 ayets - from oriental poetry, to an exegesis of the Koran from the grammatical point of view. Further, in spite of arguments between the Basra and Kufa schools, this book

by Sibaveykh was very well-received in both schools.

9. Arab linguists tried to show the difference between uttered and written forms of language. For them, sounds were divided into vowels and consonants. They were tense, after all, and open-ended. Being pronounced by raising the tongue upwards into a neutral position.

In addition, Arabian linguists compiled a number of dictionaries and other manuals, while expounding the meanings of synonyms and policemy. As to sources., a person named Al Firuzabadi compiled a dictionary of 100 volumes, although, unfortunately, this monumental work has not survived into our modern times.

10. Living in the same era, but absolutely independently of Arabs, Mahmud al Kashghari (being considered the "god of Turkology" was born in the Sintszyan province of China, A Turk by origin, his book "Türk dilinin divanı" (1073 – 1074) (The Book of the language of the Turks) opened a new pathway in linguistics. Indeed, this work of science - in the real sense of "scientific" - was based on **typology.** Partially explaining why it was to be found in the library of Ali Akber Diyarbakirli as well as its 1912 – 1915 publication in Istanbul. Assuredly, in this encyclopedic work the grammar of Turkic languages, along with their lexicology, was elucidated in the light of comparative investigation: not to mention the history of Turkish peoples and their **folklore, etymology, ethnography**. As such, M. al Kashghari, relying on his own observations, analyzed sayings, proverbs, poems and texts, simultaneously discovered general principles beneath the apparent phonetic distinctions in Turkic communication systems. In his book, therefore, he spoke of the law of harmony, whilst shedding light on the function of memes and suffixes. As to the opinion of specialists in phonetics and morphology, this volume was welcomed as essential in the field.

As Mahmud al Kashghari wrote: “I have written a book having no equal in the world. I have explained the roots of the words themselves, I have determined rules, so that my work should be an example to all. In each group I have given the derivatives deriving from the word, because wisdom is attained by simple true words.”

11. After linguistics reached its peak during the period of M. al Kashghari, this field of science suffered a heavy crisis as the centre of linguistic inquiey transferred (again) to Europe. This may be why grammar rules tend to be identified with the grammar of Latin languages. In which case, it is necessary to note that the leading position of Latin in oral practice made it impossible for everybody to understand the written version of the Latin language. A fact raising important issues of discrimination betwixt sound and letter. Furthermore, the categories of Latin grammar belonged to other languages as well. So, learning Latin meant something like memorizing logic. Each recitation of which led to Aristotle, at the same time as creating an impression that every language was rooted on one basis, while sentences were similarized with logical categories such as subject and predicate.

In 1660 “Universal and Rational Grammar” compiled by Claude Lancelot and Arnon, was published in Port Royal. Later, in the history of linguistics, this text began to be known as the Port Royal Grammar.

12. In the Renaissance period – parallel with Latin - the Greek language began to be studied. An enlargening of focus giving rise to philological investigations of classic monuments and works. Demonstably, Spanish monarch Lorenzo Hervas-y- Pandura, in his book “Catalogue of the Languages of Famous People, their Division into Dialects and their Classifications”, outlined 300 languages. Thereby introducing to readers his grammatical “characterizations” of about 40 German linguists. Concommitantly, A. Adelung (1732-1806)

in his book "Mitridat or General Linguistics" (1807-1817) interprets one text in 500 languages and dialects. All causing some critics to claim that in Europan linguistic science an unknown discipline was starting to emerge, A field wherein Germany was the focal point. It is true, of course, that in XVII – XVIII century France, linguistics also began to develop. Nonetheless, Germany took the lead with Herder, and then W.von.Humboldt, making serious attempts to reveal the essence of language.

Stressed so, from the beginning of the XVIII century until the period of W. von.Humboldt, theories like sound imitation (or phrased more technically **onomatopoetic** speculation), were widely debated. Moreover, according to this theory, words appear as a result of wave-impressions. Yet, any argument entering history on the basis of vibrational interjection is not considered a social phenomenon, but rather a natural phenomenon. An intrinsically distinct assertion. Now, it goes without saying that a language reflects the feeling of a speaker, although this is not the fundamental function of a language. What is more, this function appeared quite late in the evolution of languages. Hence, Y.G. Herder wrote in his book "On the origin of language" that people invented language in order to make their sense of Self known to their fellows. Worded alternatively, the spirits of individuals created language. From here, it becomes evident that language is not a means of intercourse bearing social importance. Instead, it is the product of Persons. (1770)

13. The fact language is largely a social phenomenon and that it primarily belongs to human beings, implies animals cannot communicate at depth. Truly, they utter noises, while following continuous verbal repetitions. Additionally, they perform movements at given commands. For example, if one says to a dog "come" or

"stop", the dog acts on the meaning of these words. Furthermore, when animals are born, they behave reflexively towards other animals. Their reflexes being non-conditioned in the frst instance, even though repeatable actions turn the majority of such responses into conditional reflexes. So, the fact all animals hearing the fearful noises of other animals physically flee, is a proof regarding reflex, not communication. Overall, a hen's, or a cock's, "gır-gır" certainly voices their feelings about an approaching fox, but does little apart from alert their fellow fouls.

The great physiologist I. P. Pavlov (1849-1936) carried out experiments on monkeys, which clearly showed the fact of turning non-conditional reflexes into conditional reflexes. Such reflexes, of course, belong to the first so-called "signal system" and are not able to perform the function of creating sound systematization bearing social meaning or social function, Indeed, they can't understand semantic meaning existing among them.

On the other hand, human beings systematically uttering sounds can understand one another's thoughts. Undoubtedly, they understand both uttered words and establish meaningful texts. This is why language sets up a "second signal system" to express events and real situations.

Atop of which human being express their individual life experiences through language, Along with different existential instances concerning today or tomorrow explained by inherited assumptions. All demnstrating animals are deprived of these sophistications.

Every human being, on the other hand, has got an ability to learn language from birth. Only later does his/her speak in this or that language - depending on the linguistic atmosphere into which he/she is thrust. Undoubtedly, after being born, children who happen to be away from their parents (or removed from their native environment), soon get accustomed to the new communication-sphere into which he/she is placed. Unarguably, he/she then learns this language surrounding him/her along with other children. As a matter of empirical fact, when returning "home" following such a separation, these children can't understand their parents. In today's world, one may observe thousands of instances of this kind. If, therefore, an Azerbaijani infant is sent to Germany for any reason, it is clear the same child will become accustomed to the German tongue and pick up this language instead of Azerbaijani.

14. In the study of language and in formulating linguistic science, the XIX century occupies a special place. Principally because this period is associated with the names of Franz Bopp (1791-1867), Rasmus Rask (1787-1832) and Jacob Grimm (1785-1863). Beyond dispute, J. Grimm separates the comparison of languages from history, although he didn't discover the "laws" of language. Nonetheless, Grimm describes the "rules" of language from an historical point of view.

Respectimg Indo-European languages, F. Bopp slightly varies from the Germanic language investigations of J. Grimm by focusing on sound and phoneme attitudes: as opposed to Grimm's morphological/ genealogical researches derived from word-formation. In himself, J. Grimm approaches language as the door to antiquity. Thusly, he examines words for their own value, as well as for the sake of learning more about the "existence of Germans" in general. In his book "Grammar of the German language" (I part, 1893), he formulates the scientific bases of German Grammar. A scholarly move that nevertheless cannot transparently expound differences between sounds and letters. Contrarily, F. Bopp in his volume "On the language and wisdom of

Indians" (1809) tried to prove Indo–European languages flowed from one and the same source: thereby framing a potential comparison of languages as an object of investigation for linguists.

Historically, the linguistics of this period entered a "Romantic" phase, instigating two directions of exploration: W.von Humboldt's language philosophy and the naturalism of young grammarians.

15. As it is impossible to deny Hegel[1] in dialectics, it is also impossible to denude the role of W. von Humboldt in linguistics. Manifestly, W. von Humboldt's (1767-1835) overview of linguistics has been widely outlined in his work "Differentiation of human language and the impact of this differentiation on the human mind" (Selected works, Berlin, 1848, 6th volume). As one may read, "Language as a whole is spirits. It develops by the laws of the spirits", Then again, "language is not the product of activity, it is the activity itself", and "language as the whole of its products differs from separately – taken speech acts". He even contends, "in a word always there is unity of both sides – there exists the unity of sound and notion", as well as "language as a whole in other spaces, and from inside, is situated within nature"[2]. A person surrounds himself, therefore, with verbal sounds in order to understand the world of things and absorb it. An understandable attitude additionally determined by language. Curiously, the great scientist saying these words describes language as a miraculous circle. For him, leaving this circle is analogous to entering another world: an enterprize expanding someone's outlook. In this view, learning a foreign language can be taken as getting a passport into other territories. "language is a thought –a creative instrument. It

---

1 Hegel wrote that, a language in a special meaning is the activity of theoretical mind, it (the language) is the outer manifestation of these activities.

2 W. von Humboldt's idea was capably developed by German scientist Leo Weisberger which brought about the creation of a new theory (see &32-37)

is the spirit of the people, it is its outer manifestation", by which the author of these words makes language a bedrock to human experience.

16. Naturalism, imitating Darwinism, considered language analogous to an organism - in that its developmental processes reflect the types of growth encountered in other natural phenomena. As a case in point, A. Schleicher, who earthed this theoretical conception, (1791-1868) found lawfulness in sound combinations themselves. Indeed, Schleicher claimed he had discovered that the principles behind Indo- European languages belonged to all the languages. What is more, Schleicher, in his work "German Language" (Stuttgart, 1869, II publication) felt he had answered the question "what is language?" As such, he stressed if one gives a widely-spread determination, a language is best seen as a thought expressed in words. This is quite correct - ... Language is the expression of ideas in sounds. It is the process of thought expressed in noises. As for this telling definition, it allows one to grasp that a language mirrors other living organisms in being created, flourishing, and suffering regress. Perhaps most curiously, Schleicher conjectured each language had been carved out of one original communication system, which had then separated into many other languages. Spending, as he did, much time and energy in looking for this universal tongue. He even penned a fabula in that highly abstract wordscape.

17. In linguistics, at the same time as naturalism (and outliving naturalism), there existed another approach to language studies called psychologism. A movement itself linked with H. Steinthal (1823-1899), and based upon Assosiative Psychology. For Steinthal, the creation of imagination through the processes of apperception, revealed psychological laws of "likening". As such, in his book "Grammar, Logics and Psychology; their Principles and Mutual

Correlations" (Berlin, 1855), he pondered on the purpose of language by writing, " .... Language is the expression of psychological spiritual movements, situations and attitudes pronounced by sounds." Added to this, Steinthal's "school of language" proclaims linguistic materials originate within people, are subordinated to wisdom, and are the product of Spirit. So, Steinthal, who approached language as the product of psychology, illustrated his view that language is a means of understanding the inner and outer world by a person's instinct. Fascinatingly, he felt imagination created self-understanding. In which case, language is the self-understanding of Spirit. Of course, the fact that the spirits of people bear individual characteristics is strongly reminiscent of language usage. Hence, A. Potebnya (1835-1891) wrote, "Language too is the form of a thought, but it is such a form that you can come across it only in language and nowhere else."

18. Beginning with the 70's in the XIX century, until the 90's, a fashion for innovation sweapt among young grammarians. These changes suggested by individual case studies, along with a possible "recovery" of Indo-European language materials. Thenceforth, grammarians cast a steely gaze on the phenomenon of continuous flux within languages. Some of them even paying serious attention to the history of minute linguistic adaptations, not to mention restoring the older forms of common communication. As a respected theoriest, H. Paul (1846-1921), explained new elements arising in a language were based on analogical associations, whilst the laws of phonetics seemed to be founded on physiological factors. Hence, having discovered all of this, young grammarians tried to discover the inner mechanisms of ever flowing language.[1]

---

1 In a sitting of the chair of comparative grammar in the Leipziq University in Germany A. Leskien (1840-1916), K.Brugmann (1849-1919), H. Osthoff (1842-1907), H.Paul (1846-1921), B. Delbrück (1842-1922) and other young grammarians not agreeing with the advanced linguists of those issues discussed. F. Zarinke ironically called them the young grammarians and since that time they have been known by this epithet.

Obviously, one never comes across conceptions expounding the inner form of a language put forth by the Romantics, W. von Humboldt or for that matter, his young follower Leo Weisgerber. Be that as it may, in H. Paul's book "The Essentials of the History of the Language" the speculative models embraced by these young grammarians were displayed in full (1880).

As mentioned above, historical studies had become the main credo of young grammarians. Partially explaining why H. Paul tried to prove the science of linguistics was nothing other than the history of a language. A "trendy" interpretation, which he himself embraced when saying:

"Besides speaking of the history of language, it would be a mistake to speak of the investigation of language. To explain language beyond history and accept this as something scietific is nothing more than absolutely wrong on the side of investigation, or the object of investigation. Going beyond the ordinary interpretation of separately taken things, we at the same time explain the connection among things and in spite of the fact that it is not clear to us, it means we stand on the ground of historical study (p.19). However, H. Paul eventually explains that his historism has nothing to do with real history. Rather, his attitude, must be understood in the context of repeated linguistic connections. This viewpoint, at the end of the XIX century in Germany, became a prominent orientation in linguistics. For that reason, young grammarians learnt exotic languages, since their main focus was the formation of historical grammar inside already existant languages.

For his part, H. Paul eventually felt forced to abstract a science beyond the history of language. And as such, he called this science "the theory of principles and methods". Therein, he studied psychological and social phenomena having nothing to do with language. Tangentially arguing, as he did, that psychological elements in cultural movements were important factors, and that psychology established the foundations of cultural studies. This "culturology" acting as a natural science. Unsurprisingly, H. Paul proceeded to exclude people's spirits, along with every other feature standing above the individual. Although, even he could not deny language existed in the speeches of individually taken as "persons": causing some pundits to hint at "posivitism" in his position. Either way, H. Paul's object of investigation was not language operating in a closed system. Instead, he proclaimed language as a "speech activity ensuring the mutual influence of individuals"

In fact, the historical surveys of these young grammarians was a method separating sound and form within their own systems, while leading them to assess historical backdrops in the light of linguistic theoriies risking intellectual atomism.

19. A potential revealation of a real essence of language at the end of the XIX century, is linked with the names of two great scientists. One of them is I.A.Baudouin de Courtenay (1845-1929), and the other is F. de Saussure (1857-1913)[1]. It is interesting to mention that both of these scholars studied at Leipzig, which was considered the epicentre of linguistics at that time. Indeed, they formulated their viewpoints there.

I. A. Baudouin de Courtenay in 1870 was at Petersburg University: occupying the Chair of Grammar. He even lectured on the theme "General Notes on Linguistics and on Language". Within this lecture he said either, "Language is the heard result of correct movements of muscles and nerves". Or as others have stated, "language is the whole of independent sounds or soundings, uniting in one whole and in the same categories joining on the basis of one language of the same people speaking this language and fitting the same conceptions of a similar kind"

In comments recorded in a minute book, we may additionally read, "Language, in the most general sense of meaning, is one of the functions of our human organism".

Thusly, the first stages of I. A. Baudouin de Courtenay's academic work appear to show he was under the influence of "Individualist Psychology". A stance, nonetheless, framed by his valuation of form, context, sound, and meaning in a language. Atop of which, sound and meaning interested him throughout his life.

20. In his 1896 article, "Humanization of Language" (written in German) I. A. Baudouin de Courtenay wrote that words were formulated sounds able to achieve contact with one another and could

---

1 I. A. Baudouin de Courtenay left senior school in Warsaw in 1866. He then went to Prague and afterwards to Vienna, Berlin, and eventually to Leipzig. By 1870 in Leipzig, he published his dissertation called "From Ancient Polish Language to the XIV century" for which he was awarded the title of Master on Linguistics and Private Associate Professor. Moreover, in 1874, at Petersburg University his work "On the Experience of Phonetics in Ryazan Dialects" earned him a Doctor's Degree. Beginning in the same year, he began lecturing in Kazan University. By 1883- 1893, he works as a professor in Yuryev (now Tartu) university. In 1893-1900 he worked in Krakow city, while in 1918 he worked at Petersburg University.

Ferdinand de Saussure studied in Leipzig in 1876-1878. There he published a book called "On the Initial System of Vowels in Indo-European Languages". After this, F.de Saussure did not write anything about more this project. By 1906-1911 - on the basis of the three courses he taught in Jenever, his followers Ch. Bally (1865-1947) and A. Sechehaye(1870-1946) - three years after their teacher's death (1916) - published "Cours de Linguistics General". In that book, F.de. Saussure is named as the founder of socio-linguistics. It is interesting to recall these two scientists knew each other cloesly. Nevertheless, by 1889, on October 16, I.A. Baudouin de Courtenay in his first letter addressed to F. de. Saussure, said: "I know, I have the right to hope that you remember our pleasant meeting in Paris seven years ago. (F. de Saussure. Notes on General Linguistics, M., 1990, p.242). Also, according to N.A. Slusareva (who interpreted this book, F. de. Saussure was mistaken by one year in this misdated letter. The fact is that the meeting took place on 1881 in December. A time during which I. A. Baudouin de Courtenay was elected as a member of the Paris Linguistic Society where he met F. de. Saussure (see: the indicated work, p. 255).

be characterized by a system. This was a gigantic step forward in the ultimate humanization of linguistic studies. It implied, after all, that the sound determination of a language is always going to be qualified. As he stressed, "The greater the physicality of particles and other parts of a language, the more pure physical life is able to boost itself" (Selected works, 1963, p.260). In the sounds of a language, therefore, and in the movements of speech organs producing expressive sounds, there are other means, which are not directly conspicuous. Features, interestingly enough, peculiar to the words, i.e. the articulated impressions of sounds in the world of connected meanings. Just here I. A. Baudouin de Courtenay adds: **"... all the words of human speech have the possibilities of expressing new meanings"**.

Intriguingly, I. A. Baudouin de Courtenay especially mentions three features in a language: phonation – speech; utterance of the words-audition, and an understanding of utterance; along with cerebration- preservation of all that belongs to a language, keeping, consideration, thought.

By 1895, I. A. Baudouin de Courtenay penned, in the introduction to his book "An Attempt to Discuss Phonetic Substitution", that in "Addition to this title, the chapter **psychophonetics** may seem a little strange. But through this I want to show in linguistics I am on the side of those orientations giving advantage to psychological factors" (the same work, p. 266).

A position expanded in his book "On the Criticism of International Artificial Languages" (1907 - again, written in German), wherein I. A. Baudouin de Courtenay determines communication in this way, "Language is not a closed organism, neither is it an inviolable ideal: rather, it is an acting instrument. (the indicated work, II part, p.140). As such, it is interesting to note that the scientist from Denmark O.

Jespersen (1860-1943) had also described language as an activity. Clearly, he saw language is a function expressing a person's thoughts and feelings.

So mentioned, our aim is not to detail the linguistic viewpoint of a great scientist like I.A. Baudouin de Courtenay, instead, the intention of this text is to explain to readers his understanding of language as a highly valued scholar. So, it would be worth mentioning the obituary authored by his disciple L.V.Shcherba (1880-1944) on the death of I. A. Baudouin de Courtenay. Herein we read, "It is true that it is difficult to say which people his science served. He worked among Russians, the Polish, and Germans, while noting his researches in Polish, Russian, Slovenian, Czech, German, French, Italian, as well as Lithuanian languages."(I. A. Baudouin's Selected works, 1963 I part, p.6).

21. For his part, Ferdinand de Saussure's ideas on language demands attention. In his book "Notes on General Linguistics" (1890)[1] he mentioned several postulates casuing an intrigued consternation among scholars. In 1894, this great French linguist penned - in one his letter written to that outstanding representative of historical comparative linguistics A. Meillet (1866-1936) – that, to his mind, a viewpoint determines an object. Namely, that without point of view it is impossible to determine an object.

Moreover, inside a number of his works, he writes: "language in all its inner parts is a regulate system, language depends upon the object it expresses, but it is free and in relation to the object that it is conditional (p.112).

---

1 F.de. Saussure, from his 1870 book, till the 10th year of the century in which we live, is still counted as a living authority due to the theses and lectures discussed as we as printed in different editions. Therein, it becomes clear he had always been a researcher, and only gradually reached his scientific conclusions. These final positions were explained in the form of a system by his disciples (1913) who published his book " The Course of Linguistique Generale".

Hence, F.de. Saussure's confrontation with speech and language-activity is expressed in the following scheme:

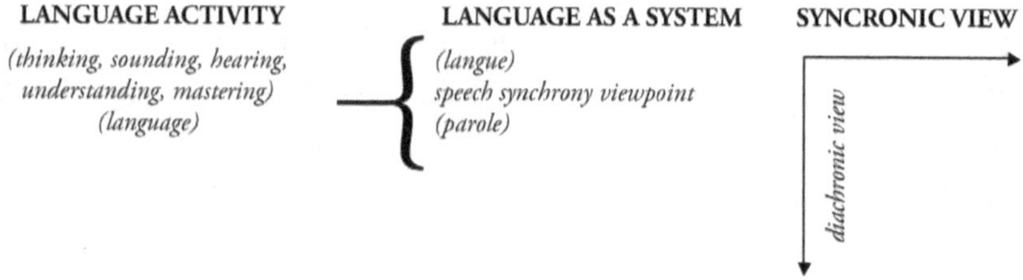

The synchron view, of course, involves learning of a language within a single time and place, but the diachronic view involves the learning of a language within several periods - systematically and comparatively[1].

Such a stance was already a jerk forward in linguistic science. Taking language as a system - in order to explain it as free and independent: not depending upon the object, In addition, it explained language as an independent phenomenon. All principles, it should be noted, still accepted by Saussure's remaining followers.

So stated, it is interesting to cite some of F.de Saussure's propositions. For instance,"Language is a system of signs, this system has its own inner structure. Equally, "It (the language) is a system of signs. In this system coordination of meaning and sound is important, besides both sides of these signs are psychological in the same degree"[2] What is more, he indicates he is descibing the French language by using the term "langue", continuing that this system is opposed with

1 In F. de Saussure's works, the French terms mentioned above are given in brackets, so that it should be clear what the author meant by them. That's why we decided to keep them as they were in the original.

speech "parole", yet both together are named **language** - which in our Azernaijani language is **"dil fəaliyyəti" (language activity)**.

Of course, language is social and constant, but speech is individual and temporary. Apart from the fact that speech requires a tongue's participation as obligatory. On the opposite side of things, intercourse does not always happen (on the model of intercourse see: Chapter 3).

Simultaneously, language may be determined thanks to its usage in intercourse, by means of real language. So F.de. Saussure turns a double comparison into firm scientific conceptions.

By doing this, F.de Saussure separates inner linguistics from outer (language) linguistics. Certainly, he attempts to show this through examples from chess-play saying: If the rules of chess represent the inner system of a language, then its outer features are mirrored by the figures used in this game. After all, playing such a game allows a physical expression of non-physical processes, which have nothing to do with the players. Herein, he concludes that a language itself can be the subject of linguistics.

22. As has been said, for F.de Saussure language signs have two sides: the side of sound or side of expression and the side expressed. The signs and its sides may be shown as follows:

Relatedly, the word "ağac" (a tree), when it acts like a sign, pushes its materiality into insignificance for linguistics - even though, the linguistic investigation of an "expresser" is of great importance. Atop of which, signs may be absolutely relative, or assumed. For example, "üç" (three) is an "absolutely assumed" figure, but "on üç" (thirteen) is a "relatively assumed" figure - because the meaning of "on

2 These quotes have been taken from F.de Saussure's second publication of the book "Course de Linguistique Generale" (Berlin,1967). Their translations were undertaken by the author.

üç" (thirteen) derives from the meaning of the figures containing the components of "on üç" (thirteen). At this juncture, it is vital to recall that the science studying the nature of signs is called **semiology.** An

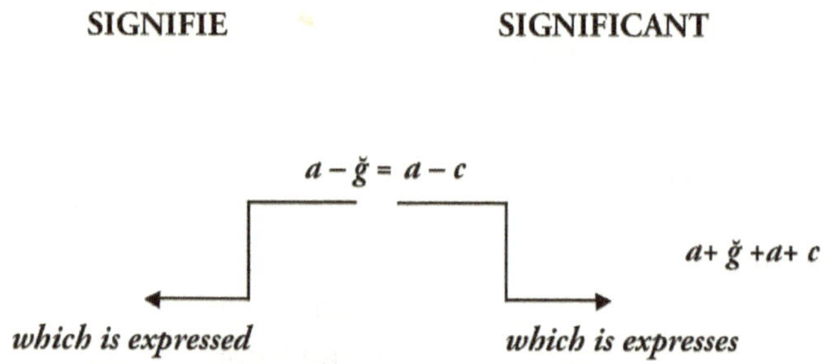

important tool for linguistics, since a language also consists of signs.[1] Furthermore, this is why linguistics is often considered a discipline within the Humanities themselves. .

Later on, F. de Saussure scrutinizes "real truth", juxtaposed to meaning, especially when it expresses **value (valuer).**

23.All leading F. de Saussure to eventually speak of **likeliness and differentiations**. Firstly "assumptions" and "differences" are features reflecting each other. Moreover, "similarity" is not "sameness". In meeting an orator, if someone says several times "yoldaşlar" (comrades) there will be differentiations in the sounds of these words. At the same time, one can't say that similarity does not exist. So, F. de Saussure writes: "In a language mechanism goes round the similarities and differentiations, the last functions (differentiations – F.V) contain the opposite side of the first ones. After a while, he continues: " **..... in**

1 F. de Saussure writes : " Language is the system of signs expressing ideas, just as to this reason he mentions that the alphabet of deaf and dumbs, symbols, forms of politeness, military signals etc. can be compared.

language only differentiations exist.... In language only differences having no positive members exist".

From here, one can attain logical results regarding obligatory linguistic elements and their **differentiations.** Further, only in these cases can language realize its function. As F. de Saussure says: **"... language is not a substance, it is a form".**

F. de Saussure, therefore, speaks of associative (paradigmatic) and straight line (syntagmatic) relations, while stressing the importance of each.

24. The examples given above show that F. de Saussure expressed an original attitude towards linguistics – and that these thoughts prompted several new orientations and trends to arise. Among them, **functional, descriptive, and structural** linguistics have become widely debated. Suggesting, overall, there has never been anyone else who shed so much light on the fundamental question "What is language?"

Indeed, the French scientist A. Martinet (1908-1999) in his book "The Unit of Linguistics" (1954, 2/3, p.123) wrote that F. de Saussure's

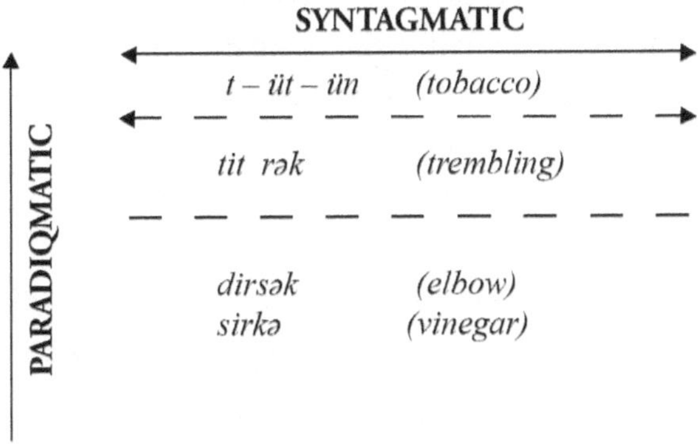

masterpiece in linguistic studies is the beginning of a new era.

25. Henceforth, the main essence of structural linguistics contains an "assumption" that a language is a complex of "attitudes". These attitudes showing themselves clearly in the phonetics and grammar of a language. If agreed, meaningful elements within language are contextualised as part of a greater whole: spelling defeat for the young grammarians. At the end of the day, structural linguistics excludes atomism, as well as physiological and psychological views, in its search for general language mechanisms. It ousts single language factors and in this way tries to show what multilvelled communication means in practice. In itself, language demands exactness, which is why those study methods employed by the natural sciences are used here. Thusly, each individually taken unit in a language is studied in relation to the rest of the units under observation. All demonstrating that language systems are not to be taken separately, but rather in relationship to every other linguistic process.

From the modern scientific perspective, if a structure is established on the principle of joining these elements together, then a "system" is the joint existence of structure and function.

26. One of the most influential voices in linguistics is the Prague school[11]. A school beginning in 1929, with the publication of a collection entitled "Travaux du Cercle Linguistigue de Prague". Overall, 8 editions of this collection were published, while only the beginning of the Second World War prevented a further run. Now, according to Prague linguists, both structural and functional orientations went side by side. In each structure, the function of the whole was easily

[1] We must mention here that Prague linguistic school in 1926 was established by famous Czech English investigator B. Matezius (1882-1945). In the formulation of this school N.S. Trubetzkoy , S.O. Karcevski (1884-1955), R.O.Jakobson (1896-1982) and others have taken active parts. V.Maltezius in his article "language and style" (Prague linguistic school, 1967,p.445) writes: " language as the system of expressions and intercourse is abstract and exists only in the ideal form".

demonstrated. That's why members of this school came to be known as **functional** linguistics.

Yet, in practical terms, the Prague school merely deepened F.de. Saussure's view on language. Its novelty stressed in separating the great master's comparisons of language and speech, language and the reality created by language, as well as diachronic and synchronic forms of communication. Fascinatingly, when they said "function" they understood the load carried by a specific language unit.

The brightest representative of the Prague school, N.S. Trubetzkoy (1890-1938), meticulously analyzing the phonetic layers of language, worked out the theory of oppositions, made an attempt to divide phonology from phonetics, and tried to establish the former as one of the Humanities. However, the latter he assiduously claimed was a science of nature (see chapter III, paragr. 21-22).

One of the most advantageous projects of the Prague school was discerning the place of sentences in the communicative process. As such, they separated two features in each sentence: **theme and rheme a**ttitudes; namely, an actual division in a sentence engineered by opposing a new thought against a known one - the result of a functional approach to sentences.

27. The second most influential school of structural linguistics in Europe was established in Copenhagen. The greatest theoretician being L. Hjelmslev (1899-1965). Now, L. Hjelmslev, together with Brondal published in 1934 a Bulletin - "Bulletin du Circle Linguistique de Copenhagae." In the pages of this bulletin were articles on linguistic theories in other institutions. All culminating, possibly, in 1939 when, together with the Prague schoolm they issued a journal called "Acta linguistica Revue Internationale Linguistigue Structurale"

For his part, L. Hjelmslev - in his theoretical work entitled "Prolegomena to a theory of language" (1953) – delved into the expressive side of the language. Indeed, he paid serious attention to Meaning. Wanting, as he did, to show form and substance as twin aspects of communication.

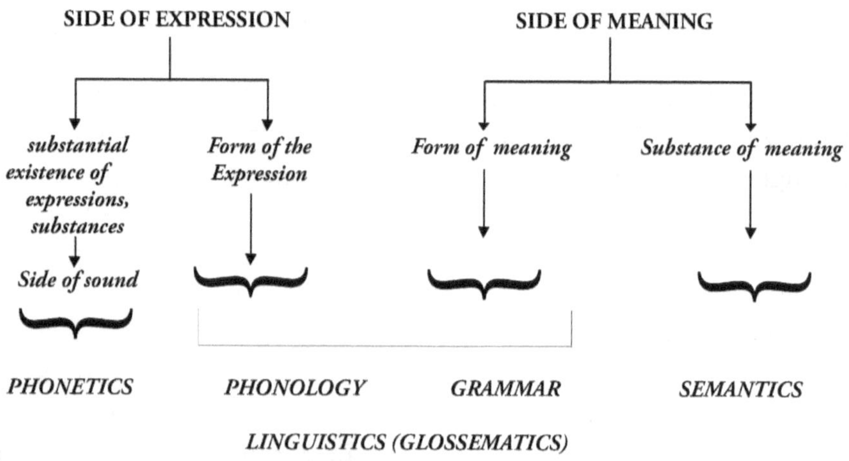

Both, the existence of expression and the existence of contents are the same for all languages. Moreover, the form of contents and expressions are closely connected with one another and are ruled over by laws of commutation. Yet, the possible change of form in expression brings forth an adaptation of contents, or the contrary. This may be why L. Hjelmslev wrote in the above mentioned work that glossemantics - being different from conventional linguistics - is not really a facet of phonetics (page79). What is more, he claims any connection between the form of meaning and substance should be named **designation**, although he calls the substance itself **designatum** (things, thoughts). To his understanding, **Form** is purely inner language, however **substance** indicates outer language aspects. In order to differentiate his views from others L. Hjelmslev then determines language like this: "It is not conglemerate with non-linguistic phenomena. It is independent, a whole sui generis **structure"**

Curiously, L. Hjelmslev's conception of "Immanent algebra" was understood as dependences (functions) among a system of notions. Here mutual dependences were taken as the main feature. At which point; one can't help quoting a sentence L. Hjelmslev used repeatedly: "Language is the structure of pure connections… it is a form or scheme not depending upon realization".

28. American Descriptivists do not resemble Copenhagenians in the deductive way they manage abstract theories, at least in the initial stages. Rather, they use inductive methods, while taking the usage of language as the concrete condition for their investigations. Conversly, American Descriptivism was formalized at Yale University, which encouraged the works of E. Sapir (1884-1939), yet also the works of L. Bloomfield (1887-1949), two extremely diverse thinkers. Those following Bloomfield (who hold behaviorist "psychological conceptions" - namely, direct experience and behavior - as a basis for conjecture, look on language as **stimulation** and **reaction**. They approach language as a special form of human behavior, which from a methodological point of view means showing that speech is the result of individual activities[21].

---

[21] It is interesting to note that both of these linguists were closely connected with German linguistics. Though E. Sapir was true to Foslers school, L. Bloomfield supported the young grammarians - for he studied at Leipzig University together with thm. Moreover, L. Bloomfield's book (which was published in 1933) on language completely reflects the views of the Americans. One must mention here that Descriptive Linguistics aimed at describing the language of ethnic groups living in America, including the languages of Indians. From this background, a big theoretical school was created.

Unarguably, Bloomfield wrote in "The Language" that "linguistics does not always act according to the form of meaning, but must act with regard to phonetic form" (p.162).

29. American Descriptivism, created by Z. Harris (1899-1992), entered a second stage through the syntactic theories of N.Chomsky (1928), a scholar who, arguably, developed an additional third stage. Indeed, in his work "Methods in Structural Linguistics" (1951), Z.Harris expressed his goal by stating that the scattering, or distribution, of language units in relation to each other establishes the main aim of descriptive linguistics. Z. Harris, who is considered the founder of "descriptive orientation", also advanced "determined language" by recording those units scattered, or depicting their surrounding environment. Hence, it is not as far from the facts to say that **phonemes** and **morphemes** cannot discriminate meaning, as it is as to claim they are specified by a break in the speech-chain, as well as by the distribution of segments during the break of a speech-chain without the participation of meaning.

In the work mentioned above, Z.Harris shows the following tasks lie before linguists:

1.In the initial stage of investigation, the smallest unit of language must be found, while not being separated from the flow of speech.

2.The separated units must be generalized in certain phoneme and morpheme groups, i.e, their distribution in language must not be obscured.

3.Each group determined as a result of distributive analysis should be widely described within its frame.

Distribution is revealed by way of substance. For example, in the words (dəng-disturbed) and (zəng-telephone ring) the consonant sounds /d / and /z / by substituting each other cause the creation of new units. The advantage of this method offered by Z. Harris is found in the evidence that, he doesn't take meaning into consideration and involves the features of every analysis.

30. The quotes from American linguists below provide the possibility to understood language in a certain period. E. Sapir, for example, states: "Language is absolutely something humane, it is not the non-instinctive system of wish and emotions expressed by the help of articulated symbols ("Language", 1921, 8).

Additionally, A. Bloch claims: "Language is the system of arbitrary sound symbols, by it helps a social group carry out joint activities ("An Outline of Linguistics Analysis", 1942, 5).

Further, E.Cassierer (1874-1945) wrote: "Language is not mechanism and not organism, neither alive nor dead. Under this term we understand physical objects. That is generally nothing " (Structuralism in Modern Linguistics. Word, 1945, I, p.110). On the same page he continues: "Language is a specificly human activity, but it should not be explained by physical, chemical and biological terms. The best and brief determination of a language has been given by W.von Humboldt "Language is not ergon, it is energia". R.Hall (1927-1997): "Language is an Institute wherein people are in mutual contacts with it - by its help arbitrary symbols are said and heard" (An Essay on Language, Philadelphia, 1968, 158).

Wjat is more, N. Chomsky declared: "After this I understand language as a net of finite and infinite sentences, their finite forms are established by the distribution of the infinite system of elements" (Syntactic structures, 1957, 13).

31. As one has seen, any determination of language by (some) American linguists proves that language is understood by different forms. But despite this determination within these determinations

there are common features, too. These shared characteristics are as follows:

1. Language is a system, for the usage of certain units - it is the whole of its necessary rules;

2. Language is arbitrary, i.e. there is no direct connection between the one who expresses, or the one who is being expressed;

3. Language consists of sounds, it is established by sounds - they are pronounced and heard;

4. Language is symbolics;

5. Language is the bearer of thoughts - people express their thoughts through a language.

As observed, these generalizations make an attempt to determine language from the inside.That's why the social side of language (and the issues of its establishment) is studied in the back plan.

32. When dealing with the famous linguist-scientist W. von Humboldt, the name of Leo Weisgerber (1899-1958) was also mentioned (see paragr. 18). Now, this linguist-philosopher had a number of interesting conjectures on linguistics. As such, it may be worthwhile to speak a bit more about him. So confessed, it is curious to recognize his article "Neoromantism in Linguistics" printed in 1930 as the publication wherein he put forth theoretical conceptions regarding the 4 stages of a languages expressive life: the language ability of mankind, the language of cultural treasures in a society; the language of each person: the applied forms of a language (p.344). Yet, close to the end of the 40's, L.Weisgerber gave precedent to the social side of language more than his inherited mother tongue. (The Leading Arrows of Understanding in Language "Wirkendes Wort, 1950/51, p.1), approached language from the position of a mother tongue ….. understood as the power of spiritual character. Similarly, perhaps,

to W.von Humboldt when unpacking the following conceptions: "language is a power in constant activity", and "it reflects a certain world outlook" as well as "it possesses an inner form". Thus, he considers language as the power of spiritual formulation and tries to liquidate notions of psychologism and sociologism existing in linquistics. Instead, he envisages language as something phenomenological. In language - by adding grammar and content-activities to sound and form, he creates a fully scientific assertion.

Undoubtedly, language worlds, together with their inner form, according to L.Weisgerber's work, generate whole spheres of comunication. Partially explaining why he looks upon language as an "intermediate world" (Zwischenwelt): the sphere of a mother tongue (muttersprachiliches Weltbild). With this in mind, his work on the "Theory of Methods in Linguistics" (1952), seems to present language as an energizing power. Indeed, he approaches language as a centre spreading light and manifesting itself in this activity.

His contention being that the things of the substantial world enter our minds by means of this intermediate world.

33. This (moral) intermediate world, by its very essence, consists of a language. More exactly, it consists of our multileveled mother tongue. As such, this meditary sphere is independent of language capacity, even though it is not a direct "reflection" of Nature. In a sense, a person grasps this process of understanding through the moral influence of a language pre-conditioned by its social features. So, built around each individual is a sphere of values and orientations, which manifest themselves in a form divided between different language collectives.

All causing suppoters of this theory to contend that the transference of language capacity (Sprachinhalt) to the intermediate

Language collective ***(Sprachgemeinschaff)*** ***(Dinge der Aussenwelt)***	------------------ 0 ------------------ ***Intermediate world*** ***(Zwischenwelt)*** ***Moral existence*** ***(Geistige Gegenstände)*** ***Contents (Inhalte)***	***thing of the surrounding world***

world is achieved through an inner form (innere form) of the language collective. Interestingly, L. Weisgerber rejects energy conceptions of the speech act as "psychological assumption", preferring to apply F. de Saussure's notions and explain it as an active power - which, in itself, reflects any investigation of language capacity. At the end of the day, neoromantism suggests language is learnt from the inside. A stance hinted at by Humboldt and timidly applied by the young grammarians. For L. Weisgerber, however, this concept acquired a new meaning.

Members of language collectives, of course, depend on language operating around separately taken individuals as a reality. After all, a mother tongue gains its existence in this way. It seems as if points of some initial force manifest themselves as a power, formulating morality, creating culture and vivifying history. In this way, mother tongue seems to have carried out its function, while opening a way back to the language collective at the same time as turning the world into the product of morality.

This may be why L. Weisgerber speaks of strong mutual contacts between mother tongue and language collectives. From these comparisons, he discovers two humane laws of language. As to the law of a language collective, humankind, without exception (even though continuously under the influence of natural laws), is divided into language collectives. Therein, the laws of mother tongue show if a person is morally formed by her ministrations, and in this way join the thought and activity-worlds of one language collective together.

The contents expressed by language substitutes traditional meaning (lexis) and functional (grammar) conceptions, because the meaning of words and the functions of their forms are very complicated. Besides their grammatical investigation ousts meaning and function from a language and allows thinking to express itself in the outer world. As L. Weisgerber suggests, they are the constructors of language contents, as well as the "moral world of freedom" surrounding language. The word " Onkel" (uncle), on one hand, reflects the systematization of sounds, whilst on the other hand, it reflects the intermediate world (the moral existence in a language), the bark of thought. If there was a further third hand, it would express existing things (Vaterbruder), father's brother (Mutterbruder) mother's brother etc. in a model.

Sounding	*Intermediate world* *Moral existence* *The content of the word*	*Outer world, things, objects*
Onkel *language collective*	*The bark of thought*	*Vaterbruder* *Mutterbruder* *Mann der Vaterschwester* *Mann der utterschwester*

34. Taking as a basis for reflection the contents in a language - in the intermediate world, L. Weisgerber takes this language as an intermediate sphere in itself. Simultaneously, both sounding and contents belong to the language therein. Moreover, the means of expression in a language would establish unity between them. Sound (layt) an object (gegenstand) and a thing (zaxe), as attitudes, could be visualized by the great scientist like this

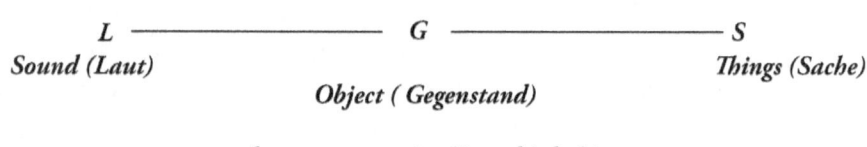

L* ——— *G* ——— *S

Sound (Laut) ***Things (Sache)***

Object (Gegenstand)

language capacity (Sprachinhalt)
dil (Sprache)

For L. Weisgerber, language is a power in activity. It rules over the movements of a people. Indeed, they are morally purified by certain possibilities inherent within mother tongue and can master the correct way to behave in reality through her influences. All depending on which of the aforementioned symbols happen to be revealed first in the field of language investigations. Certainly, exploring sounding (lautbezogen), contents (inhaltbezogen) and things (sachbezogen) systematically, L.Weisgerber, associates the distribution of words across an alphabetical line with the sounding of words. Thereby, he takes the grouping of things as an extra linguistic factor too. Explaining his thoughts further, L. Weisgerber writes that the differentiation in a Germanic sentence (Treten Sie mir nicht auf die Fusse // Beine, Zehen//

is not the differentiation of " ayaq" (foot), " qıç" (leg), " barmaq" (finger), since this differentiation comes from the differentiation of a morally intermediate world.

35. Each exploration undertaken by L. Weisgerber is done in order to prepare recipients of mother tongue in grammatical uses of language, along with the inductive role at school. In this sense, scientific grammar is best understanding as language (energia) in a stage of transition, while school grammar could be seen as a subject wherein the essence of language is learnt. Nonetheless, from a language viewpoint, these issues must be put side-by-side with fields of wanting, capability, and increase, or completely subordinated to them. Only in this latter case (in the widest sense of meaning), can it help the development of mother tongue. If in science, therefore, "the grammar period" was put to an end in school "a certain form of language instruction" –grammar instruction would itself end.

In the 40's, L. Weisgerber, while discriminating between the spiritual and sound aspects of language, was already preparing for that time (in the 50's), when he started speaking about a threefold linquistic comparison –sounding, contents, and activity. Later on, he put forth a fourfold comparison: form, contents, function, and activity. In conformity with this position, he then distinguished 4 types of investigation. A fact discovered in his contention that any perspective arising from form must not only involve sounding but also contents. Indeed, if the union of form and contents establishes the object of grammar-learning in language (as ergon), the angle of activity through function takes language as energia. This initial proposition contains the wording of the world, but the second propostion approaches language as a point of existence. Altogether, L. Weisgerber's language instruction reflects the following stages, as well as these concomitant features:

1. Stage	side of sound (lautliche Seite)	moral (spiritual) side (geistliche Seite)

2 . Stage	learning of sounding (lautbezogene Betrachtung)	learning of the cont (inhaltbezoge Betrachtung)	linguistic energetic view (sprachwissen-schaftliche Betrachtung)

3. Stage	learning of form	learning of the contfunctional view		learning of the impact
	(gestaltbezogene Betrachtung)	(inhaltbezogene Betrachtung)	(leistungsbezogene Betrachtung)	(wirkungbezogene Betrachtung)

36. For L. Weisgerber grammar is not an aim in itself. Rather, it is the transition period of an aim. Language being an acting power continuously ensuring the lives of collectives are a means of passed over. Unquestionably, functionality must free language from statistic isolation and artifical hypostasia, following which it must take to the world. What is more, for L.Weisgerber, linguisitc pressures establish liner principles due to every mother tongue in the world expressing things through words. From the methodical point of view, his central notion is that statistic language proves the energetic polar opposite from linguistic contents. Its subject (in the language collective) is the wording process for the world around us.

The primary function of language is reflecting the world through a mother tongue. Any transition to the 4th stage allows the impact aspect of language (in spite of the importance of its initial function) to make a direct association. Indeed, when grammar gives importance to the impact circle of a language and functionaity involves the “world” via the aspect of impact ….. allowing life to return to the field of linguistics. A field longing to reveal in the whole of life's processes in terms of a languages participation in language collectives. Thence, the impact of language begins from the moment of wording the world in itself. This is why, in every walk-of -life, one comes across the active inference of language. In the lives of word-creaters, as well as within the work of certain collectives associated with language, the reflexive influence of language is conspicuously felt.

Since formality determines meaning and function, the transition of learning associated with content can be explained by the intermediate world. Atop of which, a functional look at language attains language-value inside the aspect of methodical language impact. Hence, L. Weisgerber stated that an impact circle of a mother tongue included all in the values that mother tongue exhibited in a system.

All implying the connecting function and aspect of impact within language is explained by the fact that if one describes content by function (and without impact), one attract a "language region". In this way, within grammatical investigations, scholars can hardly seperate language capacity from the surrounding world. If function and impact, therefore, serve to indicate the limits of content - at the same time as function and impact stand upon content - then there appears to be a threat of circularity.

37. One must note, the researches of Sapir-Whorf centered around perceptions that language has a strong influence in establishing a language outlook. Unsurprisingly, for this scholar, language and household are taken as parts of a common science – anthropology. Assertions marking this study as a possible manifestation of a people's culture. As we may read, "Language and culture", or "language and people" tangentaiily connect with conceptions spread across Germany by L. Weisgerber. Yet, Sapir-Whorf takes as his basis W.

von Humboldt's theory of "language (not as an ergon), as an energia". Additional influences on his work including F. de Saussure's notion "language is a system of signs", and J. Trier's (1894-1970), "theory of semantic fields". Never forgetting L. Weisgerber remained faithful to his teacher W. von Humbolt's words, "structuralism is the most common and most eminent characteristic feature". All in all, this stance draws attentions to the features of ethnolinguistics. Creating, thereby, a new trend echoing Humbolt. A fashion, as it has been said, finding foot within the four–volumed work "The Power Fusions of the German language" (Düsseldorf 1949 – 1950) and – especially - in the second volume of this series, "The World of the German language" For his part, L. Weisgerger vastly develops these formulations. An achievement proved through extracted comments like: "A linguist must look upon language not as a completed, unmovable structure, in other words not as ergon. Rather he must look upon language as energia and taking it as a structure (always being a power in movement) determines and renovates it's first and most important function: language being the power of moral structure, creating the intermediate world of thought as one of the fusions of human morality and of thinking". In the "moral reality" of this intermediate world, a person's conscious actions are reflected back to them. Here we encounter a transference to a "product of the spirits" in our real world - which has been taken as the only basis for existence after the period of W. von Humboldt. Moreover, acting by this principle, it is possible to determine future approaches within dynamic language investigation by making it is necessary to approach language as a power creating culture. After all, language is an important factor in the creation of culture and it takes part in every social formulation. This principle condition reveals language as the vital creative power in history, involving, as it does, the active creation of people and their moral stimulations. (p. 7-8) L.Weisberger, for instance, when taking language as a social phenomenon, regards it as a social form of understanding. Indeed, it is the leading power. It creates notions, configures objective reality, and establishes objects for human beings. As the lexics, grammar, and syntax of language reflect values and traditions, language is considered a cultural phenomenon.

38. Gifted authorities including L. V. Shcherba – L. R. Zinder – Y. S. Maslov all concur. Yet, as a disciple of I. A. Baudouin de Courtenay the originality of L. B. Shcherba shines through. Mainly due to the fact he widely interpreted the issues of general linguistics in two of his works: "Three Aspects of Language Phenomena and Experience in Linguistics" (1931), and "The Further Duties of Linguistics" (1945)

Of couse, academician L. V. Shcherba - being different from F. de Saussure - discriminates three aspects of scrutiny: language itself (processes of speaking and hearing); language materials (things that are spoken and written in a language), dictionary and systems which linguistics attains from grammar. The first notion can't be imagined without a system, namely, without grammar and a lexicon. However, a dictionary and grammar show themselves in the language materials. So, L. V. Shcherba - who approaches language as a system – is adamant it as a social product. In this regard, L. V.Shcherba writes "Language system and language materials are different sides of language activity given only in experiments, because it is clear that unless language materials are understandable, it is dead and understanding is not possible. (Three aspects..., p. 26). Clearly, L.V.Shcherba's generalizations on language are grounded in concrete observations. He even compares the languages of weakly developed tribes: their jestures and all kinds of affectations as a primary problem.

In the rich heritage of his science, the theory of phonemes

occupies an important place. But when generalizing his statements pm this matter L. V. Shcherba's approach to language as a system applaudes vivid spoken language (especially the role of passive and active grammar) in teaching language.

39. For their parts, L. R. Zinder (1904-1995) and Y. S. Maslov (1909-1990) - being influenced by L. V. Shcherba - develop their teacher's thoughts on language. As such, Y. S. Maslov in his book ("Introduction to Linguistics", M., 1987) writes, "Each language is the product of this or that collective and that's why it is a social – historic phenomenon. Each language is an important condition for the development of human development, as to its tenderness and perfection it is a charming (strange) world of intercourse, an immeasurable means in the formulation and delivering of our thoughts to the other". as well as "Each language for the expression of thoughts is established from the sounds which a person pronounces. Each language consists of individually taken elements, an ordinary saying in each language in the composition of other utterances is fractured into the other elements, and repeated in the other combinations. In each language such repeated elements - in large quantities - have been represented and a system of quick rules exists by means of which these elements unite in the words expressing meaning" (p.4)

Further thoughts specify, "Language exists as a vivid language, because it is in activity. Its activity is possible only in speech, utterances and in speech acts" (p.10). Later he writes, "Speech is the form of existence of language. Language is in action and directly it is given in speech".

40. The other follower of Shcherba, namely L. R. Zinder, has also got an interesting attitude to language. In his masterpiece "General phonetics" (M.,1979, 2), L. R. Zinder wrote, "Language is a means

of communication among people. It is a means to dispatch one man's thought to the other man. As to its structure, language is a system of signs characterized by the mode of expression and contents. The thought and emotion etcetera given in the first term, if represented, serves as a form to the existence of thought, emotion etcetera of the second term. The side of sound is peculiar to the plan of expression. It is important for the dispatching and reception of information" (p.6)

A little later, L. R. Zinder wrote, "If a language does not express a thought, it is nothing - unless it is turned to a substantial being, it can never exist" (p.6). Without doubt, L. R. Zinder's meditations caused serious interest. Assurely, he also points out that a language uses definable sounds and, accordingly, can carry out this function, "Occasionally, language should not be a language of pure sounds; one can say that the fact there are expressive sides to a language possessing natural sounds is merely its inseparable feature" (p.5)

41. M. Kazimbey (1802 – 1870) in his many – sided thoughts on language, conceived it as one of the fusions between people's history and culture. Thus, he stated, "The richest source of existential information, the mysterious rig – rags is but language". Curiously, M. Kazimbey - based on his linguistic explorations - uncovered links marking a hidden relationship of languages (especially of Turkic languages), on the phonetic, lexical, and syntactic, level. Indeed, M. Kazimbey in his book, "The General Grammar of Turkic – Tatar Language" (1846 (2)) determines language as a means of communication: explaining the position Turkic languages occupied in world culture, while insistently suggesting that Russians learn more aboit this language group. As such, he deepens general research by his reports, speeches, and articles (a letter to the editor of the journal "Sovremennik", 1952, № 12 etc). Indeed, he repeatedly mentions the

impact of Eastern Europe on linguistic studies. An assertion founded on the importance of etymological analysis, as well as his personal insistence that the self–belonging of a language should be proved as a result of depth scrutiny within language. (His inquiry into whether Chuvash is a Turkic language or not, is a clear proof of this practice).

42. On the other hand, B. Chobanzadeh (1893 – 1937), who came to Azerbaijan at the beginning of the 20's, was an extremely well–prepared linguist. As a recognized scholar, he made a series of interesting comments on the creation of language, along with its social nature. Irrefutably, B. Chobanzadeh felt language was associated with social forces and denied it was a product of the brains of individual people. Moreover, its formulation, Chobanzadeh postulates, is in the ancient East. Partially explaining, for him, the roots of Indian, as well as Arabic languages - especially with respect to the importance of the school of Alexandria (Iskenderiye). Indeed, he proudly names M. Kashkarly as the first prominent Turkologist of the East, while like M. Kazimbey, B. Chobanzadeh, he also demands that a linguist thoroughly knows the language he investigates as an insider. After all, a true scholar never bases his understanding on historically established laws within that language alone.

43. Obviously, A. Akhundov (1932) is one of the scientists closely engaged with the essence of linguistics. In his book "General Linguistics" he even tries to give answers to the questions "What is language?" and "If language is the treasure of the masses, is it the only means of thought for them?" (70)

By determining language as a purely social phenomenon, he contends it bears national features but not international ones. For A. Akhundov, language is determined by functional. Alongside which he notes when one initially begins to learn a language, one gets a dictionary and grammar books of that language. As we may read, "It appears that a language consists of words and grammar?" ..... although he equally hints a person needs inherited texts by saying, "Maybe language consists, somehow, of those texts?". Taken together, one must be able to communicate in a language and must understand what is said in this language: "Namely language, in fact, consists of speech activity, or more correctly speaking, it consists of speech acts" (70).

As may be seen, A. Akhundov answers "What is language?" by claiming –as a social phenomenon – language is a means of communication and a treasure of the people. Namely, he indicates that language (as an indicator of moral being) has a unique system and structure.

44. In this small summary, explanations of language, its essence, system, and structure, along with all the thoughts on linguistics since the time this science was established, have been both outlined and surveyed. Henceforth, it becomes clear that linguistics is an extremely complicated and rarefied undertaking. Indeed, it is associated with the interactions of individuals and society (being a mass of individuals), in an abstract as well as a concrete manner. Indeed, one observes its "material" manifestation in speech, when it acts as a part of complicated processes like thinking–speaking-hearing-understanding and so on. In addition, this summar recounts current opinions, not to mention written researches on linguistics in an attempt to enable readers to participate in any discussion on issues surrounding this vital aspect of human existence. What is more, every language feature mentioned herein is intended to introduce the twin streams of phonetics and phonology to anyone preparing to acclimatize themselves with the titbits of this science. Taking the Azerbaijani language as the focus of attention,

however, it may prove necessary to talk about it a little further.

After all, this book is not focused on language per se, but, concretely speaking, on the Azerbaijani, English, and Russian languages.

2. ON THE AZERBAIJANI LANGUAGE

In itself, the Azerbaijanian language belongs to the oghuz-seljug semi-group of the oghuz group of Turkish languages. As such, it is nearer to Turkiye (Turkish), Turkmen and the Gagauz languages than other variants. At present, more than 50 millon Azerbaijanians speak this tongue. An often forgotten fact, until one bears in mind that more than 35 million Azerbaijanians live in South Azerbaijan (Iran), whereas only 9 million azerbaijanians live in Northern Azerbaijan. Perhaps one also needs t recall that Azerbaijanians have spread across the worls in an international diaspera. Digging deeper, the Azerbaijanian language is undubtedly one of the Turkic languages having ancient written records. The first written manuscript being "Kitabi Dədə Qorqud" (The Book of Father Gorgud), discovered by the german orientalist A. F. Diez in 1815 inside a Dresden library. A little later, other copies of this saga were found. Hence, academician V.M. Zhirmunski felt compelled to speak about "Kitabi Dədə Qorqud" while trying to prove certain chapters of this saga reached back to the V-VI centuries.

As we may read in the section of the Saga "Dirsa Khan,s son Bughaj Khan declares his lady hey..."

Xan qızı, yerimdən turayınmı?

Daughter of Khan, shall I get up?

Yaqan, la boğazından tutayınmı?
Shall I catch you on the throat?
Qaba öncəm altına salayımmı?
Shall I kick you down?
Qara polat uz qılıcım ölümə alayınmı?
Will you be under my feet thrown?
Öz gedəndən başuni kəsəyinmi?
Shall I cut your head off?
Can tatlusın sana bildirəyinmi?
Shall I tell you that I kill you?
Alca canun yer üzünə dökəyinmi?
Shall I shed your blood on the earth?
Xan qızı, səbəbi nədir, degil mana.
Daughter of Khan, I don't know why
Qatı qəzəb edərəm şimdi sana, - dedi.
I am angry at you - to find the reason I try.

Reading these lines it is not difficult to see how close they are to today's language. This is why the prominent scientist A. Demirchizade called this saga a real Azerbaijani "monument". Assuredly, he claimed, after the VIII-IX centuries, this saga had been properly composed in Azerbaijan.

2. Moreover, famous linguist H. Mirzazadeh's understanding of written specimens of these works (whose authors are known to us), contended they could be found in the Azerbaijani language of the XIII century. These are two gazels of I. Hasanoghlu.[3]

Ss he wrote, "Bashımdan getmedi Hərgiz sənünnən içdiğün badə" (I can not forget the wine which I drank with you) as if he was our contemporary. Now, in the XIV century, the great Nasimi (1369-1417) penned.

3 H. Mirzazadeh, the historical grammar of the Azerbaijani language, Baku, 1980, p.6.

Ey Nəsimi, sübhdəm billah şu yarım xoşmı
Ey Nasimi, is my beloved since morning happy?
Şol həbibim, dilbərim, aləmdə varım xoşmıdır.
For she is my doctor, my beauty, is she happy?
Ey yüzi gül, ləbləri mərcanımız,
You, whose face is like flower,whose lips tender
Ey gözi nərgis, şəhi məstanımız.
You, my beauty, you whose waist is slender.

Equally, the regal figure and outstanding poet, Commander Shah Ismayil Khatai (1486-1524), who wrote his creative works in the XVI century, reads as if his lines had been written by a present day lyricist

Qış getdi yenə bahar gəldi,
Winter passed away spring came
Gül bitdi və laləzar gəldi.
Flowers grew, all in flowers became
Quşlar qamusu fəğana düşdü,
All the birds began to shed tears
Eşq odu yenə bu canə düşdü.
Flame of love just me scare
Sərvin yenə tutdu damənin su,
Your figure is tall as a tall tree
Sərv üstə oxudu faxtə gu- gu.
On a tall tree a bird sang thee.

M. Fuzuli (1494-1556) wrote:

Könlüm açılır zülfi-pərişanını görgəc.
I feel you seeing your sad face
(gülər qönçə-yəni dodaq), (smiling bud-lips)
Nitqim tutulur qönçəyi-xəndanını görgəc.

I can't speak seeing your flower-like lips
Baxdıqca sənə qan saçılır didələrimdən,
Looking at you,I shed not tears but blood
Bağrım dəlinir navəki-müjganını görgəc.
My heart breaks, seeing your state
(kirpiklərin oxu, ox kimi kirpik)
(my lashes are like arrows, an arrow is like my eye lashes)

Saib Tabrizi (1601-1676) in very pure Azerbaijani wrote:
Torpaqdan ayrılanlar bir gün düşər torpağa,
Those who have separated from land, one day will go into land
Xalqa söykən hər zaman, düşməyəsən ayağa.
Rely on the people, be proud, understand?
Dünya mənim gözümdə bir otaqlı xanədir,
The world in my eyes is a one-roomed cell
Insan həmin xanədə qiymətli dürdanədir.
A man is a treasure in it, this is, what I always tell.

3. In the XVI-XVII centuries, oral folk literature flourished, All shedding light on an epic saga known as "Koroghlu", which was composed around this time. Interestingly, the language of this saga is mellow, being written purely in the language of the people. Here both the language of poetry and narration peculiar to the language of the sagas is richly displayed.

Koroghly addressing Nigar says:
Hansı dağların qarısan,
Of which mountains are you snow,
Hansı bağların barısan,
Of which rivers do you flow

Nigar, Koroghlu yarısan,
Nigar's wife of Koroghlu
Bilir külli aləm səni.
It's known to all fully

4. Molla Panah Vaqif (1717-1797) is additionally known for his mellow language and ahighly developed style in Azerbaijanian poetry. Thus, a stanza from his poem " Durnalar" (cranes) provocatively reads:

Mən sevmişəm ala gözün sürməsin,
I have loved the antimony of your nice eyes,
Bədnəzər kəsibən, ziyan verməsin,
That evil eyes, which harm you may die.
Sağın gəzin, laçın gözü görməsin,
Be caucious in the sky, when flying,
Qorxuram səfnizi poza,durnalar.
Let your line not be sparse in the sky.

G.B. Zakir(1784-1857) also wrote in the style of Vagif:
Laçın yatağıdır bizim məkanlar,
Our lands are the lands of falcons,
Yavaş-yavaş gedin səsiniz anlar,
Walk silently in the fields along.
Qorxuram toxuna ötən zamanlar,
The trees they have lighted on,
Sürbəniz dağılıb çaşa, durnalar.
I wish you not to scatter of cranes!

S.A. Nabati (1812-1878) penned:
Səba, məndən söylə o gül-üzarə,
Morning, tell that garden of flowers,
Bülbül Gülüstana gəlsin, gəlməsin?
Nightingale should come to the garden or not?
Bu hicran düşkünü, illər xəstəsi.
Me, missing you badly, mad for you,
Yanına dərmana gəlsin, gəlməsin?
Should come for a remedy or should I not?
Mən qurbanı olum, ənbər tellərin,
I may victimize myself for your scented hair,
Qönçə dodaqların, püstə dillərin,
You've bud-like lips, tongue's a pistachio.
O lalə rüxsarın, mişkin xalların,
To the poppy –like chicks, to the light of the moles,
Oduna pərvanə gəlsin, gəlməsin?
Moths should come or should they not?

Curiously, Ashiq Alesger (1821-1926) created such worthy specimens of poety that they became examples of versification on a global scale, once more openly showing the beauty of the Azerbaijanian language:
Qışda dağlar ağ geyinər, yaz qara,
Mountains wear white in winter, but in spring just black.
Sağ dəstinlə ağ kağıza yaz qara,
With your hand, on white paper write black
Əsər yellər, qəhr eləyər yaz qara,
Spring will come, winds will blow, winds black,
Daşar çaylar, gələr daşlar çata-çat.
Rivers flood, stones will come in cracks.

Seyid Azim Shirvani (1835-1888) sang:
Füqaralar yanıban zülm oduna oldu kabab,
The poor people, burnt in the flame of a yoke, became kababs,
Bir tərəfdən elədi zəlzələ Şirvani xərab....
And earthquakes took place in Shirvan making it very bad...

M. A. Sabir (1862-1911) in the poem "Ağacların bəhsi"
(The arguments of trees) uses all the mellowness of Azerbaijanian verse .....
Alma, palıd, şam ağacı hal ilə,
Apple and oak and fir tree one day,
Eylədilər bəhs bu minval ilə.
Argued and with the words with which they play.
Başladı tərifə palıd qamətin.
Oak tree praised its thick stem,
Öydü özün, zorbalığın, halətin,
Praised its branches, leaves and all, then,
Canlıcadır, zorbacadır baldırım,
It said to it can be equal, just nothing
ındıra bilməz məni heç ildırım...
Can't break it either wind or lightning...

Mahammad Hadi (1879-1920) crooned:
Cəhanə gəlmədən məqsəd nədir insanə, bilməm ki?
Why does a man come into this world, what's the aim,
I don't know?
Həqiqətmi bu xilqət, yoxsa bir əfsanə, bilməm ki?
Whether its false or true, or just the same, I don't know?

Husseyn Javid (1882 -1944) lamented:
Bax qızdırmış günəş.
See, the sun has heated.
Utanıb qaçmaq istəyir.. guya
Being ashamed, of your state every day,
O da qızğın sənin zəlalətinə.
Being angry at your state, it's become hot.
O da küskün sənin bu halətinə.(" Şeyx Sənan")
He has hurt you, wants to run away ("SheykhSanan")

6. Ahmad Javad (1893-1937), in his poem "Dilimiz" (Our language) severely criticises writers who have fallen under the influence of Persian and Arabic, demanding that they should point out the tenderness of their own language:

"Od" yetmədi yağdı "atəş" başına
"Flame" was not enough "fire" was shot on your head
"Siyah" qondurdular "qara" qaşına
With the black was died up - your brow, instead.
Alınır "dilləri" "zəban" verilir.
Your language's been taken away - "zaban"[41]
has just given it to you
Ismarlanıb "boran" "yağmur" kəsilir.
Instead of our "boran"[52] used again "yağmur"[63] too.
"Ağları" bəyaza, "sarısı" " zerdə",
They called "aghi"[74] bayaz[85] and "sari"[96] "zerde"[107]

4 [1] zaban,in persian means language
5 [2] boran – rain in Azerbaijani language
6 [3] yağmur – rain in Persian language
7 [4] ağ – white.
8 [5] beyaz in Turkish white
9 [6] sari yellow in Azerbaijani terms
10 [7] zerda- Persian word for yellow

Döndü, can dayanmaz bu "ağır" dərdə.
It's hard this torture to bear
Dəyişdi hər şeyi "bum" oldu " bayquş".
Everything changed today "bum"[118] *became a "bayquş"*[129]
Elbisi geyildi, "paltar" qaldı boş.
All the deserts dressed green, naked remained a thick bush.

7. Nabi Khazri (1926) intoned,
Ana dili (mother tongue)
Səni şəfəq bildim bu cahanda mən,
I thought you in this world were a sun rise
Bəzən şimşək olub qəzəblə çaxdın.
Now you were nervous, but now wise
İlk dəfə dünyaya göz açanda mən,
When in our country, opened your eyes
Qəlbimə günəşin özüylə axdın
You flowed into the heart together with the sun
Ana gözlərindən süzən nur kimi
Believe, I can't ever substitute you in any other tongue,
Hopdun ürəyimə sən gilə-gilə
Just nothing, you absorbed into heart and soul,
Hər kəlmən, hər sözün bəzənməyibmi?
Have they not adorned you, my words of all?
Mehriban anamın təbəssümilə
By the kind mother's smile
Ucalır bağçadan bülbülün səsi
Rises a nightingale's voice for a while
Çay susur, əsməyir çəməndə yel də.

11 [8] bum – owl in Persian
12 [9] bayquş – owl in Azerbaijini

Rivers stop running, ceases the wind
Nə qədər doğmadır onun nəğməsi,
Mother's son's too kind, and sweet
Bülbül də elə bil ötür bu dildə.
Nightingale just sing in mother's tongue.

8. And here is M.Shahriyar (1904-1988) decrying,
Bir uçaydım bu çırpınan yelinən,
I wish, I flew with this beating wind
Bağlaşaydım dağdan aşan selinən,
I wish, I joined the coming flood, and
Ağlaşaydım uzaq düşən elinən,
I wish, I wept with the people of my separated land
Bir görəydim ayrılığı kim saldı?
I wish, I know who separated us
Ölkəmizdə kim qırıldı, kim qaldı?
Or which of them died or perished alas?

Here are specimens of one branch of Azerbaijanian written literature and poetry, which have a history of more than a thousand years. All in all, making Azerbaijanian a mighty weapon in the hands of native writers. Tangemtially, of course, this also demonstrates the linguistic advantages of Azerbaijanian s a mother tongue in its competition with languages considered more influential for global patterns of communication. Quite apart from the evidence herein of Azerbaijanian as an examplary language in the field of poetry and art.

9. On the invincibility of Azerbaijanian as a language, friends and even enemies have mouthed significant words in admiration of its capacities.

Thus, educated people in Azerbaijan have valued their language and praised it highly:

For instance, N.Narimanov commented: "Mother tongue. The kind existence declaring its remedial influence in that language, which has made you hear the lullaby in that language, when you were still in a cradle. In the form of harmony and tenderness, in the depth of the spirits it has presented you with caring".

Furhtermore, M.J.Pishevari eulogized, "Our language with the sagas, stories, narratives and speeches may compete with the languages of the largest countries of the world.

....Azerbaijani language is so strong, so natural, that even if the arabic and percian languages are excluded out of it, it is still possible with the remaining (purely) Azerbaijani words to write and express the largest thoughts and supreme aims with it".

10. One of the most enlighted people, H.Zardabi, wrote: "Language is such a thing that it is impossible to keep it in its own position. As soon as, extra things are created and the instruments changed, the amount of new words shall increase day-by-day. An increase of such words won´t bring any harm to the language, but instead it shall bring good to it".

The poet-innovator R.Rza (1910-1980), used to say this, "The law of diffusion (absobation) of the physical world exists in language too. This is observed in the field of language. There is no more, or less, developed language that could not profit from other languages".

Not only separately taken words, sometimes the forms of expression too, may transfer from one language into the other ...

Each language has its own form, taste and salt: its words, experssoins, utterances; its own self–belonging features. These tongues are (occasionally) conspicuous, sometimes subtle. When one touches upon these details, they frustrate the seeker.

What is more, the prominent Azerbaijanian poet Sabir Rustamkhanly (1946), in his poem "Sagh ol ana dilim" (Thank you, my mother tongue), tenderly expresses the feelings of patriotism:

"Sağ ol, ana dili"
"Thank you, my mother tongue"
Sağ ol ana dilim, ana öyüdüm,
Thank you my mother tongue, mother's admonishment,
Füzuli eşqindən divanə dilim.
My language being mad with love for Fuzuli,
Ürəyim başına nəfəs dərmədən,
Being in the bottom of my heart, taking no breath,
Fırlanıb kül olan pərvanə dilim.
Moving around it as a moth and turning to ash my language.
Üstünə yürüyürdü Quran dilləri
The languages of Koran ran to you,
Peyğəmbər dilləri, qanun dilləri...
The languages of Profetes, of the laws too...
Qapılar dalında qoydular səni,
You were kept behind locked doors
Haqq dedin, dabandan soydular səni,
You wanted justice, they peeled you from their heels.
Ancaq məhv olmadın, anam, can dilim,
But you did not perish, dear, mother tongue
Ordular sarsıdan qəhrəman dilim....
My hero language, my mother, my son...

11. It has been said of the Azerbaijani language:

"The language of Transcaucasion Tatars (Azerbaijanis) vaguely differs from the Osmanli (Turkic) language and with this language (with the Azerbaijani language) as with the French language in Europe, you can walk the whole of Acia" (Bestuzhev Marlinskiy, Полное собрание сочeнeний. Изд, 4-ое, t. 1, cast II, SPb, 1847, p.114).

"I have tried to learn in the Tatari (Azerbaijani) language **in Acia.** From M.Y.Lermontov´s letter to S.A.Rayevski in 1837.

Prominent traveller and folklorist, August von Gaksthausen, in the middle of the last century recorded: Armenians wrote their works in the Azerbaijani language but not in their own language, because this language in the south of the Caucasus, among the people, is the language of trade, information and mutual understanding. In this respect, it can be compared with French in Europe. It is specifically the language of poetry… prominent armenian poets in order to spread their works widely use the same tatar (Azerbaijani) language (Way notes, СПб, 1857, the 2 part p.52).

Russian scientist, P.A.Falev, in 1916, after his travels to Transcaucasia and Azerbaijan, penned in his account (which he published as a result of his journey), that it is not only in Azerbaijan, but also the whole people of Transcaucasia, spoke in the Azerbaijani language. (Известия АН, 1917, p.171).

12. These numerous examples have set forth - without reflecting the extraordinary distribution of sounds and without considering the molding of intonation - the factors proving a unique **tenderness** and richness to the Azerbaijani language. Moreover, these instances reflect the attained expressions, occurances and zig-zags of intercourse. Yet, what is the feature that enriches this language from inside: the factors making the phonetic structure so unusual? At this point,

any investigation into the phonetic structure of Azerbaijani, or its phonological sizes (This term belongs to R.Rza – F.Y) demands a careful analysis.

Without going into arbitrary details, scholars tend to speak of general features of the Azerbaijani language.

13. Firstly, let´s note that this language - in its distribution of vowels, or **consonants,** or visa versa, observes **harmony**. In speech, among the sense groups, a vowel is usually marked with the word vowel and is indicated by the symbol (V), while a consonant is indicated with the symbol (C) or consists of the alternation of consonant with (C), or vowel with (V). Hence, let´s review two lines of B.Vahabzade´s (1925-2009) poetry from the poem "Ana dili" (Mother tongue):

Ana dilim, səndədir xalqın əqli hikməti;

V + C + V + C + V + C + V + C + C + V + C + C + V + C + V + C / C+V+C+C+V+C+V+C+C+V/C+V+C+C+V+C+V

Translation: My mother tongue. The people´s wisdom and truth is in you

Ürəklərə yol açan Füzulinin sənəti,

V + C + V + C + C + V + C + V + / C + V + C + V + C + V + C / C+V+C+V+C+V+C+V+C+C+V+C+V+C+V//

Translation: The art of Fuzuli opening ways to (my) heart too,

In these two lines (in all in 5 places) within the word two consonants have come one after another. In two of them, as the suffixes begining with consonants joined to the ones which began with consonant sounds, this event has taken place (sən – dədir, ürək – lərə) (it is in you,to the hearts), but the other words are borrowed words from other languages: (xalq, əql, hikmət)) (people,wisdom,truth).

Additionally, in one place two consonants in the word function have come side-by-side. (Füzulinin sənəti), or (art of Fizuli). In all the rest of the cases (in these two lines - 63 times - there are junctions of vowel and consonants): the features of which we have mentioned above ….. in full force.

14. As a comparison, let´s analyse two lines of the German poet Heinrich Heine (1797-1856) "Səni pəncərədə görəndə" ("when I see you at the window") /Wenn ich an deinem House, des Morgens vorübergehe//

CVC, VC:VC:CV CVC/ CVC: CVCCV CCVCC: CVC VCV →CC VV//

/So freuts mich du liebe kleine, wenn ich dich am Frenster sche// CVCC VCC CVCC VCVCV CC VCV/CVC VC CVC VC CV CCCVC CVV//.

From the 77 vowel- consonant combinations in 14 (CC) (or CCC), consonant combinations are repeated. Interestingly, 7 of them have been used within the wording, and besides, used a single time in the form of (CCC). It´s true, of course, in 7 of these combinations 3 consonants have been used in the morpheme junctions (morgen+s vorüber + gehe, freut+s), but in the fourth within the morpheme (mor+gens, f+reuts, k+leine, Fen+s+ter). In the seven remaining cases consonant systematization has been observed in the word border.

/an{ + } deine m {+}h ause, des {+} mor gen + s}+ vorü- be r+g ehe, freuts+mich, ı ch+di ch, a m+f ents + e r+s ehe//

As we see the phonetic structure-feature, this makes the Azerbaijani language tender, so musical, that in one vowel nest several consonants cannot be applied. Contradiction this, in the German language, one vowel nest and 2 or more consonants may be considered an ordinary case.

15. The second distribution-feature distinguishing Azerbaijani as a language is that its words have two peaks. One of these peaks comes

at the beginning of a word (or is situated in the first root vowel), while the second is associated with a stressed vowel. The first vowel of the word root - if we are to use the terminology of R. Jakobson - is called Sondervokal. All meaning the first vowel of the word is rooted in the harmony, whereas the following vowels and consonants are rooted in the same harmony. Let´s comare:

ata-lar-dan: üz-üm-ü, isti – ni

(from "The fathers:my face, the heat")

A vowel, coming at the head of the word, determines the harmony of the vowels and consonants coming afterwards. In linguistic science, this is called the law of **synharmony.** But in the German language, a vowel by the suffixes joining the word inclines to the vowel in its articulalion, which in germanistics is called an Umlautisation event.

(der) Mann - (man)

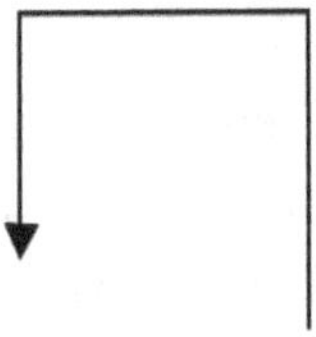

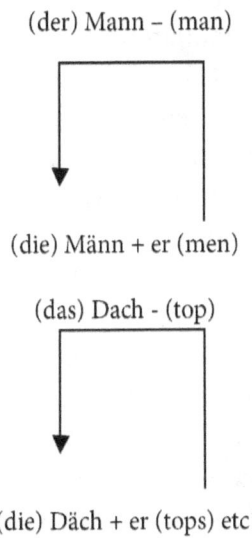

(die) Männ + er (men)

(das) Dach - (top)

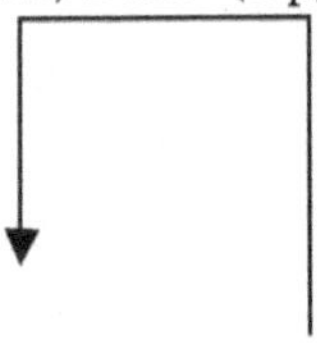

(die) Däch + er (tops) etc1

So, the essence of peak I establishes a basis for the law of synharmony – due to the fact that if the first vowel of the root of the word is thick, then the following vowels and consonants must aslo be thick. Indeed, if they are thin, then they must be followed by thin vowels. Moreover, if they are pronounced by lips, they must be lip-vowels and consonants. Other words, not obeying these rules, are borrewed words. On top of which it is hardly infrequent these days to find borrowed words, such as /naümid/ (hopeles), /bisavad/ (without education), substituted by Azerbaijani words - and are used as "ümüdsüz", "savadsız".(without hope, uneducated)

16. The second peak of Azerbaijani words is established by a stressed syllable. In words where the law of synharmony is strictly observed, then the influence of the stress weakens. Thus, the law of synharmony separately regulates the bark of a word. In which case, the word acting together with the law of synharmony is easily pronounced, double peaks, and mutually regulate each portion. For example,

Adam – adamlar - adamlardan etc.

(a man-men-from men)

One of the peaks begins, whilst the second completes. Furthermore, in cases where the synharmony of these peaks break (and the word isn´t an aboriginal Azerbaijani word), this process is abundantly clear. For instance,

Opera, musiqi, traktor, etc.

(Opera, music, tractor) etc.

It is apparent from these examples, that both peaks have been violated. This is why neither the stress, nor the first vowel of the root of the word, can act according to this general rule. Also, this is why one can´t consider such words as native Azerbaijani words. Most probably, these words (after exercising the process of adaptation) either accept the double peaks, or new words are created in Azerbaijani. Certainly, until recent times, words like "münasibət" (attitude), and əlaqə (link), were used in Azerbaijani. Nowadays, /ilgi/ (link) is more often used because newly established words with double-peaks are obeyed.

As is known, neither German nor Slavic languages, posses such features.

17. The third structural feature of the distribution of words in narration, transformation, and roundabouts, is associated with the place of the stress.

There is no doubt that the distribution of words in a sentence depends on the theme and rheme ruling over the actual devision-relations. The function of the sentence, and the demands of the speech-conditions by words revealing the sentence, or narration, comes at the beginning. Let´s see the examples:

1. /Anar mağazadan **kitab** aldı//(Anar bought a book from the book shop).

2. /Mağazadan Anar **kitab** aldı// (It was from the shop that Anar bought a book).

3. /Anar kitabı **mağazadan** aldı// (Anar bought the book from the bookshop).

4. Mağazadan kitabı **Anar** aldı// (It was Anar who bought a book from the bookshop).

The comparison of these examples shows that the distribution in each one of them depends on the thought being told, instead of the said idea. Among them, the first and the second ones may substitue each other, but none of them can be positioned in the 3-rd or 4-th place. This is because in each of these sentences the narrated thought, as well as the word distribution obeying this narration, must be taken in association with the preceding word - and depending upon this situation, it must be explained.

In the 1st sentence, it is said Anar goes to the shop, he buys nothing, accept a book. In the second sentence, (approximately) a thought nearer to the first sentence, it is expressed this is why the first and the second sentences can be indicated as variants of the same sentences. After all, they express the same thought. However, in both cases the main problem is that it was Anar who bought a book from the bookshop, whereas in the third sentence it is expressed that Anar didn´t buy a book from anywhere else but from the shop. In the third sentence, buying a book (from the bookshop) by Anar, is strongly stressed. Interestingly, in all these sentences each sentence-stress directly falls on the word coming before the predicate. Of course, here one is deal with neutral and normal speech style[1].

From here, we can conclude that narrative and transference-stress directly falls on the word coming before the predicate.

18. The numerated facts above are features drawing attention away from any functional viewpoints. Now let us look at its separately taken strata from the inside and explain its structural lines. Firstly, one must mention that the phonological system of Azerbaijani consists of 9 vowels and 23 consonants. So, when comparing them with proper consonants and vowels from the Russion and German languages, one can come to the following generalizations.

As is apparent from this table, Azerbaijani vowels are more in number than Russian vowels but two times less than vowels in German[1]. At first look, it may seem this fewer number of vowels damages intercourse. After all, the possibilities of expression within language becomeing a great deal poorer. Yet, Azerbaijani and Russian

[1] In linguistic literature it is claimed that by artificially putting stresses on any word one expresses logical understanding. But it should not be forgotten that any change of stress in this way means goin from real speech.

1 Here we show the general lines for the all-rounded information see secton 3.

manage with 6 or 9 vowels to satisfy those who speak in these languages, while German does works with 17 vowels. That´s why inexperienced people (especialy phrase-mongers) at the same time as analyzing languages, repeatedly speak of the advantages of this or that language, while hardly praising those languages to the hilt. However, authorities know that the language of a people is (for that people) an unsubstitutable moral treasure.

Hence, praising one language highly at the comparative expense of other languages makes no moral sense at all. Quite simply, one language in comparsion with another exhibits a wide sphere of usage or not.

19. When comparing, therefore, Azerbaijani consonants with the consonants of German and Russian, one attains interesting results.

Each table making it clear that Azerbaijani has 23 consonants, compared to the German language wherein there are 23, while in the Russian language there are 37 consonants. The consonants peculiar to each of these languages in the schemes above are given in crumb lines. So, if one says, generally, that the language having fewer vowels there are more consonants or viser-versa, there is a germ of truth.

Azerbaijani language

b, p, d,t, g, k, h, ͡c
v, f, z, s, γ, x, j, ͡z
ş ʒ, h,m, n, l, r

German language

b, p, t, g, k, tʃ, tş, pf,
v, f, z, s, x, ş, j, ʃ, n,
m, n, l, p, r, η

Russian language

b, p, d, t, g, k
b´, p´, d´, f´, g´, k´,
v, f, z, s, x, j,tʃ, ʒ , ʃ
v´, f´, z´, s´, x´, tʃ´,
ʃ,ʒ´
m, n, l, r
m´, n´, l´, r´

It is important to note that issues surrounding vowels and consonants will be dealt with in further writings. Here, it is enough to give the number difference (see chapter III).

20. Grammatical features drawing one's attention in the morphological layer of the Azerbaijani language are as follows: the names have cases (nouns have 6 cases), they take plural forms (singular and plural forms), and status of belonging /kitabım, kitabın, kitabı, kitabımız, kitabınız, kitabları/ (my book, your book, his book, our books, your books, their books).

Verbs change as to the tense and time. Also, they are transitive and intransitive, exhibit transference and intransference, as well as having reflexive and comparative forms. In addition, they have moods, active and passive voice forms, and the urgative form.

Adjectives and adverbs change as to degress, pronouns change as to person and case forms, while numerals take plural forms.

21. As to syntactic structure and coorelalions, the Azerbaijani

language is associated with a group of syntactic languages, which is why in Azerbaijani the link of adjoining has been more widely spread and the link of government is relevant.

Adjoining links	Government	yaxşı oğlan yaxşı qız		yaxşı oğlanlar yaxşı qızlar	
	Agreement	Kitab Kitabdan kitabsız	oxuyuram	kitaba ona tərəf ordan	baxıram
	Adjoining links	o oxuyur mən yazıram adam gəlir it hürür		onlar oxuyurlar biz yazırıq adamlar gəlirlər itlər hürür etc	
		good boy bood girl		good boys bood girls	

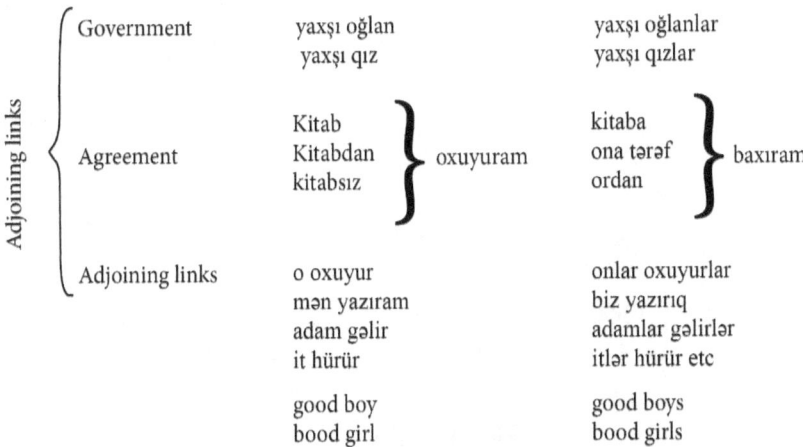

The Agreement links may often be broken:

22. In later chapters of this book, the phonetic structure of the Azerbaijani language and its phonological features are explored in greater depth. This task is undertaken to explain those means ensuring the sounding of Azerbaijani through concrete examples. Atop of this, the system of vowels and consonants of this language, its system of stresses and syllable models, including prosody and intonational, features are further contextualized.

II Chapter

PHONETIC STRUCTURE AND PHONOLOGICAL SYSTEM OF THE AZERBAIJANI LANGUAGE

II.1.THEORETICAL PROBLEMS OF AZERBAIJANI PHONETICS

The phonetic structure and the phonological establishment of the Azerbaijani language has been a topic in a number of investigations – each one differing in viewpoint. Indeed, determinations of phoneme invention, along with the discovery of paradigmatic and syntagmatic coorolations, have attracted the attention of not only linguists, but also people from other professions. Here one may especially mention A. Damirchizadeh and A. Akhundov. Never to forget, of course, native linguists such as F. Kazimov, S. Sadygov, T. Hidayatzadeh, A. Alekberov, F. Jalilov and others, who by their serious scientific explorations have greatly enriched Azerbaijani phonetics. If one then adds those authors of separately taken articles, dissertations and books, one can immediately see how well researched Azerbaijani phonetics and phonology have been[1]. As for his objective attitude

1 The existing literature on the phonetics and phonology of the Azerbaijani language have been written colligatedly by the authors of the work "Experimental phonetics. Baku, I, 1980, II, 1981" we don't indicate it here.

regarding scientific facts, A. Akhundov′s monography "The system of phonemes of the Azerbaijani language" (1973) has continually inspired specialists. The reason to this being Akhundov's statistical methoology when examining the usage (frequent or not), of phonemes and the probability of lawfulness of their appearances. As to this study, an appeal has been made to the founder of modern linguistics F. de.Saussure. Indeed, his approach to modern phonology uncovers a number of unsatisfactory considerations, especially when incautious scholars forget that in a language not only sounds exist, but also flow of sounds which are pronounced; their main attention given only to pronounciation of esolated sounds. At the same time one must say isolated sounds are not initially given. "in comparison with sounds, syllables have been given directly" (F.de Saussure, 1976, 86). Namely, "in the search of his principles – he goes on saying – if phonology gives advantage to the isolated sounds, this is contradictory to the sound mind; as soon as we come face to face with double-sided combinations, phonology remains helpless. In order to understand what is happening within the sound combinations it is necessary to create such a phonology here that a sound should be approached as mathematical equality in relation with sound combinations" (p.87). Thusly, N.S.Trubetzkoy said of no less importance is the lawfulness of phoneme combinations for the characterization of language structure (N.S.Trubetzkoy, 1960, p. 284). This points to theoretical issues raised in the works of A. Akundov, which still prove extremely valuable for Azerbaijani linguistics.

2. In Azerbaijani linguistics, those who separate phonetics from phonology try to investigate language units by using the method of double-comparison with "mutual ties". However, they don't pay necessary attention to the coarticulatory features of descrete flow in speech - as in a chain of speech, while ignoring mutual impact for

speech units. Especially, perhaps, when making generalizations respecting the means of experimental investigation methods widely applied in modern linguistics, and without which it is impossible to achieve serious scentifie successes. Their difficiencies can equally be explained by the fact that language units in speech act not in the form of isolation from one another, but appear organically linked with one another. These unit-morphemes, lexemes, etcetera (having meanings and free usage potentials in language) are the unity of adjoining two or more morphemes along a straight line.[16] This is why - while learning the phonetic structure and phonological system -phoneme combinations draw our attention in any modern research schemata.

3. The investigation of law objectivities in the phoneme-combinations by typological comparative methods has great importance for the science of linguistics. Through this approach, one can reveal genetic ties. Additionally, one can point out the self-belongingness of this or that for linguistics. As an example, in the Azerbaijani language, while two or three consonants cannot come at the head of words, in the German language this is ordinary.

All elucidating why words such as /ʃprot/ (sprot), /ʃtraf/ (fine), /ʃpris/ (stringe) etcetera are of German origin beyond any doubt.

As for law objectivities in the phoneme-combinations, this is of great importance to the sphere of application - mostly directed to practical issues of confrontative and contrastive linguistics.

When learning other languages than our mother tongue, those factors causing obstacles are discerned through the system and structural differences among languages. After all, these differences are encountered by recognizing mother tongue, while operating

---

16 In the Azerbaijani language the word with one phoneme is only /o/ (he, she,it). But in the German language / Ei/-is a one-phonemed word, which means an egg. There are also many one-phonemed words, having grammatical meaning. The suffixes of case are an example to this.

with distinctons between other language units and potential points of linguistic contact. This can be explained by the existence of self-belonging laws of adjoining betwixt each language. In other words, one can say in this confrontation of languages, not only paradigmatic differences but equally syntagmatic contrasts show themselves. For example, in the German and Azerbaijani languages, phoneme /h/ is existent. One may say their acoustic and articutalory features are also similar. Moreover, this phoneme is a pharyngal consonant. It is voiceless and constrictive - but as to usage, there are differences between them. For the usage of the /h/ phoneme in the Azerbaijani language there is no notable limitation. Indeed, it may come at the beginning, in the middle, or at the end of words. Compare in this case /həm, hökm, həkim, baha, səhər, vəhşi, şah, silah/ in English (also, a sentence, a doctor, expensive, morning, wild, shah, weapon) and so on. But in the German language, the usage of this consonant is restrictive. It cannot act as a syllabic, morpheme and as the last element of words. On the other hand, within the syllable, its coming after a vowel is impossible. Sometimes in the manifestation of phonemes (which we think resemble each other from acoustic and articulatory viewpoints), these differences are observed.[17] Yet, in the Azerbaijani language, there exists the phoneme /o/ while in Russian the phoneme /o/ (beginning with the element like (u)) acquires a difthongoid character. So stated, in the Azerbaijani language, the phoneme /o/ has no such feature. In any confrontation of the phonemes of these two languages, therefore, the

17 In applied phonology, when learning other languages than the mother tongue, two types of thoughts exist. Firstly, the idea that in learning the foregoing phonemes (having resemblance to the mother tongue) the appearing obstacles reguire more training. For example, Azerbaijanians find difficulties in learning the Russian /o/. The reason is that the Russian /o/ is diphthongoid. As to the second conception, difficulties appear in learning those phonemes not existing in the mother tongue. For example, the Russian phoneme "ц" /ts/ does not exist in Azerbaijani. That's why Azerbaijanians learn it with difficulty. However, supporters of the first idea are right because aquiring the habit of possessing phonological features is not as difficult as all that. Indeed, when learning phonemes which do not exist in Azerbaijani, a person should be very attentive.

differences appearing in linguistic literature are known as **contrasts.**

4. Contrasts appear not only in the confrontation of different languages, in the comparision of phoneme systems, but additionally in language units: including their coordination with one another. As such, the field of science studying the differences between mother tongue and the language we are learning is generally discussed under the name of **contrastive linguisties**. What is more, the science revealing resemblances together with differences is called **confrontative linguistics.**

In the 18th and 19th paragraphs of chapter 1 Russian and Azerbaijani consonants and vowels were introduced. Following this, it becomes clear from their confrontation that the Azerbaijani consonants /ə/, /g/, /ğ/ neither exist in Russian or German. Besides, the soft consonants of Russian do not exist in any other language. Whereas, the German diphthongs, /pf/, /ɔ / phonemes do not exist in Azerbaijani or Russian either. These are the contrasts emerging in any comparison between those systems. Yet, in all three languages vowel /à/ exists. In spite of the short /à/ in German, an open syllable and at the end of a word cannot arise. For the vowel /à/ in the other languages there is no such limitation. Curiously, this differentiation in the usage of this phoneme is not in the system of phonemes, but rather with the possibilities of entering such a combination. As far as resemblances are concerned, one meets them at every step. For example, there are sonants in all three languages: among the other consonants, however, it is easier to find these resemblances.

5. Let's note that the phonetic establishment and phonological systems of Azerbaijani (from the stance of methods in general linguistics, as well as theories) have not been studied at an appropriate level. One can´t consider therefore, the dimention used in any

determination of phoneme composition in this language as satisfactory. So confessed, every analysis seems one-sided or contradictory. In addition, dictionaries of orthoepia and orthophonia have not been published up until now. In which case, any results attained are based on isolated sounds, or their mechanical confrontations. Hence, from the viewpoint of modern linguistics, the prosodies and intonation of Azerbaijani have only been vaguely and superficially studied. Thence, the investigation of phonemes, along with their study within combinations (a study of the factors undergoing change from differing positions) is necessary to uncover further language trajectories. At this juncture alone, wiil it be possible to determine differences and resemblances in comparison with other languages.

In order to archieve the above-mentioned aims, it is vital for phoneme composition to be determined. In reality, moreover, in order to point out the essence of things - and their systematic attitudes to one another -these things themselves must be clear. In other words, the status of each phoneme in Azerbaijani must be deduced. This means to answer the questions, "How many phonemes are there in Azerbaijani?", or "Is this, or that. sound a phoneme, or a variant of other phonemes?" a framework must be built. Otherwise, determining the functional duties of language sounds, which later form a basis for other linguists to distinguish them as phonology - and separate them from phonetics – remains difficult (N.S.Trubetzkoy).

6. When determining the phoneme composition of a language, therefore, modern linguistic literature uses several strategies. All demanding that one expands on some of them, because the phonemes of Azerbaijani are determined by these methods:

a) **The ability of sounds to differentiate meanings in words**. As such, the works of I.A. Baudouin de Courtenay develop rubrics in this regard, which are unendingly followed by his admirers. His method contending that when kvaziomonyms confront two words (wherein vowels or consonats juxtapose), differentiation occurs on the substantial bark. Moreover, if this differentiation is associated with a difference in meaning, then that vowel or consonant needs to be considered as a different phoneme. Examples being, /at-it / (a horse-a dog), /baş-qaş/ (head-brow), /daş-döş/ (a stone- a brest)" etcetera. After all, it is known that differentiations between these words are based on the sounds (a-i, b-g, a-ö). This is why the supporters of this principle, without proof or evidence, take these vowel and consonant combinations as evidence of its efficacy.

Factually, this issue was defined by N.S.Trubetzkoy and L.Hjelmslev, who defended sets of "special rules" when determining this process. For his part, L.Hjelmslev wrote that a change made in the mode of expression ..... can make a change in the plan of meaning. So, in any plan of meaning one can speak of phoneme differentiation. Interestingly, Hjelmslev called this rubric the principle of commutation. In the case of H.S.Trubetzkoy, he too (approximately) approved of this overall framwwork. For him, two sounds can act as a phoneme only when they are members of phonological confrontation (opposition), namely they can establish kvaziomonyms. Not sufficiently differing from the Prague and Denmark Structural Linguistic Schools, therefore, the American Descriptive School explained any phoneme interdependence of sounds through the assistance of minimal parity, as /bir-pir/ (one- sanctury). A little later, American scholars - who include distribution in their work - come to the decision that only sounds in an irregular position can be taken as different phonemes. However, sounds embracing each other's position can be different variants of one another, since these sounds possess the function of completing one another.

Alongside this, the followers of American phonologists, being true to the traditions of London phoneticians (when grouping sounds according to the phonemes worked out by D. Jones), do not forget the principles of acoustic and articulatory closeness. So, in the opinion of Americans linguists, two sounds being near to each other in acoustic and articulatory features - if they take part in the distribution of completion with each other – may be approached as different phonemes of the same variants.

In the words, "kül-kəl" (ash-bufallo) [k'°] and [k′] sounds resist each other's position. But despite these sounding differentiations, there is an acoustic and articulatory nearness between them. Altough, when all said and done, they do not differentiate the meaning of these given words. This is carried out by the vowels. That′s why they are different variants of one phoneme.

The defect in this view (exposed above), is in the fact it takes mechanical sound oppositions as speaking of those sounds that differentiate meanings. Expressed so, it is surprising the linguistic status of a language unit - having no meaning - is determined by semantics outside of semantices. If things went on like this, of course, linguists would not take into their accounts that synonyms and homonyms exist. On the other hand, as has been mentioned before, what can be said about the essence of things - which is not clear to anyone? Either way, F.Veysalov (Veysalli), 1980,1990) is a source with much to offer on this topic.

b) Phonological investigations based upon İ.A. Baudouin de Courtenay's outpourings, as well as allied phonetic researches, brougt about the formation of two contradictory schools of thought. One of them is associated with the name of academican L.V.Shcherba, while the other with the name of N.F.Jakovlev. Now, if the school of Shcherba takes concrete language materials (especially in vivid speech), as a basis for research, then Jakovlev's school prefers explanations of language arising from written sources - thereby giving importance to the identity of the morpheme of a word. In fact, both of these schools use conceptual schemes surrounding morphemes. Indeed, Shcherba, in his Masters Dissertation in 1912 ("Quantiative and Qualitative features of Russian vowels"), attempts to prove the phonemity of any sound using morphological principles. For instance, in the Russian word forms "**voda**" and "**vodu**", the seperation of the sounds "a" and "u" (at the end) bear a morphological function. A task, as it were, allowing them to claim independence for phonemes thanks to the help of morphological analysis. As such, Shcherba seemed to show the unique importance of morphological principles by this. Certainly, those sounds - with the help of morphological borders - separate themselves from the speech act by means of morphemes linked with meaning (expression of grammatical subject and object).

It is more correct, no doubt, to name the morphological principle of Shcherba's school as morphologism, whilst the method of investigation proposed by Jakovlev's school is best designated as morphemematism. By discriminating between these two schools in this manner, it (nonetheless) becomes evident that drawing the word-stock into any linguistic analysis is crucial. Revealing, thereby, that Moscvites bewilderingly exclude borrowed words from general analysis. Contrarily, the school inspired by Shcherba proudly proclaims, "not a single word must be kept aside" and takes borrowed words as a simple fact of language. Clearly, it´s truth that Germans pronounce the word Xarkov (Kharcov) in conformity with the character of their language. At the beginning of this word, they use the mediolinguial constrictive voiceless sound /ç/. A sound that doesn´t act as a phoneme in the Russian language. That´s why in the pronounciation of Germans, any destinguishing phonemes enter the correlative confrontation in a **weak** position. Even though, considering it as a borrowed word, this is telling and not necessarily true. Despite this fact, however, the above word is markedly different. It has already been adapted into the language. Obviously, by phonetic standards, the laws of language reign in the majority of cases. Hence, it is hard to find a word to substitute it. And as such, one shouldn't keep any word away from investigation having branded it with the term "borrowing".

As far as the concept of "position" for the Moscovites is concerned, there is no serious innovation at work. Indeed, Shcherba frequently stressed the fact that a phoneme can reveal its independence only in an independent situation. This means consonants before vowels, and vowels in the stressed position, are more clearly pronounced: namely their qualities in these positions undergo very vague changes and sometimes no changes at all take place (for example: as in the letter "o" in the Azerbaijani language)

When speaking of these two schools, the concept of "position" for Moscovites is regarded as an all-rounded stance - appreciated as a special service to linguistics.

b) Taking the above – mentioned issues into consideration, one conjectures it necessary to deal with this problem generally. Certainly, one of the leaders of the Moscow phonological school, A.A. Reformatsky (1900-1984), doesn't call the state of usage of a phoneme a "position". Rather, this debatable viewpoint is adopted by a number of global phonologists! Be that as it may, differing from them, A.A. Reformatsky devides his position into two parts: the so-called **strong** and **weak** positions. A stance peculiar to many of the scholars inspired by him. Yet, his position is reflexive and individual. After all, it is obviously seen that while the strong position is acceptable in realization of those functions of the phoneme itself, a weak position in this respect is not suitable.

This scientist, who takes the understanding of phonemes and a discrimination of features of meaning as a firm basis, then splinters these positions into two. From this perseptive, any understanding of a strong position is regarded as one in which a phoneme acts in its capacity. Namely, it should not be dependent on position. Nonetheless, from the viewpoint of linguistic understanding, in this weak position a phoneme loses its qualities and falls under the dependence of its position. This is why it does not act in the form of variety or variations. As such, one needs to consider the highly instructive examples in Russian wherein existent pairs /mal-myal/ (мал-мял) and /myl- mil/ (мыл-мил) speak volumes.

As to A.A. Reformatsky, in the word pairs "мал- мил" (mal-myal) if one drops /m/ the consonant remains in the form "ал" (which can be considered as a short form of the word "алый" (red) as well as the word "ил" (means "лил"), wherein it is assumed there is no significant change in the sounding of the vowel. Accordingly, they are the main colourings of the vowels /a/ and /u/. Even though, in the words "мял" and "мыл" (myal,myl) - by omitting the first consonant - one may create words non-existing in Russian. Indeed, within Russian such words cannot exist. Acting from this principle, A.A. Reformatsky describes the vowels [æ] and [ы] as variations of phonemes /a / and /I / all significative of a strong position in which confrontation of the phoneme is in vigour. Clearly, alongside being different in themselves, they differentiate the meaningful units in the language. What is more, being manifestly different from them, phonemes in (significative) weak positions posses the same sounding: namely they are neither different nor differentiate others. This usually indicates itself through a closed correlative sentence. Thus, phoneme equivalent is neutralized. For example, in Russian at the end of the words, voiced consonants overlap voiceless consonants. Compare /lug/ and luk /luk/. Indeed, voiceless consonants before voiced consonants become similarized. Compare: /lug bı/ – (luq bı) and /luk bı/ – (luk bı). It may so happen that the members subjected to comparison manifest themselves in the quality of a third sound. Certainly, comparisons in Russian like "gol" (goal) (in football) are said as "kol". Contrariwise, in the unstressed syllable, (before stressed and after stressed syllables) it is /_ л _/, but (in the second unstressed syllable) it is pronounced as /_ ə_/ . Simply compare then, (sлma pлimala sлma) – (I fished the sturgeon myself) – as it is spoken in the name of a woman.

As to the Moscow school of linguistics, significative strong or weak positions do not refer to an individually taken phoneme. Instead, they refer to the comparison of more than two phonemes, which then manifest themselves in strong positions, although in weak positions they are neutralized in general variants.

In fact, the position of "neutralization" was first mentioned by N.S.Trubetzkoy himself. A term denoting the distinction of phonemes entering correlative confrontation in a weak position. Voiced and voiceless consonants of such confrontations, in this respect, don't differentiate at the end of words - and for this reason words in German tend to concentrate on both features within themselves. Hence, N.S.Trubetzkoy labelled the phonological status of a consonant taking part in this neutralization as an archiphoneme. Later on, the Moscovites called it a "mixed phoneme", or "hypophoneme". In some sources, the sounds used are addressed as a "line of phonemes".

Intriguingly, Moscovite versions and colourings are not associated with meanings ….. and that's why ordinary speakers of the language can't guess at its depths. Atop of which, variants being connected with meaning aid the creation of homophones.

Of course, it is impossible to agree with these views, because each sound in fact represents a certain phoneme - and in concrete speech acts as its manifestation.

c) N.S.Trubetzkoy in order to prove his views on phonemes of sounds indicated 4 rules:

1) In Language, two sounds occuring within one and the same environment (without distinguisting their intellectual meaning), can be substituted. In this sense, they are the facultative variants of one phoneme. For example, in German (r) and (R) sounds indicate this point. The first one is a forelingual consonant, although the second one is a uvula consonant. In other words, a sound that can easily be used instead of the other (also, the word does not lose its self-belongingness). Compare, [fy: ren] and [fu: Ren] etcetera. Here one can´t agree with Trubetzkoy, because the same person doesn´t use both of them in his speech. Indeed, one gives advantage to one of them, but not the other. Stated so, within one language - in different stylistic shades (and depending upon society, dialect and culture), phoneme variation shows itself. For instance, one hears in the speech of the older generation: / yaxşı bir yemək yeyək/ (let,s eat with appétite), /qazzı-qazı danışmaq/ (speak with pathos), /əəəla cavab/ (a goood answer), /nəticələri əlan edirik/ (declare the results) and so on. Besides this, in the language of individually taken persons, if one adds up some patalogical errors, one can create a wide prospect of facullative shades. Some people, after all, pronounce /ş / with a fizzing sound and /s / with a hissing sound.

2) Without changing meaning, or damaging their identity, if

two words occur in the same position (yet can´t be substituted with one another), they must be understood as a phonetic manifestation of two different phonemes. In fact, in the fifth paragraph of this chapter, the essence of such a phenomena is uncovered. For the time being, however, one or two illustrations will suffice. Compare: in german /Lippe/ – (lips), /Lappe/ – (duster), with the Russian /dom/ (haus) – /tot/(that one), and the Azerbaijani /diş / (dent) – /daş/ (stone) etcetera.

3. Two sounds having articulatory and acoustic nearness - even if never appearing within the same phonetic environment - must be taken as combinatory variants of one phoneme. In the Korean language (at the end of a word), neither the sound [r] not [s] occurs. However, in this position [l] they act, since [r] being nearer to the sound [l] they perform as a variant of one phoneme. Yet, in Russian, consonant "ö" and the "ä" vowel come between the soft consonants, whereas "o" and "a" are not used in this position. That´s why, from the phonological viewpoint, the "ö" and "o" vowels act as variants of one phoneme. Although, "ä" and "a" function as the variants of other phonemes. Here the crucial roleplays have their acoustic and articulatory nearness, along with the ability to substitute one another. Hence, the sounds coming in the same position, as well as the sound which can´t (possibly) come in the same position, can act in combinatory variants of the same phoneme therein. Phrased differently, when they are able to establish phonological oppositions. For example, in the Japanese language, the sound "d" comes at the beginning of a word, but the sound "p" is never used in this position. Thus, it is possible to approach them as variants of one phoneme. All meanng, they are the only voiced backlingual consonants with such a resemblance to each other that the features make them different from any other phonemes.

4) In spite of two sounds more or less meeting the reguirements

of the third rule, it is still impossible to describe them as variants of one phoneme. Especially if they follow each other as memebers of a one sound combination. Indeed, in a position wherein two sounds occur without the accompaniment of the other, it is impossible to consider them as variants of one phoneme. For instance, in English, [r] comes only before a vowel, yet [æ] comes only before the consonants. Moreover, [r] is a non-explosive consonant, whereas [ə] - being pronounced with an exclusively non-shaded expression (and with the opening of the mouth in an uncertain form), might be considered as the combinatory variant of one phoneme. However, this is impossible, due to the fact letters in "profession" [prəfeʃn] [r] and [e] follow each other, while in other words like perfection [pəfekʃn] only one of them, "ə", is acting.

7) Contrastingly, phoneme composition in Azerbaijani is determined by the method of work within the pairs, along with sound position. This is why Azerbaijani phonologist, F. A. Kazimov (1925-1989), argued Azerbaijani vowels (in a strong position) take to the root of a word (F. Kazimov, 1952, 295). For his part, A. A. Akhundov (specifying Kazimov's claim), shows that vowels in a strong position allow the first syllable of a word-root to arise. He also gives advantage to minimal pairs. As we may read, "In the Azerbaijani language too - as it is in the other languages, in order to determine the vowel phoneme, we use qvazihomonyms (words discriminated from one another by minimal sound shade- F. V)". Namely, words only differing by one vowel are chosen and then opposed. At this point, such vowels are considered as different phonemes. However, if one doesn´t attain different words, these vowels are not actually different phonemes. Instead, they are "artificially" designated different phonemes, or considered different variants of the same phoneme (Akhundov, 1973,

46). Here, the main idea is an association of phonetic differentiations with the differentiations of meaning. Besides, it must be remembered suffixes are not used as minimal pairities. In which case, this method may "belong" to those words differing from one another respecting one vowel, or one consonant. Thusly, in phoneme combinations (and in diphthongs and affricats), the borders of phonemes are determined by a "belonging" of their parts to different constituent elements of the overall ensable (N.S.Trubetzkoy, 1960, 63).

As far as any determination of independence with consonants is concerned, Kazimov conciders the consonant in a word-root as strong, but a consonant used in the suffixes as weak (F.Kazimov, 1958, 49). This being the case, A. Akhundov contends a strong position is the position, which comes before a vowel (A.Akhundov, 1973, 46). Furthermore, he exclaims the phonemity of consonants coming side-by side needs to be determined by their "belonging" to the same morpheme, or to different morphemes.

8) Radical scholars, however, consider the methods enumerated above as giving insufficient grounds for the determination of phoneme composition in any language. Before everything else, one must mention that work with kvazihomonyms demands a certain imagination regarding the phoneme composition of these words. Really, if one associates the distinction between words with the sounds /a/ and /i/ , vowels in the words /daş/ (a stone) and /diş/ (tooth) this merely means one is relying on associative psychology, while happening to know their differences beforehand. Assuredly, those who speak of an association of meanings through the participation of vowels seem to have forgotten principles of freedom and conditionality respecting language signs.

As for the principle containing the main essence of F.de Saussure´s languistic instruction, there isn't a direct connection between names and the meanings, which they express. On the contrary, words like /daş/ (stone) and /dish/ (tooth), are notions basically differing from each other. What is more, this distinction derives from their inner ontological distinction. It´s true, of course, that their differentiations from each other arises before our eyes. Although, they might not differentiate as distinctly as in language. That´s why it´s enought to set hononyms as an example. After all, don´t polysemantic words in their phoneme compositions differ from one another? Compare, /ayaq/ (foot), /stolun ayağı/ (the foot of the table), /adamın ayağı/ (the foot of a person), /heyvanın ayağı/ (the foot of an animal) etcetera. As one may see, it not always necessary to look for differentiations in every language-notion. For this reason context and other means exist. So, relying on these desciptions, one can´t accept the claim that phonemes - as units differentiating meanings – are existential. Herein a strange logic evolves. All accept, surely, that separately-taken phonemes do not express any meaning. Indeed, the majority of scholars accept this. Therefore, a question emegers, "How it is meaningless units are taken together with meanings?" At the end of the day, it is an illusion to say the meaning of the word /daş/ (a stone) has taken meaning from the phoneme /d+a+ş/. Those who suppose meaning-distinctions of phonemes in the words /bir/ (one) and /pir/ (sanctury) do not associate them with phonemes themselves, but rather identify them with differential features (as voicelessness and voicelness). So, it is a recurrent problem among scholars who contend that phoneme and differential features (while being concentrated in one phoneme, that the phoneme is a unit standing above them), differentiates words and word forms. Sometimes, they can be equal to one-another regarding function, yet, as to the structure, they belong to quite different levels.

Thus, differentiations between words being closer to one another (in phonetic features) emerge out of a serious concern. Indeed, can any approach to the words as /pul-mul/, /ʃey-mey/, /gır-mız/ reveal concepts surrounding kvazihomonyms? Well, at least it is clear that the words coming on the second side of such constructions do not possess any lexical meaning. Therefore, if one approaches them from a purely phonetic viewpoint, one can see that together with those consonants on the first side, those which are found on the second side are the consonants creating such an utter contrast. But in spite of this, one must not take these words as words having independent meanings - though if one takes them in the separated form from the construction, both of the words "mey" and "mız" act as independent words. Hence, the above mentioned words give us grounds to approach them as **kvazihomonyms.**

Nə zaman? (when), nə et - what to do	İsmin yönlük halında (in Dat.case of noun) qoşma (post position)
Bəzən(sometimes) bəzən(adorn up)	ilə (in a year) ilə (with)
Həmişə-(always) geyin (dress)	günə- (in a day) kimi (as)
Hərdən(seldom) daran (comb)	aya (in a month) qədər (till)

The most difficult feature of quazihomonyms is that most of the examples taken as minimal pairs do not belong to the same semantic group. It is for this reason that their quazihomonity causes such great doubt. Therefore, lets examine the following examples.

Of course, it is impossible to transfer the words noted above from one column into the other, i.e as they enter separately taken paradigms, their syntagmatics preserve their freedom and independence. So to list, or correlate, the above-mentioned words is not correct at all. Together with entering different word groups, they also carry out different syntactic functions. Thence, to differentiate them, both a wide surrounding and text are required. So understood, it is impossible for phoneme variants to substitute each other within one and the same word. In Russian for instance, "e" and "э" do not act as variants to each other. Even though, when one is used instead of the other, the word preserves its meaning. Simply, it is impossible for them to be used in one and the same word. However, to determine words following one another by syllable dimention is fraught with serious difficulties - each syllable being, in itself, a phonetic unit that can´t be taken as a basis for being phonologically independent. In Azerbaijani, to really determine the syllable borders of "doğrudan"(reəly), "bicaq"(knaif), "pişik"(kat) – **(doghrdan, p´cax, p´sik)** is far from easy.. In ordinary speech, after all, the vowel existing in the first or second syllable suffers serious reduction - maybe even breaking and falling from the chain of speech. In this case, how can a syllable border help us?

In order to determine the phonological independence of sounds, the most reliable measure is morphological dimention.

When speaking about the position of a unit - wherein its phonological status is not clear - it is inappropriate to enforce scientific categories. Analogously, a person must be known in order for others to speak about his position in the society. This becomes possible, moreover, if such a position exists in the abstract mind in the form of a model. Hence, before proving the position of a sound, the phonemity of the sound itself needs to be established. Only then can the features which a phoneme exhibits be explained. And as such, the explicative method of investigation, and its advantages, are manifestly before our eyes.

Taking the above mentioned features as a basis from which to prove whether a sound is a phoneme or not, is debatable. Either way, its morphological function demands examination. A mammoth task also determining the phoneme composition of the Azerbaijani language. By this determination of phoneme composition, of course, the same principle shall be explored as a potential universal measure.

9) In the book "Modern Azerbaijani language" (1978) it is said there are 9 vowels and 24 consonants in this tongue. As a calculation, these figures were evidently reached without proof and, apparently, this thesis is based on the work of a retired scholar, A.Demirchizadeh. However, those morphological dimentions ensuring the independence of Azerbaijani phonemes, suggest a number of hypotheses. First of all, the problems of speech sounds, as well as the ability to separate them from a speech chain - through the help of morphological borders - enters discussion. Certainly, acoustic physics and experimental phonetics demonstrated long ago that those units considered inseperable from the entire speech chain (either by acoustic, or by means of articulatory criteria) cannot actually be divided in this manner. Indeed, the only means to splinter the speech chain being linguistic dimention. Namely, only with the help of a morphological border can one separate this or that sound from the flow of speech. In order to prove this contention, let's consult these examples. On the left-hand side, indicated inseperable

words are listed, while on the right hand side units, which have become seperated from morphological compositions are indicated. In other words, those remaining on the right side of the segment units.
Compare

/gala/ (tower,wall)	gal/a (I wish he stayed) mood expressing
/ajı/ (a bear)	/aj/i/ (moon) the case form (I see the moon)
/o/ (he, third person singular)	/o/ as a separate word "he"
/dolu/ (hail)	/dol/u (full of a pail)
belə (demonstrative pronoun)	/bel/ə/(to the spade) case form
/iti/ (blunt)	/it/i/ case form of the word (dog)
/kürü/ (caviar)	/Kür/ü/ case form of the river /Kur/
/dosab/ (sweet extract prepared from grapes)	/dol/ab/ (winding round one´s finger)
/guyrug/ (tale of horse, dog etc.)	/gorug/ (preservation)
/zoghal/ (corneal)	/udz/al/ (grow higher)
/bəzək/ (a type of bird)	/bəzə/k/ (decoration)
/ucal/ (be higher)	/ucal/t/ (make him higher, transitive form)
/jazır/ (3. Person singular) he writes	/jaz(m)ır/ (the negation of the verb write) does't write
/inan/ (believe)	/ana/n/ (your mother)
/imam/ (religious rank)	/inam/ (belief)
/ana/ (mother)	/ana/sı/ (his,her mother)
/yaşamag/ (to live)	/yaşa/t/mag/ (to make one live)
/tıxamag/ (to peg)	/tıxa/c/ (a peg)
/tutmag/ (to catch)	/tuta/g/ (a holder)
/gucaglamag/ (to embrace)	/gucagla/ş/mag/ (to embrace mutually)

/gaynamag/ (to boil)	/gajna/r/ (boiling)
/oxumag/(to read)	/oxu /j/ur/ (he reads)

One can increase the number of examples easily. Yet, the essence of this working principle can´t be made pursuasive by these illustrations alone. Clearly, in the examples given on the left hand side, it is impossible to separate the word composition of this or that sound. Regardless, those words given on the right hand side (by the help of morphological boundaries) could easily achieve this goal. It´s true, of course, that from the word "ajı" (a bear) which means a wild animal, it is impossible to separate any sound by morphological means. Equally, the word /maj aj/ı/ (May, month) doesn´t create any difficulty when separating the last vowel. As such, the vowel /I / if separately – expresses a grammatical meaning. It indicates the possessive case of nouns. At the same time, this vowel is not "belonged" by this word, but has a "family" throughout Azerbaijani nouns. Hence, it´s unity with this meaning gives it a certain independence. Interestingly, the same sound having gained independence in this system of language - getting its status from phonological features - can preserve and keep its acoustic and articulatory nearness by the realization of forms in all other cases. Basically, the vowel /ı/ in a speech act (as an independent phoneme) seperates itself through the help of these aforementioned morphological means from speech flow. Though it is "impossible", this phonemes achieves functional "wholeness", while its phonological load is understood as /ı/ and stands in opposition to the other sounds of the language. From these functional features words used as separators in the terms /ayı/ (bear) and /maı aı/ı (may moonth), reveal the last vowel used never acts as a different phoneme. Truly speaking, in Azerbaijani it is impossible to find such words in which their sound bark is differentiated just with this vowel. As Acad. L.V.Shcherba wrote: "Each phoneme is determined by the differentation of the phonemes of other languages. By this all the phonemes of every language create a monosystem of confrontation in which each member is determined both by individually-taken phonemes and by different systems of confrontations between their different groups" (L.V.Shcherba, 1937, p. 17). So, by means of morphological dimention we show the seperation of the vowels /a, ə, i, u, ı) from the speech chain and by this one may determine their level of independence. As far as the vowel /o/ is spoken of, one must say its meaning with the functional link is before our eyes. Certainly, in Azerbaijani, this phoneme acts as a word. In order, therefore, to prove that this phoneme is an inseperable discreet unit, it is enough to confront the vowels which one has separated by the morphological means above. There is not a word in the Azerbaijani language, in which from the beginning, to the middle or from the end, the vowels mentioned can pass such a morphological boundary.

10) Only the vowels /ö/ and /e/ (acting according to these morphological principles) cannot be separated from the act of speech. In the first place, this is explaned by the fact that the vowels /ö/ and /e/ can´t perform as word forming suffixes. Herein belongs the vowel /o/ too. None of these three vowels, neither from the right, nor from the left, can be separated as to the morphological boundary. So, what s to be done? Before answering this question, one feels the necessity to get closely acquainted with the problem and then apply scientific materials. Indeed, G.P. Melnikov - who studied vocalism and synharmonism, conjectures that any problems inside Turkic languages are often associated with these very issues. Thus, in Azerbaijani (standard

language) - among the affixes from the open vowels. where only /a/ and /ə/ occur - open sounds pronounced by ones lips participate. For narrow vowels, there is no such restriction. Put in other words, /ı, i, u, ü/ have been widely represented by affixes (F.A.Kazimov, 1954, 96: G.P.Melnikov, 1962, 53). In order to prove this idea Melnikov presents some facts.

In Turkic languages, synharmonism serves as the phonetic establishment of a word. That´s why in the differentiation of a word, it plays a subsidery role. After all, it could be said that an antropophonic hiearchy exists, whereby the realization of possibilities in language functions - along with the most important substances (antropophonemic features), are used for functinal confrontations. For differetiations of the vowels, language still uses a number of different acoustic oppositions. However, the remaning phonetic means are directed to ensure synharmonic functions. From such a stance, G.P.Melnikov seems to advocate a very confused conclusion, saying that the usage of phonemes /a/ and /ə/ is because the suffixes (/do, dö/) have been mixed up in the language. In other words, for G.P.Melnikov, if there were suffixes (/do-dö/), then a confusion in meaning might arise (G.P.Melnikov, 1965). As such, one suspects G.P.Melnikov puts forth a doubtful problem. Clearly, there is one reason why (/do-dö/) suffixes can´t be use, while these forms of the vowels can´t come at the end of the final syllables. But suffixes, as is known, join the root of words. To leave aside the law regarding a restriction of distribution and to run after substance, means to divert ones attention from the problem. Oddly, G.P.Melnikov - who considers "darkness"(qaranlıq) and (wideness) (enlilik) a firm acoustic feature - then tries to explain his point through the existence of contrasts. As for the pair /a-ə/ and /a-e/ only the first term is used as an /a-e/ pair mixes up the suffixes.

For example, /-de/ may mix with its eqvivalent /-di/. In accordance with this, one should say this explanation isn’t satisfactory. When all said and done, at the lower levels of language (when the distingiushing features are not strict enough) this function is carried out by other functions. For instance, in German - within the middle gender - the nominative case, as well as the possessive, are virtually the same. Certainly, Germans never mix those forms because both the text and the environment don´t give any possiblity of doing this. Also, in Azerbaijani, even if distinguishing suffixes were impossible, text and environment would not let them become confused.

In Azerbaijani, the vowel /ı/ comes at the head of a word. An event G.P.Melnikov tries to explain by saying the vowel /i/ is sufficiently different from acoustic and articulatory viewpoints. In fact, this is due to the work of distribution. Another way to explore things, therefore, is to stress that those phonemes unable to separate from the flow of speech with the help of morphological dimentions appears a more fruitful avenue for research.

Let´s take the verb root /et/ (do). Here it is a fact that the vowel /e/ cannot seperate from the_consonant /t/. Additionally, let us take the verb mentioned above as an example. Now, the analysis of the morphological structure of the word shows that the consonant /t/ (on both sides) is separated by morphological boundaries. Gaining independence this way, the same consonant in the word /et/ - and in other words like /t/ - can separate with the help of the same boundary. As such, it seems to have preserved and safeguarded its independence. Its independent consonant /t/ in all other cases - even if it is linked with meaning - neither by grammatical nor lexical means, has the right to leave the speech chain. So, in the words /et/ and /öt/ the independence of the consonant is admitted, namely in these words ability to be seperated from /e/ and /ö/. In linguistic literature this is called **division with remainder principe** (L.L.Bulanin, 1970).

11) These are clear examples of the separation of consonants from the speech chain with the help of morphological bounderies. Hence, it becomes obvious that from the consonants /n, m, r, j, l, s, t, dj, g, gh, ş, b, k/ in Azerbaijani words (both sides seperating into morphological bounderies) each unit bears grammatical meaning. Nevertheless, it´s difficult to show the independence of the following consonants, since /z, p, tş, zj, d, v, f, h, x, kh/ (acting according to the principle of division with a remainder) prove they can also be seperated in such words as /atş, və, dəf, göl, həm, az, lap, lax, gızj, tak) (hungry,and,a drum,lake,also,little,just,spoiled,paralized,only etc).

As far as the words /əmmək/ (to suck), /illik/ (yearly), /əlli/ (with hand) etcetera are concerned, the consonants used in them can´t be taken as long consonants. This is because a morphological boundary passes between them. Compare: /əl-li/ (with hand): /boksçu bir əlli vuruşurdu/-(a boxer fought with one hand), /əmmək/ (to suck): /ana uşağı əmizdirir/ – (mother makes the child suck); / illik/ (yearly) : / bir illik dana əti daha dadlı olur? – (The meat of a one year calf is tastier) and so on. Indeed, Azerbaijani words such as /saat/ (a watch), /maaş/ (wage), /maarif/ (enlightment), /amma/ (but), /əlli/ (fifty), / səkkiz/ (eight), /baqqal/ (grocery), /saqqal/ – (beard) take the usage of homogenic grafems to indicate the usage of long vowels: or the usage of consonant phonemes in them to mean they fall under the influence of writing. In reality, words like this prove the length or shortness of the vowel reguiring serious investigation. But here one is satisfied with the fact that in vivid speach they are pronounced in long variants. To gather this, it is enough to hear a speaker attentively. In real speech, after all, one does not hear /a:/, /l:/, /k:/, /m:/, /g:/ etcetera.

Undoubtedly, nobody in ordinary speech pronounces /ma:ʃ, am:a/. So, taking the existience of minimal pairs, those who tried to prove they were long varients would like to say /sa:t-sat/, /mə:dəni- mədəni/ even though such confrontations of different language levels would not bear close examination. In order to show the length of a vowel /u:/ they would need to use confrontations of words like /oxumur// or oxumu:r?. But it is a well-known problem that in the second case the lenght of a vowel derives from the reguirement of intonation within an interrogative sentence. Namely, to establish the lenght of the vowel used, one would need to raise an introgative question in order to discriminate its phonetic features. But these are linguistic phonomena of diffferent levels; one serves to express the sentence, while the other serves to express the communicative type of interrogative sentence. Thus in modern Azerbaijani (from the viewpoint of pronounciation), the existence of long phonemes is under suspicion.

12) Among the phonetic structure of Azerbaijani and the means surrounding its phonological system, - and among its language units - the law of synharmony, stress and intonation, determination of their role in phoneme combinations, as well as syllable establishment, syntagm and stress, which organically move together with word order in sentences. Moreover, word, syntagmatic and sentence differences in the distribution of intonational features (depending on the communicative type of sentence), inculding the creation of systematization in narration, together with segment units, are the features that occupy important roles in phonetic and phonological investigations during the latest periods.

II.2.PHONETICS OF THE AZERBAIJANI LANGUAGE. ITS OBJECT, SUBJECT, AIMS AND DUTIES

The science studying the substantial features of communication - sounding, hearing, and understanding: features in complexity, although not linked with each other from initial observations of a language system - is called phonetics. Depending on the aims and duties of this study, it is possible to learn about the substantial existence of communication from different perspectives: history (here, the transformation of language as a means of communication in this or that stage of history, and the changes taking place in its phonetic structure must be recorded), historical-comparative (changes taking place in the historical phonetic establishment, being either investigaled in different time functions, or compared with the past period of either relative or non relative languages), synchrone (a way learning the phonetic establishment of phonetics from the viewpoint of one period of time, both yesterday and today), applied (the place of phonetics in the explorations directed to improving life conditions of a people - together with other fields of science such as economics, culture, communication, literature, pedagogics, technigues, kibernetics), along with those examinations undertaking the role of confrontative and contrastive researches into consideration in language learning, are all aspects of this pursuit. On one hand, it is possible to take such different features separately: acoustic (at this time the acoustic nature of what is said and what is heard is in a leading position), articulatory (physiological mechanism of what is said, or what is heard), functional (the place in a language system respecting the system of units which is said or heard: their duty, their attitudes to other language units and other issues) and academically unveil them. Yet, no matter what these differences are, in the centre of all phonetic investications is the means of the language itself: its features of unification, the creation of these means of communication (word, sentence, intonation etcetera) each awaiting investigation/ What is more, prosody and features of intonation still demand research. Besides this, phonetics may be considered the conformity between writing and speech[18] along with the contradictions between them.

2. The object of this science of phonetics is vivid speaking and sound speech. We learn vivid language by means of objective (apparatus – tape-recorders, ossillography, kinoroentken, spectrography syntezator and analizator) and subjective (a scholars ears, generalizations) aids. Equally, by inquiring into the speech of the people as a language collective. Furthermore, one discovers the subject of phonetics – as the substantial existence of intercourse, its phonological system and the objective laws of distribution of the units establishing them. One more thing is worth mentioning, speech, being a many-branched process, can be the object of investigation in a number of sciences. So confessed, it can be the object of investigation in physiology (to learn the movements of hearing and speaking organs of the speaker and the hearer, to study the general activity of the human organism), acouctics (investigation of acoustic nature of what has been said or heard), psychology (the state of communication in the psychological activity of a person), linguistics (function of language units, their mutual coordination, their distinctions) and speech in other, artisitc, fields.

18 When we say "speech" we take into consideration the notion of "oral speech".

3) The fact that language is the most important means of intercourse implies that the mother tongue of a people can be arranged into language units able to create language blocks in conformity with context and speech conditions: and that they should be able to use these principles of their distribution correctly. By this statement, alongside the phonetic attitudes making obstacles in the choice of a phoneme, morphological, semantic, and syntactic relations, it is apparent supplimentary issues should equally be considered. Each proving that speech – as well as the language it is organially associated with – are in real terms inseperable. Substantially, this also means any reflection of the language units of speech, the articulalion of sounds systematically by a speaker, and hearingl, as well as understanding what has been said by a listener, are intricately interconnected. If this were not the case, then language could not exist as a means of intercourse. Either in a natural forms like Greek, Latin, German, English or artificial ones such as Volapyc, Ideo, and Esperanto.

4) After F. de Saussure, language scientists approached communication as a system of signs. But signs in essence - are understood by different organs of sense in differing ways. Hence, the science dealing with signs is called semiotics. Unsurprisingly, supporters of Saussure contend the sign system of a language includes lingiustics along with semiotics. Although, one must not forget that language signs are different from the signs surrounding us. They consist, in fact, of signs established by the sounds which people can pronounce, hear, and understand. Furthermore, these written signs have been compiled by individual scribes compelled through necessity to send messages to distant places during the historical stages of society.

Any compiling of an alphabet, therefore, is one of the most important problems standing before phoneticians. An alphabet, after all, is only considered complete when it is able to reflect the phonetic establishment of a language correctly. Now, the equivalent of a phoneme in writing is called grapheme. The ideal being that writing possesses the graphic equivalent of each phoneme. In this way, people, in order to establish alphabets, have gone through intense language processes. As a case in point, Azerbaijani even used runes (old forms of grapheme) existing in old Turkic languages at various stages. Nonetheless, the greatest written source "Kitabi Dədə Qorqud"(The Book of Father Gorgud) has reached us in the Arabic alphabet. After the religion of Islam made Turk's obey its edicts, this ideology made these cultures accept their alphabet too. Consequently, Turks were forcibly made to accept the Arabic alphabet, which from a phonetical viewpoint does not fit Azerbaijani. Hence, the enlighted, educated inteligensia of Azerbaijan have repeatedly spoken about this matter. Indeed, in 1929, Azerbaijani's transfered from the Arabic alphabet to the Latin one - which seemed to be more suitable to native alphabetical systems. Unfortunalely, however, this did not last long. So, after 1939, Azerbaijani's were obliged to accept a half Latin and half Cyrilic alphabet. A good move, nevertheless, in that this transfer to a quasi-Latin script reflected favourable social conditions.

5) Conditionality is one of the most important features of language. After all, there is no direct connection between what is expressed and the method of expression (words created by the imitation of sounds are an exception). For example, the word /ot/ (grass) in Azerbaijani, and /o/ and /t/ in their sound systamatization have nothing to do with the notions they express. However, it might so happen that the sound systematization could also be established by sound combinations as in /otş/, /oş/, /og/ etc.

But as a result of historical development, the word stating the notion /ot/ (grass) has been formulated from the phoneme systematization of /o/ and /t/, while in modern usage its indication is in another form of Azerbaijani. One not considered satisfactory by all of its speakers. So, if there is little association between the word and the notion it expresses (from the very establishment of this language), then the accurate expression of this notion as an accepted word is vital. Moreover, this **conditionality** and **arbitarity** belong to most words in a language. Tellingly. the second feature of these signs is their **descreteness. In other words,** language signs are largely inseparable from even splintered sounds. Here one speaks of language behaving in units at a certain level of establishment. For instance, the word /ot/ (grass) neither from a lexical, nor from a morphological stance, can be divided into a smaller segment than itself. Needless to say, from a phonolgical viewpoint this word is the systematization of the phonemes /o/ and /t/ -and can be (theoretically) divided. Here one notices a feature pecular to these signs, which is associated with their being **unilatiral** and **bilateral.** Hence, morphemes and lexemes are bilateral - in that they have both an expresser at the same time as belonging to something expressed. Thusly, in the word /ot/ alongside expressing a plant growing in a meadow, there is a /o + t/ systematization of sounds expressing this plant. Yet, neither /o/, nor /t/ can be explained in this way. As in all the other phonetic units, its initial function is to discriminate between words and word-forms. Overall, this is enough for them to be discerned in full. In which case, the most important tasks standing before phonetics is to investigate the characteric-features of a language, to determine their place among other languages, and to point out those factors discriminating such sounds. Undoubtedly, such a study of the nature and function of phonetic units shouldn´t be forgetten. However, together with this enterprize it must equally be recalled that phonetics studies delve into the meaning of soundings, as well as the expression of that sounding. At the end of the day, everything in a language serves the expression of meaning. Besides this, phonetics investigates objective laws of sounding and hearing of these meaningful units.

III. 3. THE CHARACTERIZATION OF PHONETIC UNITS

1)Phonetic structure in Azerbaijani reflects its phonetic prospect. It was even argued that all the phonetic units in the phonological system must have phonetic implications. Namely, a substantial side, wherein they can be discerned so as to be discriminated from others. Certainly, on the basis of inner rules and laws of language, they contacted with each other, thereby creating a chain-like systematization in the manner already mentioned. However, sounds have no individual meaning at all on a phonological level. Indeed, they are abstractions and generalized in the phonemes representing them. Regardless, classic phonetics identifies phonemes with specific sounds. Indeed, each phoneme was associated with a sound and vice versa. Yet, following the creation of phonology, tendencies to determine sounds as existing entities having their physical pecularities, (envisaging phonemes as functional units manifesting in them) were strengthened.

Of course, if one approaches any phoneme individually, one cannot determine its entire meaning. Pointedly, in the word /ot/ (grass) neither the vowel /o/ nor the consonant /t/ has any meaning if taken separately. Clearly, they have no direct connection with the notion of / ot/ (grass). Nevertheless, discerning this word with /at, it ət/ (a horse, a dog, meat) remains very important. Otherwise there will be communal confusion. Herein, the self-beloningness of phonetic units manifesting themselves in order to be discriminated - and to discriminate - claims attention. It could be aid, perhaps, that the inner establishment of a language may pictured in modern parlance as a multi-storied building. The lower layer of this construction establishing the phonetic structure, while the upper storey allows a syntactic layer to be built. Phonetic structural units, therefore, serve the establishment and creation of the other levels. So, phonetic units in the sound bark of the upper layers often repeat, admittedly, even though they never lose their independence. For example, /ata/, /atalar/, /atalardan/, (father, fathers, from fathers). Truly, it may happen that one phonetic unit, or morhpeme, can express a word, or even a sentence. Let´s compare phoneme /o/ as opposed to other vowels, although at the same time /o/ is a morpheme (as a personal pronoun in the third person singular), as a word /mən, sən, o/ (I, you, he) in the paradigm. It is even a sentence in answer to the question ?gələn kimdir? (who is coming?) – /o/ (he). Contrarily then, its functionality is manfold.

Phoneme systematization by establishing units in the upper layer creates the possibility of discrimination. This is obvious by the way usage-distinction of such phoneme systematization additionally plays an important role. In the Azerbaijani language /d/, /ə/, /n/ phonemes are distributed in this manner to manifest constructons like (dən) (grain), which are then employed as a morpheme, a suffix /dan-dən/, and even as a food product wherein /dən, duz, düyü/ (grain, salt, rice) is used.

No doubt, the distributions of these phonemes in the forms of / dnə, ədn, ndə/ can´t establish a whole word. Indeed, from all three forms not a single word is genereated. However, in English the word "ənd" is possible. Moreover, as part of an objective law in phoneme combinations. In themselves, phonetic layers have got specific connections with other layers, which in modern linguistics are called a hierarchic attitudes. Namely, there exists an attitude of dependence on one another. All meaning that phonetic units - in order to communicate - must must hold commerce with units of upper layers. The rule being these upper layers must consist of at least one phonetic unit, otherwise communication can´t take place. And tellingly, from the phonetical point of view, there can´t be any communication expressed at zero: or having non-substantial existence. Now, let´s apply the following instances in order to see how phonetic units show themselves in the hiearchic attitude related to other layers of language: /Türkün dili hünər dilidir// (The Turkic language is a language of courage).

Layers of structure	**Units**
Syntactic level	1 sentence
Lexic level	3 words (one is repeated)
Morphological level	7 morpheme (one is repeated)
Phonological level	10 phoneme (4 of them are repeated:/r/ –three times, /i/ 5 times, /n 2 times)

One must mention that for language bearers having no linguistic preparation, the smallest unit is a word. In themselves, they do not choose units smaller than words and in fact are indifferent to them.

2) The phonetic units considered above are called segment units. As such, they are distributed one after another along a straight line as descreet units. Assuredly, once they are put in opposition to the units spread along this straight line they are known as a supersegment. Putting them, in other words, in a chain of speech even though supersegment units have no place in the flow of speech, since as a whole they establish prosody and mould intonation in the language units to which they belong. It is for this reason that second units

cannot act in an isolated form. Rather, they need a bearing, which is the distribution of segment units. In the expression, (Türkün dili) (the language of the Turk) /t, ü, r, k, n, n, d, l/ phonemes making links of different kinds have created this systematization. In their phoneme system, repetition takes place in a manner one can show:

/t/, /ü /, /r/, /k/, /ü /, /n/, /d/, /i/, /l/

Firstly, the paradigmatic and syntagmatic analysis of this expression shows that in Azerbaijani 8 phonemes (numerated above) have been used by the speaker. However, from them only /i/ has been repeated three times, while the rest of the phonemes have been chosen once. Needless to say, this distribution, in itself, can´t establish that expression. After all, for that supersegment means ensuring their syntagmatic unity-prosody and intonation. Yet, that stress which is the constituent part of intonation becomes a more active process. If, therefore, we complete the expression and say /Türkün dili hünər dilidir// (The language of the Turk is the language of courage), then we shall see that among them there is a pause. Furthermore, a pause dividing speech into smaller phonetic units-syntagms. But sentence stress together with intonation of the syntagms as /türkün dili/ and / hünər dilidir/ transforing them into a whole also creates a sentence being a means of intercourse. Indeed, a pause makes speech inteligible and fluent, depending upon the place and function sentences of a different lenght embody.

III.4.CONTRADICTIONS BETWEEN WRITING AND SPEECH.

1) Though phonetics has not chosen written speech as an object, it investigates the links and contradictions between written form and verbal sound. First of all, it must be mentioned that oral speech it is not determined by any governing law. Instead, each language has its own norms of pronunciation and these norms reflect in them the language activity of a Society. Divertion from these norms, of course, are not welcomed by members of that Society. Indeed, these diversions may appear as a result of dialects, idiolect accents, and under the influence of foreign languages. Pronounciation, or hearing rules formulated by a historical collective - and to be considered as satisfactory for all members of this collective – establish the orphoepic norms of a language. Thus, a norm is usually regulated by this or that investigator and directed towards one orientation. As to modern Azerbaijani pronunciation, norms in the middle of words reflect the fact that the sounds /dz/ are changed to /zh/ at the end of words, while the sounds /b/ and /p/ accordingly are changed into /v/ and /f/ - each one accepted as a diversion from the norm. Against it, rules of writing are approved by the State, whilst serious attention is paid to their implementation. At schools, within written works, those who make more mistakes than the norm get "bad" marks and are not transferred into a further class. Moreover, on the pages of newspapers, books, and journals, the rules

of writing are seriously obayed. All causing some to say these written laws should be called orthographics (writing correctly). Yet, there is an individual character for each language when taken seperately. An instance discovered in the German tradition of writing nouns in capital letters. Additionally, a one syllable grapheme /h/ indicates the lenght of that vowel. Nonetheess, in Azerbaijani, this grapheme can indicate both the consonants /h/ and /x/

Compare:

/səhər/ (morning) but only /halva/ (xalva) or, /halva/ etc.

2) It should be worthwhile indicating the following distinctions which are observed in writing: illustrating

In writing		**In speech**	
Rəgs	baʃına	/rəks/,	/ baʃ'na/
Dost	gənd	/dos/,	/gənt^{h}/
Bıçag	piʃik	/p'tʃax/,	/p^{i}ʃik/
Çıxıb	qızlar	/tʃ'xıḅ/,	/gızzar/
Çiçək	gülümsündü	/tʃ^{i}tʃək'/,	/g^{ü}l^{ü}ms^{ü}ndi/
Süd	düʃük	/süt^{h}/,	/d^{ü}ʃük/

Here, one may easily increase the number of examples, although a readers attention needs to be draw to one side of the problem by indicating that the written form does not fit this speech at all. Interestingly, a reader can get additional examples from A. Afandizade´s book "Orthographics – orthoepia...dictionary" (Baku, 1989).

3) Now, modern Azerbaijani orthographics is based upon phonetic, morphological, and historical-traditional principles. As for phonetic principles, there is not a notable distinction between the written and

oral forms of the language. Today. Azerbaijani's write the words "tam", "daş", "qaş", "saman"("taste", "stone", "brows", "strows") in the way they are pronounced. Even though such words compose a very little part of our stock. Generally, of course, it is difficult to find any language in the world where only phonetic principles dominate. Yet, in the majority of languages, there are a group of words, which (without depending on their duties, their age, or place of birth), are written by all the beares of that language and pronounced in the same order.

Nonetheless, in language there are words and word-combinations, which at the boundary of morpheme and words, undergo some changes within sentences. Consequently, there appears to be a distinction between writing and speaking. In such caces it is important to pay attention to the similarity of the morphemes. At present, one can say /işliyir, ağlıyır/ /works/,/cries/ but one writes "işləyir" and "ağlayır". From this, it is clear that the variants of the suffix "la-lə" exit only in two forms. Its written form reflecting morpholgical princípes. Indeed, with the application of morphological rules, historical-traditional principles must usually be obayed. Today though, one says /məllim/, /a teacher/ while one writes "müəllim", because these words are reborrowed words in Azerbaijani and in their writing the rule of the language from which the word originated is kept. Clearly, most words written with an apostrophy are words of this type. Overall, in words borrowed from Arabic, Persian, and European languages, the writing rules of these languages are at least relatively observed.

4) The scholarly description of such a sceintific basis for language - depending upon the aim - may be grounded in different speech styles. Certainly, if one has presented the aim of learning the phonetic establishment of literary language, then such researches must absolutely rely upon the speech style of the literary language in

question, as well as the literary norms of pronuncation. But recalling the usage of Azerbaijani in diverse fields, one must chose a proper speech style. Hence, if one adds stydying different dialects, idiolects, trades, professions, and separately-taken groups, it is not diffilcult to understand how complex this undertaking is: how sophisticated and varied it is.

Also, when speaking of the norms of literary language, until recently specialists pursued this work under the name of Orthoepics: begining with individually taken segment units, up to the word, word-combinations, a sentence, and even pronouncations. Curiously, in order to prove if it was really so, it was not necessary to go too far. Certainly, in the above-mentioned book by the well-known linguist A.Afandizadeh, Orthoepics is understood in this manner. Of the 140-150 pages of his book, an acquaintence with given rules is spread out. Frankly speaking, such a perspective is monolateral and does not meet the requirements of modern language studies, while the author simply seems unaware he has mixed two issues up. Hence, his investigation is engaged in the phonetic establishment of language by trying to determine the phoneme systematization of the words in language. Simultaneously, he seeks out those features and utterances of the words (the phoneme compositions of which are already known), to uncover this and that phoneme within a word or expression. So, let´s suppose that the question interesting us has been put in this form: tısbağa, tüfəng, dəmirdən, əsəbiləşmək (tortoise, a gun, from the iron, to get angry etcetera), forcing researchers to ask how the phoneme compositions of these words are revealed? In answer to this question (in the words of A.Afandizadeh) one is told "that in the unstressed syllables of the words vowels /ı, i, u, ü/ sometimes they become shortened (weak), but we seem to divert from the question" (p. 140).

A question, of course, begging another question. From another angle, if one inquires, "How are the vowels pronounced in this or that word", then it is possible to agree A.Afandizadeh's answer given above.

On a personal note, taking these double features into consideration in "Experimental Phonetics" (Baku, BDU. 1980, p, 27-31) one's own innovations in Azerbaijani linguistics were put forth regarding the necessary discrimination between two fields of science - instead of orphoepics: **orthoepics and orthophonics**.

5. Now, orthoepics includes a determination of phoneme-composition of words in a language, the determination of intonation establishing the phonetic self-beloningness of phonological confrontations of sentences (being units of communication), and a determination of syllable models of language. For example, in the word /daʃ/ (a stone) there are three phonemes – /d/, /a), / ʃ/), and in the word /gül/ (a flower) there are three phonemes too – /g/, /ü/, /l/. Yet, how each of them is said in these words is not an issue for orphoepics. Rather, orthoepics appoints phoneme inventars in the words and investigates them. Differently from orphoepics, orphophonics is a field of science, which studies individually-taken phonemes in identifible phonetic positions - including changes undergone by the influence of stress or intonation.

Through utterance, one pays attention to the phoneme composition of the word one makes (albeit with an artificial pronunciation) - as if one pronounces individually taken phonemes having no connections with one-another. Nevertheless, any phoneme falling under the influence of its position, or the attitudes of neighbouring phonemes, surrenders to prosody-intonation moulding its activities. So, in the words "gül"(a flower), "gülək"(let us laugh) and others, the labiolized pronunciation of the first consonant is paramount. One must say /_k°_/ - the lips protruding in the pronunciation of the first consonant. This is created by the influence of the vowel /ü/ coming after it. On the other hand, at the end of the word [l′] it should become a little voiceless, even though [k′] the transition from construction to an explosive needs to be pronounced as a [ç] like in the German. These indicated features, of course, are not peculiar to any of the phonemes within Azerbaijani. Phrased alternatively, in the phoneme system of Azerbaijani the libialized, or (non-libiazed) sounds becoming voiceless in the sonorous, Moreover, any transition of the mediolingual consonant [k] to constriction refutes confrontation. But their articulation without the aforementioned features may mean the violation of norms of pronunciation and a wrong sounding in the ears. Thus, orthophonia systematizizes and explores prononciation features in accordance with speech, while phonological concerns confrontation language.

6) Those who speak in dialects, when speaking in literary language, act according to their articulatory habits and give special colourings or variety to the **orthophonic rules** of language. As a result of this, a few changes in the orthophonic layer take place. Changes, which may violate the existing harmony of the phoneme system. For instance, in the Gakh region of the Azerbaijani Republic, the sounds /r/ and /l/ may substitute each others place. Compare, /partal, şarval/ (dresses, trousers) etcetera. Now, the phonetic establishment of a language is grounded on the features that emerge during speech and those orphophonic rules applicable. And this, in its turn, has an influence on the phoneme system of a language. All giving a basis for separation between orphoepics and orphophonics - both on a theoretical, as well as practical level.

Hence, it is necessary to mention that in different regions of Azerbaijan, deviations from the norms of literary language are often associated with both orthoepics and orthophonics.

Additionally, in the North-West regions of the Azerbaijani Republic, instead of the phonemes /o/ and /ə/ one very often hears /u/, /ü/. For example, the word /uʃag/ (a child) is pronounced as /oʃax/, while the word /özü/ (himself,herself) sounds /üzü/ and so on. This is orphoepic deviation, although saying the word /gülək/ (let's laugh) as /küłək/ is the result of **orthophonic** deviation.

7) Any distinction of **orthoepics with orthophonics** is of great importance in teaching a foreign language. Indeed, when learning a second language, or struggling with other languages, with varying degress of success are usually associated with a lack of distinction between these two disciplines. Sometimes it happens that a language-learner knows the phoneme composition of a language quite well. Also he or she knows relatively well the acoustic and articulatory features of the phonemes used in a word. However, if the features of vivid speech are unclear, then mistakes occur. As I.A. Baudouin de Courtenay said, the intention of a speakers pronunciation is not always parallel with the acoustic effect. In which case, the existing orthoepic dictionaries do not reflect the variant features of phonemes as they should.

Orthophonics requires the development of new articutation habits along with automatization, because these fresh skills are basically different. Thusly, in order to achieve results, long term training is required. This is why learning situations in a different language must be examined in the light of mother tongue. Furthermore, at every step, it is necessary to rely on mother tongue to assimilate the dissimilar features from the learnt language. Sadly, one needs to mention that any exploration of phonetic establishment or phonological systems, may prove more difficult to undersatand, since the issues of prosodics and intonation are grounded on subjetive observations.

Recently, widely-spread experimental phonetics research has created possibilities to uncover all of the changes taking place in vivid speech. Although, strangely, Azerbaijani has been investigated very little. All in all, one can name only a handful of studies. Among them, the two-volume book called "Experimental phonetics" - supervised by the author of this work – (Baku, I volume, 1980, II volume, 1981) alone stands out.

By using modern experimental, investigative, methods, in this book some of the **orthophonic** features of Azerbaijani are numerated.

We may devide them into the following groups:

1)The fact that phonemes undergo strong reduction. This especially shows itself in narrow vowels: Compare (gülümsündü, slindi, yğışdılar, tmurcuxladı)(smiled,rubbed off, gathered together, shot into buds) etc.

2)Prolongation of the vowels in the syllables coming before stressed syllables, Compare, /ma: rif, şa:kir, ə:la, tu:fan, şö:lə, tə:nə, i:lə, sü:ni/ (enlightment, Shakir **(name), very good**, flame,reproach, with, artificial) etcetera. As can be seen, the syllable being open shows its impact on the prolongation of the vowels. Tellingly, most of these words are borrowed words from other languages.

3)At the end of the words, labial vowels suffer delabializations. They are pronounced either without the participation of the lips, or are pronounced with a very weak labialization. Compare (göründi, uduzdı, sovusşdı) (was seen, lost, escaped) etc.

4) In the open vowels /a/ and /ə/ it can be said the closed syllables are substituted by their closed equivalents. Compare, /iʃliyir, baʃlıyır/ (he works, begins) etc.

5)Sonants become voiceless at the end of the words. Compare, / nar, tural/ (pomegranate, Tural) etcetera. This most of all shows itself with consonants /r/ and /l/.

6)Occlusive-plosive voiceless consonants at the end of a word (when coming before the stressed vowel), are pronounced with aspiration. In order to believe the facticity of this statement, it is enough to bring the palm of the hand near to ones lips. By this action the powerful stream of air touching ones inside hand shall prove those consonants are explosives, and at the same time, that they are pronounced with aspiration. Thereby, one shows some orthophonic features. Yet, any determination of these features through systematizing them, inclusion within text-books, learning correct Azerbaijani, or vivid background, takes the science of phonetics out of banal situations into the central debates inside modern lingiustics.

It becomes clear from above that between speech and writing, between their smallest unit-grapheme and phoneme there is no direct connection. So, in order to reflect the real prospect of vivid language and give orthophonic features, signs for transcription are used[19]. Now, in linguistic literature three types of transcription are indicated. By **phonetic, phonologic transcription,** one shows the phoneme composition of a pronounced word, as well as noting what phonemes

19 Both the grammatical and scientific investigations of global linguistics use signs compiled by the International Phonetic Association - on the basis of latin graphics. Below we introduce discreet and diacritic signs used for transcription.

Phonemes:
Vowels: /a, o, u, ı, e, x, y, ø, i/
Consonants: /b, p, v, f, d, t, z, s, ʃ, tʃ, dž, ʒ , ħ , k, γ, g, x, h, j, m, n, l, r)

Diacritic signs
(:-) shows the length of the phoneme
(.) – sign of semi-length

(°) is written under the voiced consonant and indicates voiceless

Note: (h) is written above the occlusive-plosive voiceless consonant and expresses the aspirated pronunciation (°). It shows labialization. «/« - indicates a short pause and is put between the syntagms. «//« - indicates a big pause and is put among the sentences. «¿ -¿» indicates that the sentence is pronounced by the intonation of an interrogative sentence. (ʹ) – indicates stress - one shows a word, two-indicates a syntagm, 3 shows a sentence (→). In the pronunciation of a phoneme tongue is protruded (←) tongue moves back etc.

participate therein. An example being in Azerbaijani, wherein the word /xətt/ (a line) exhibits three phonemes /x/, /ə/, /t/, but in the word /qənd/ (sugar) four phonemes /g/, /ə/, /n/, /t/ exist. However, in the phonetic transcription for both of these words one finds a mark at the end for the pronunciation of the consonant /t/ with a special transcription sign. Such signs in phonetic literature are called **diacritic signs**. Needless to say, in phonomorphological transcriptions the morpheme composition of a word is indicated without undergoing any changes. In spite of the fact that words such as, “dost”, “dostlar”, “dostum” (a friend, friends, my friend) etcetera hang lose. Moroever, /dos/, /doslar/, /dossum/ are written in their first forms because scholars try to indicate that originally they all came from the word “dost”. Nonetheless, phonomorphological transcription is more important for flective languages. Clearly, in Russian, if one transcribes the words “вода”, “воды” (water) from this viewpoint, one is sure to write the root consonant in two ways – (a/0) because two types of vowels come at the root of these words, while the vowel /o/ must be kept because in the existing form there is an /o/ vowel morpheme. Yet, if this vowel falls into an unstressed position, it changes its quality, thereafter turning to /a/. So, alongside the transformation of a word by way of a phonetic change, it is also important to indicate from what morpheme it has been derived. Certainly, in language learning, phonetic transcription it is of great importance due to the fact a person must master vivid language and not leave out the smallest orthophonic feature. This situalion is equally observed in any scientific investigation of language.

III.5. ATTITUDE OF PHONETICS TO OTHER SCIENCES

1) Any language study dealing with sounds is organically linked with the Humanities - especially with other fields of linguistic science. Curiouly, such a study must necessarily be associated with the exact sciences as well. Much has been written, therefore, on the connection of morphology, lexicology, syntax and semantics with phonetics in linguistic literature. Indeed, phonetics is closely connected with lagopedics, syrdopedagogics, phoniatrics, affyzation of speech, psychology, acoustics, physiology, pedagogics (field of language instruction) and so on. Their wide explanations also becoming a special theme. About this, one has written a great deal (F.Y.Veysalov, 1980; F.Y.Veysalov, 1989).

Be that as it may, one would like to draw attention to those fields of science, which are widely studied nowadays. Information theory, for instance, and cybernetics have actualized the science of phonetics. Indeed, a number of undertakings can´t do a thing without phonetics. Sending information with little expenditure across long distances and improving systems of communication requires the exploration of sound-composition by mathematical means. Additionally, when dispatching information to a listener, choosing the units composing the substantial sides of information and their distribution, as well as acoustic differences in the structure of signals, phonetics plays a vital role. Furthermore, transmitting signals a long or short distance is of serious importance. Perhaps particularly when messages bridge languages. An issue, which may become an obslacle regarding the sent information. For example, in German, if instead of /ʃta:t′/ (govrement) /ʃtat/ (a city) is given, this will immediately create a misunderstanding in dispatching. Or in the Azerbaijani language, a prolonging of the last vowel at the end of a sentence may show it as a question. Compare, /′sən kitab ox′′′ujursan// or ?sən kitab ox′′′ujursa:n¿(you read a book,you read a book?). From a phonetics stance, distinguishing between two communication-units is often based on the pronolonging of the vowel of the last syllable. If one does not obey this rule, it will not be clear if the sent information is a question or an answer. So, turning language signs to electric currency, to send information long distance (in telephone talks, letegraph or by telex etcetera), not only segments, but also concrete acoustic features of the supersegment units must be taken into consideration.

2) The rule of confrontation in communication techniques with the information given (by the combination of certain distinguishing signals) is called a code. However, the process in itself is named encoding. In the reception of information the process of determination as to where the signal systematization begins, and where it ends, is called decoding. If encoding is based on two different signal systematizations, this is called double-coding. That said, if it is based on three different signal systematizations it is called threefold coding. For instance, in the Morse alphabet threefold coding is used: full stop, long signal and pause. The phonemes, which are used in this alphabet are given as simple, but those used a few times are given with their (code) combinations. Compare:

e – (·), a – (· –), t – (–), m - (– –), i – (··), g – (– ··), r – (·–·), etcetera. In this way, one may give the sentence /Atam mat etmir// (My father doesn't mate) as follows

/.$\underline{a}$ /$\underline{t}$/.$\underline{a}$ / $\underline{m}$ – /$\underline{m}$ –/.$\underline{a}$ / $\underline{t}$ /e/ $\underline{t}$ /–$\underline{m}$ / $\underline{t}$ /i/.$\underline{r}$.//

3) Measuring the quantity of this sent information is at present one of the issues drawing scholarly attention. How much information to give, along with its uncertainty, is helped by mathematical methods, which very easily calculate the problems involved. Also, it is possible to calculate the real load of each language-unit in a word: whether a sentence, or in whole speech.

The calculation of uncertainty within this information (this is called scientific enthropics according to the theory of probability), is applied by Cybernetics, while the theory of information – along with an active interference by the theory of probability into linguistics - has all been made possible in recent times.

If one agrees, therefore, with the thought that there are 32 phonemes in Azerbaijani (the author doesn't take occlusive-polosive consonant "k`" as a seperate phoneme), then each phoneme is applied in this language by the same probability. Meaning, of course, the probability of appearance of each phoneme in Azerbaijani.

$M \frac{\log 32}{\log m} - \frac{Ho}{\log m} M$ by the expenditure of the elementary signals will be equal to Ho = log 32 = 5 binary1 digit. Tellingly, in such a case, if one takes the condition of usage as similar, then the probability of generating each phoneme is as much as that. Now, if one gathers all these phonemes in a box and if one wants to make words with the same probability of occurance, then the probability of occurance of each of them will be equal 1/32 to further, if one calculates this with a logarithm using base 2 then we shall get the following figures:

$$\log 32 = 2 \cdot 2 \cdot 2 \cdot 2 \cdot 2 = 5 \text{ binary digit}$$

However, as it is known in vivid speech, the probability of occurances for all the phonemes is not the same. Indeed, there are lexical morphological, syntactical and phonotactical factors impacting on them. So, taking all this into account, together with the maximum enthropy of the phonemes Azerbaijani, (Ho = 5 binary digits) as the first, and the second and other conditional enthropies can be calculated as follows:

$$Ho = \log 32; H_1 = -P_1 \log P_1 - P_2 \log P_2 - \ldots. - P_{32} \log P_{32}$$

Here Ho = 5 binary digit, H_1 = 4,35 binary digits, H_2 = 3,52 binary digits, H_3 = 3,01 binary digits.

4) Obviously, one must mention here that Azerbaijani - from this perspective - has not been studied at all. Yet, research into these issues might speed up the problem of automatic translation, while enabling intercourse with a machine. As such, it is worthwhile to mention one more topic here. In language, since there is a "maximum enthropy" there is also a minimum enthropy. All demanding a calculation of minimum enthropy too. Hence, specialists record that the maximum enthropy of a phoneme Ho can never be less than the minimum enthropy, namely, Ho (maximum enthropy) is always bigger than

From another angle, it can be much nearer when demanded.

Hence, it may be nearer. Minimum enthropy dispatches more information to maximum enthropy (Ho = log n and states that a phoneme dispatches more information). R=1- *Hoo / Ho*

The relativity of minimum enthropy in accordance with maximum enthropy shows the difference in how little one unit of relativity actually is. Certainly, K.Shennon calls this the norm or excess of language. Interestingly, A.M.Yaglom (1921-2007) and I.M.Yaglom

(1921-1988) as brothers in their work "Veroyatnost i Informasiya" (Probability and Information) (M.1973, p.245), claim one can say the abudance of information in language is apporoximately equal to 50 percent. If one retells this a little roughly, it means 50 persent of the choice in sounds used in a text are determined by their own structure, while only a few percent of them are occasional. For the reason, if even prepositions and conjunctions are missing in a telegram, even if there are some mistakes in a text, it is not diffilcult to understand written materials. Moreover, in oral speech any redundancy of information can be substituted with the help of paralinguistic movements and by supersegmentative means.

5)In German, English and French, which are the most investigated languages in the world, the frequency of the usage of letters has been widely examined. Thus, it is clear that all those languages take advantage of the Latin alphabet. In the Latin alphabet, of course, there are 26 letters. During calculalion, one more is added to this, which is the vacancy among words. So if one acts according to a 27 letters frequency of usage, then of each letter is 4,76 binary digits: Ho = log 27 ≈ 4,76 binary digits. However, for each language a seperatelytaken investigation is needed, since the usage of letters in these language are different. For instance, in German the medium length of a word is more than it is in English or French, in which vacancies among the words naturally influence differentiations. Indeed, in German and English "W"and "K" have more frequency of usage than French, although in French the frequency of usage regarding "W"and "K" is equal, one may say, to neel. Also, «TH» as a letter combination in English and » «SCH» in German are more often used. In German, after the letter "C" it can be said the letter "H" always arises, while in English and French this would be quite unusual. This information (taken from a book of by the Yaglom brothers), is very interesting.

Language	English	German	French	Spanish
H_1	4,03	4,00	3,96	3,98 binary digits

As one can see, in these four Europian languages - in all cases -- the medium usage probability (enthropy), is theoretically a great deal lower than the probability of the usage of each letter in Latin (compare: p.93). On the other hand, within these languages the probability of usage regarding these letters does not greatly differ from one another.

At this point, of course, it would be worthwhile making one more comparison. If one takes into consideration the fact there are 32 letters in Russian, one may equally see that in Russian - and in Azerbaijani too - the probability of the usage of each letter is log 32 =5 binary digits. Namely, in comparison with the Latin alphabet, it is approximately 0, 25 percent more. Fascinatinly, one can derive such a conclusion that from the viewpoint of mathematical calculation, because the Latin alphabet is less ecomonic then Azerbaijani. Moreover, in Russian, any machine calculation of a text - having 30 thousand two or three lettered letter combinations - gave the following result (Text has been taken from L.N.Tolstoy´s novel "War or peace")

Ho	H1	H2	H3
log 32 = 5	4, 35	3,52	3,01

So, by the application of mathematical investigation, one may calculate not only the usage of phonemes, but also the probability of usage of letters in a text very precisely - which in its turn speeds up the solution for a number of technical problems: the production of typing machines, the management of complex machines, and the improvement of communication systems etcetera.

CHAPTER III
A COMMUNICATIVE MODEL OF INTERCOURSE AND ITS COMPONENTS[20][1]

III.1. ON THE COMMUNICATIVE MODEL OF INTERCOURSE

a) Intercourse is a complicated process. In which case, clearly presenting a model of its processes is not only a problem for linguists, but also an issue for all those who are involved with speech activities. Undoutedly, psychologists and physiologists require such a model in order to discover the psychological and physiological basis of intercourse. Furthermore, the technical sciences - especially automatic translation, automatic recognition of speech signals as well as characters - and new fields of knowledge (like information theory), demand this model to develop an analogue of intercourse. So, it is clear that this type of modeling is considered a special stage in modern science. Indeed, through a model of intercourse, one seems to have visualized the polysided process of speech. Hence, when one says a "model of intercourse" this phrase is generally understood to mean a

---

20 [1] Towards the writing of this chapter, the author published an article in 1980 called "Experimental phonetics" - see the inner rights of the publishing house BSU. This section has the same name and author. However, the third and the fourth chapters of the same section have been rewritten. Indeed, today's achievements in phonetics have been discussed herein.

scheme reflecting the process of speaking, how hearing takes place, and how one understands such an information flow.

b) Language as a means of intercourse is successful due to the fact it encodes language units generated by a human being, which are then received by another human being who decodes them. When one looks at this model, it is useful to recall the triumph of modern communication systems. Indeed, the units within phonological layers of language seek normalization in sounds. From this, the speech apparatus of a human being has been both moulded as a result of historical process, along with the (achieved) pronunciation of this or that sound. To reflect reality, the senses produce character-expressions and pictures of things created in the brain. As a result of these complicated activities within the nervous system, the movements of active organs linked to the speech apparatus (taking different forms above the glottal vacancy of the voice), manifest vibrations through the vocal-cords, systematize the sounds, and eventually hit the airwaves. Hence this long evolutive process is made concrete. Curiously, one may observe the opposite orientation of this process in the second component of communication – wherein one listens. These airwaves, depending upon the frequency and power of the voice, reach the ear of a listener, the sounds enter the ears of this other human being, turn into mechanical processes, rush up the nerves, which then turn this information in the centre of hearing into meaningful awareness. Thus, sent information is understood, while the communicative function of language is implemented.

c) In this model of intercourse, it is necessary to distinguish four components from one another.

1. The linguistic basis of intercourse;
2. The articulatory basis of the intercourse;

3. The acoustic basis of the intercourse;
4. The perceptive basis of intercourse
(see picture 1)

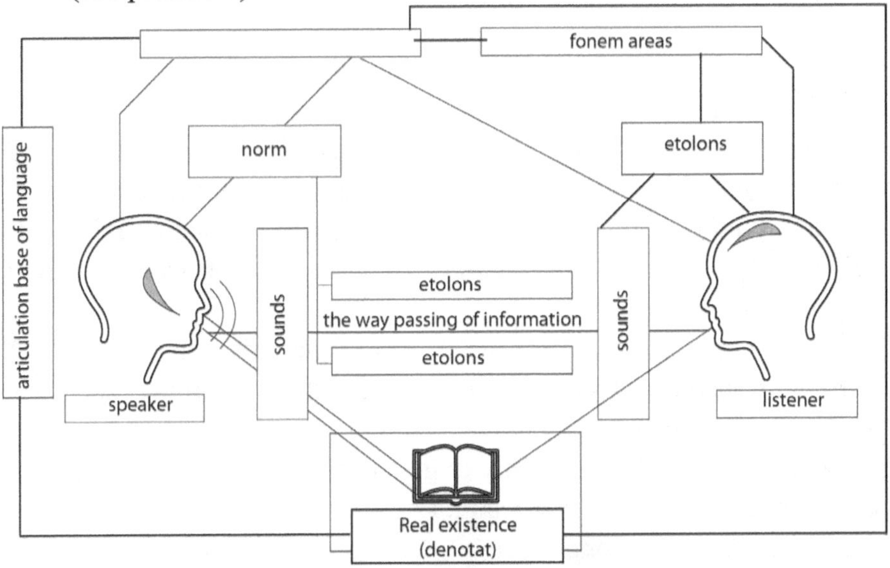

Picture 1. Model of intercourse

Now, it is necessary to deal with each of them separately.

III. 2. LINGUISTIC BASIS OF THE INTERCOURSE

1) Herein one shall deal with language signs taking part in the process of intercourse. Initially, a single sign is opposed with the other in this paradigm. What is more, distinction is based on one of several features, while the confrontation of units displays the same differential features in paradigmatics, mutual ties in syntagmaties and a diapozon of opposition from the viewpoint of an expanded variety of differential symbols. Simultaneously, other integral symbols enter too.

	/ t^0 /			/ d^0 /			/ s^0 /
/ t /	/ $t^{\cdot}$ /		/ d /	/ $d^{\cdot}$ /		/ s /	/ $s^{\cdot}$ /
	/ t^h /			/ d^h /			/ s^h /

As we see the /t/ and /d/ phonemes in syntagmaties act in several variants, but their paradigmatic confrontation is in vigour: conditioned, even though not going beyond the boarder of one phoneme. Indeed, [t] and [a] in the speech chain are labialized soft, while hard variants enter the oppositive attitude.

2) For intercourse to take place, the main condition is that together (with the speaker), a listener should possess the same linguistic basis. Obviously, if a person of avarage personality says in his native tongue the sentence /dun dirsjre goola/ (I go to lesson), he, or she, will not be understood by those who cannot speak this language. Thusly, the most important component for a linguistic basis is the norm. A rule revealing that norms are regulated by the system.

A language unit, or a language phenomenon beyond the system, can't enter a norm. In themselves, there is no distinction between forelingual consonants with respect to labialization. However, forelingual consonants before the vowels /ø/, /ü/, /o/, /i/ are labialized. So, this feature, not being peculiar to the system from a paradigmatic viewpoint, shows itself on a syntagmatic level. Hence, a norm is associated with the activity of a language unit within the speech chain. Clearly, a norm regulates speech.

3) Phonemes in the process of intercourse are not used separately, in the isolated form

In very rare cases, in this or that language, information is given by only one phoneme: by its realization through the type of intonation.

For example, in Azerbaijani, the question, "Who is reading?" (Kim oxuyur?) /He/ (O)[21] is an interesting case (A.A.Reformatsky, 1967. 28). To this statement, the answer is only one phoneme /o/ (he), which has been realized as a sentence. In Azerbaijani, under certain circumstances, one sees that a single phoneme may be used as a morpheme, word, or even as a sentence. The fact that in Azerbaijani a phoneme can occasionally act as a morpheme additionally illustrates cases wherein the dative and possessive cases, the mood of the verbs, equally multitask. Assuredy, in German, the suffixes of plurality and case suffixes [ə] and as a uniting sign like [s] exhibit many roles. What is more, in Russian the suffixes of case and plurality generate separate words. As such, one may come across /i, a, u, v) working in this manner. Usually, of course, morphemes, as well as sentences, are the systematization of a number of phrases. This is why the phonemes contacting one another in a chain of speech undergo serious changes: not only in terms of quality, but also regarding the phoneme, stress and intonation, neighbouring phonemes (including sociolinguistic development of the speaking person) - each one playing great role. Assuredly, in sentences such as /Səməd acı-acı gülümsündü/ (Samed smiled bitterly), there are 11 phonemes, each one of which has been arranged one after another. From them /ü/ appears three times, /s/ twice, /æ/ twice, /m/ twice, /d/ twice, /a/ twice – even though repeated. Indeed, the usage positions of these phonemes are quite different. For instance, the phoneme /s/ is employed for the first time in front of a sentence, before the unstressed /æ/ is applied. Yet, when it appears for a second time, it is used after the consonant /m/ and before the unstressed /ü/. Undoubtedly, the difference between these two /_s_/ is great. They are distinguished from each other (acoustically), although

21 In this respect, the example mentioned by A.A.Reformatsky is very interesting. Two men from Rome argue: who can say or write the shortest sentence? The first states and writes: /Eo rus/ (I go to the village). The other answers: /I/ (i)" (Go).

from the phonological viewpoint each of them represent one and the same phoneme. Moreover, they both carry out one function - the function of the phoneme /s/.

Conversly, the same phonemes may undergo changes that take into consideration the person who realizes those phonemes through specific individual features. Indeed, L. R. Zinder names the first type of change as combinatory change. He even calls the second type of change an individual change (L.R. Zinder, 1960).

4) Phonology is the constituent part of phonetics

Learning of mutual connections between articulated sounds from a speaker, and the units which a listener understands, has always been one of the most important questions occupying linguists. All meaning, in each of these sounds, classic phonetics distinguished between three aspects, even though the activity of speech organs was considered the main cause in establishing speech sounds. That's why the articulatory side of speech was considered as primary, while the acoustic aspect was seen as secondary -as the result of physical movements producing the speech act. Acoustics, therefore, not agrecing with this schema, insisted on saying the essence of things was more important than their appearance. Hence, the far reaching arguments between those studying acoustics and physiologists deviated from discovering the essence, or functional aspects, of sound. Instead, they tried to examine articulations as pure sounds. Thus, O.Jespersen from Danmark wrote: "Both of the sides in themselves are not in the right position, but both of them together are right" (O. Jespersen, 1925, p. 75).

Undeniably, many facts are known regarding the so-called secondary importance of acoustics in the history of linguistics. Beyond doubt, G.Forchhammer (1865-1974) noted that speech sounds are nothing more than the area of articulation within organs of speech. This is why, G.Forchhammer equally calls his ideas (on the establishment of sounds), a turning point in linguistics. And as such, he removes phonetics from linguistics, while suggesting one substitutes it with "ialetics" (gr. Ialein – danışmaq (to speak) (G. Forchhammer, 1924).

From these thoughts, O.Jespersen becomes clear that to clarify which of them is more important for science is absurd - because both of them are significant (O. Jespersen, 1925).

So, the acoustic effect, which results from the movement of organs of speech, is an important condition respecting the realization of the communicative function in a language.

5) It is necessary, of course, to mention that the articulatory aspect (until the beginning of the XX century) had played a leading role in research. On the whole, this aspect -especially in "Germany based" psychology - was a dominant trend[22]. Unsurprisingly then, the Englishman A.Sweet (1906) and the German E.Siversin (1850-1932), reference (E. Sievers, 1876), wrote their first works under the influence of psychology. In opposition to this, Russian thinkers began to study language sounds from an acoustic position. Assuredly, in the works of A.T.Thomson (1919), L.V.Shcherba (1974), and V.A.Bogoroditsky (1930), readers are given a vast amount of information on the acoustic features of speech sounds. Indeed, they attempt to show mutual ties between articulatory aspects of sound with openly acoustic aspects. Therefore, these authors demonstrate that the discovery of primary data (on this or that aspect) is not a theoretical question. Rather, they

22 In Europe, one of the first founders of laboratory based experimental phonetics, P. Calzia, may be indicated as an example. It is interesting to note that such an attitude to phonetics is also found in the works of another representative of the Hamburg school H.H.Wangler. He and his teacher P.Calzia, take phonetics as an independent science not associated with other subjects and think it to be an applied science. It's true that in his last publication H.H.Wangler tries to associate phonetics with phonology (H.H.Wängler, 1972).

envisage it as offering a practical solution to each question - depending on the aim of research (E.Fischer Jorgensen, 1962. 615).

For his part, E.F.Jorgensen (1911-2010) - from Danmark – shows that despite recent "thorough" examinations of language sounds, all three aspects need to be considered obligatory. As such, he names them, articulatory, acoustic and perspective aspects.

As to the thoughts of modern linguists like R.Jakobson and M.Halle (amongst others), each seems to claim understanding is first, while the articulatory aspect is last. However, the acoustic element dominates the middle. Certainly, R.Jakobson and his collegues came to this decision as a result of acoustic analysis.

Perhaps this makes it clear why these primary aspects of sound can't help touching on the province of phonetics as a science. An overlap implying the independence of phonetics and its place among the Humanities or exact sciences still causes serious disputes. "Viewpoint determines the object of science" says F. de Saussure, taking the distinctions attained as a result of this confrontational basis. Even though the great scientist forgets the substantial grounding of such discerments.

Yet, increasing technical develpments in experimental phonetics appears to prove its close relation to the natural sciences. A statement testified by fact that experimental phonetics was usually headed by doctors, physiologists and acousticians, not linguists (O. von Essen, 1964). As for the thinking of W. Kuhlman, it is clear that investigated sounds are either in the googling of a cock, or as a part of human sentences (W.Kuhlman, 1937. 79).

6) Provocatively, F. de Saussure's disciple N.S.Trubetzkoy - remaining true to the thoughts of his teacher – made an attempt to prove the existence of 2 subjects suggested by speech sounds. He

noted that one of these subjects was directed at the speech act, while the other one seemed directed to language itself. Obviously, the first assertion is close to the natural sciences, its mode of investigation, and methodology. Contrastingly, this second approach is allied to the social sciences. So, for Trubetskoy, each of these sciences demanded its own self-belonging objects, modes of inquirey, as well as forms of experiment, which is why he spoke of phonetics and phonology as distinct and independent sciences. However, H.S.Trubetskoy's conceptualizations never really came to full fruition (N.S.Trubetzkoy, 1960).

As mentioned above, a language manifests itself in speech. Indeed, only speech can be an object in the phonetic structure of a spoken language. In which case, all the laws of language can be scrutinized, then generalized. Primaily then, learning speech sounds is not distinguishable from acoustics. Unless, of course, phonetics wants to be the subject of acoustics, or physiology. Taking, thereby, the linguistic aspect as its basis.

7) Stated so, studies arising from the physiological side, wherein a speaker, or hearer, merely engages in intercourse is of no use whatsoever. After all, phonetics is interested in a physiological account of organs as they speak, in the hearing and listening processes, as well as of speech sounds themselves. Of course, a person can produce sounds like roaring, crying, whispering and shouting, but these do not serve the interests of intercourse. Moreover, a person hearing these sounds may understand thm in part, but not as a whole. Clearly, human ears don't grasp these noises as a complex. Therefore, phonetics, when seen as a part of linguistics, tends to focus on the fact that any research into these human charcteristics from an acoustic point of view (pronounced from substantial barks) distinguishes one

text from another (maximum) text through the discrenments of an interviewer. However, phonetics, as a subject, is simply interested in discovering objective principles. As far as phonology is concerned, it makes phonetic differentiation the same topic, but can't differentiate between inherent similarities. All this approach can do is to expound bases. Below, are examples one has taken from different languages to demonstrate this.

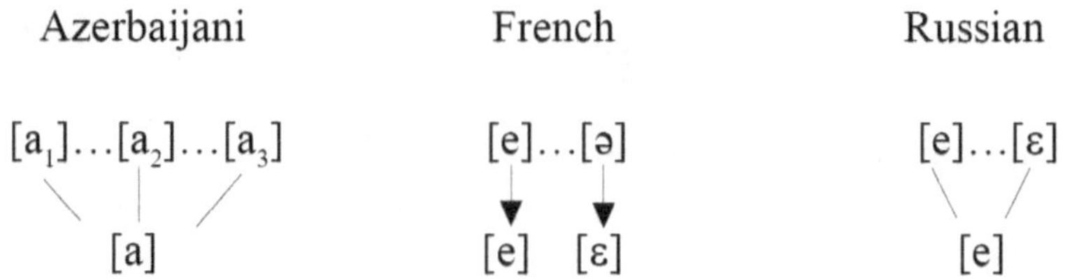

Now, N.S.Trubetzkoy and his followers in 1926 (the year in which the Prague Linguistic School began its activity - starting with the Hague Linguistic School Congress of 1928), suggested the sound side of language should form an independent science. However, one can see the roots of this assunption in the works of I.A. Baudouin de Courtenay, L.V.Shcherba and even in the works of English scholar D. Jones. Indeed, for these scientists the majority of sounds (either said or heard), are limited in sound meanings due to sounds and word-forms discriminating between each other. So, without relying accepted epithets (a sound system unit of language, phoneme, phonological unit, sound imagination, sound type, or sound family, etcetera), they more or less opposed phonetics to phonology. Yet, one should recall that I.A. Baudouin de Courtenay had already separated these two aspects from one another. The first he called antropophonetics and the second psychophonetics (I.A. Baudouin de Courtenay, 1963).

8) Of course, the terms phonetics and phonology were still used

in the literature until N.S.Trubetzkoy's contribution. All shedding a different light on the works of F.de Saussure, wherein his dialectic between phonetics – understood as historical sound changes in the system of a language – and the same pursuit as phonology - a science based on the physiology of sounds is not always robust. Certainly, O.Ernst looked upon phonetics as a motor affirming the act of speech, but envisaged phonology as a science exploring causes, which were historically created[23].

9) At present, a few supporters of N.S.Trubetskoy's thoughts are still to be found[24] (Изв. АН СССР, 1952. 53). Yet, if one really agrees with N.S.Trubetskoy, it becomes impossible to explain a number of phenomena emerging within intercourse. For example, in Russian, the vowel /o/ is diphtongized in its pronunciation. Moreover, this modern literary pronunciation is considered normal, even though in the phonological system this feature can't be understood as relevant. After all, in the Russian system of vowels there is no confrontation of diphtongized, or non-diphtongized, phonemes. Another example is discovered in Azerbaijani wherein, at the end of the word /r/, this morpheme effectively becomes voiceless. Indeed, in Azerbaijani, sonorous phonemes do not create opposition between the voiced and voiceless character of phonemes. Rather, the devoiced form of [r] must be grasped as a norm of pronunciation. Compare: /nar/ (pome – granite), /gar/ (snow) etcetera.

10) So, there are sound-events, which do not belong to the

---

23 N.S.Trubetzkoy, waiting for comparison with F. de Saussure's work "parole and language", tried to prove that each of them were fields of learning. Certainly, N.S.Trubetskoy, by carriing out phonological investigations supposed he had discovered a new field of science. Associated with this, S.Bergsveinsson points that the learning oppositional systems of phonology - and their systematic descriptions - has at least a history of 800 years (S.Bergsveinsson, 1942. 59–64).

24 In 1952–1953, "The news of the department of language and literature" in the Academy of Sciences in the USSR, held (journal based) discussions proving that these scientists were monolateral in their viewpoint. Hence, the thought that phonetics and phonology were independent fields of science was dismissed.

phonological system of a language, bearing, as they do, a purely phonetic character. Nonetheless, without these sound-events phonology can't exist. All this, once again, shows that any strict confrontation of phonetics with phonology may be depicted visually as the dykhotomik principles of F. de Saussure. Possibly prompting, in its turn, E. Coseriu (being one of the greatest linguists of the present time), to say that instead of speaking about dykhotomic principles, one needs to engage with trikhotomic description of language structure. A model showing it is necessary to remain aware of the norm between parole and langue. Obviously, speech is the systematization of sounds in language. Yet, in the systematization of these sounds there exists a series of objective laws referred to as a norm, although this "norm" depends upon the system. Either way, a norm is the whole of all the variants - albeit in a system of phonemes (units of language), in reflection.

11) Contended so, it could be said all linguists are monolateral in one sense. Also, it can be stated that language sounds are constitutive in understanding these units. For example: /gala/ (a tower) consists of the systematization of four phonemes. In this word, therefore, in the first place stands /g/ in the second /a/ and accordingly in the third and fourth places stand /l/ as well as /a/. Hence, by this systematization the established word enables an understanding of the object. Sometimes, no doubt, phonemes are looked upon as discriminative units. But it is necessary to mention that phonemes (correctly perceived), allow one word to be differentiated from the other. As far as discrimination of individually taken phonemes is concerned, the basis of this discrimination establishes the features, which characterize them.

Language sounds do not act as a physical phenomenon in the intercourse, but rather as elements possessing a certain function. Each of them having a certain load. So, the sounds serving to dispatch information - and make them understand from the physical point of view - possess numerous variations. Thusly, these differences (variety) are the form of realization of such units - existing in limited quantities - within a language. Moreover, arising out of this numerous variety, one discovers 30–40 language units are disceranable from only functional viewpoint. Clearly, this functional aspect alone can possibly answer the main questions of linguistics (including phonetics), wherein physical sounds - being different in a language - are determined with reference to the form of a unit. Or, potentially, this can solve questions regarding these sounds when they resemble each-other, although they are understood as two different units. Either way, in order to (theoretically) answer these two questions, linguistics need to concur on the conception of phonemes.

12) Obviously, in the classic literature of linguistics, language sounds are described differently. This is because classic linguists were loth to explain the active causes of different sounds used in speech as one or two units (phonemes) from functional viewpoints.

Partially, these linguists approached sounds from a postion of physical differentiations. As such, A.Thomson - who had the extraordinary ability of feeling different forms of pronunciation regarded the Russian sound "ı" as a pivotal case in point. However, even he didn't understand the reason why he could show that this /_ı_/ (having different prononciations) could act as one unit.

13) Only I.A. Baudouin de Courtenay, being Polish by nationality, although having carried out his researches in Kazan and Petersbourg universities (and who belonged to the psychological branch of yuanggrammatism), ventured to suggest a conception of the phoneme in full. So, in his book, "An Attemt to the Theory of Phonetic Alternation" (I.A.Baudouin de Courtenaye, 1985), this scholar

indicated several types of alternations in phonemes. Unsurprisingly then, this work influenced the foundation of the Moscow Linguistic School. Additionally, in his other work I.A. Baudouin de Courtenay defined each sound as the whole of an articulatory movement and acoustic impression. As such, he declared a phoneme was an "impression" existing in the conscious of a human being and never really fitting the intention of a speaker. This is why I.A. Baudouin de Courtenay discusses two aspects of learning a sound composition (see p. 102).

14) It needs to be added that the Petersbourg disciple of I.A. Baudouin de Courtenay is L.V.Shcherba. At the beginning of the century, Shcherba carried out investigations in the laboratory of the French Monk Rousseau. After returning to his own country, Shcherba wrote his famous book "Quanitative and Qualitative Features of the Vowels of the Russian Language" (L.V.Shcherba, 1912). Furthermore, in this work, which was his Masters Dissertation, Shcherba works out a firm theory of phonemes. As such, L.V.Shcherba more or less founds experimental phonetics in Russia.

Interestingly, on the sixth page of this aforementioned book, L.V.Shcherba writes that phonemes (including the sound composition of a language) have independence, along with autonomy. Unarguably, this concept is the cornerstone of his phonology. In which case, one needs to explain what this "autonomy" is. In Azerbaijani, there are words like /gâ$_1$la$_2$/ and /gâ$_1$la$_2$/. /_a$_2$ /. Now, the second word is seperated by a morphological boundary from the former word. All hinting that the first word /_a$_2$ / cannot be separated in a similar manner. Namely, both /_a$_2$ / have no meaning when examined separately, because these words insure formation in different forms within the words indicated. Conversely, in the words /âyâza/ (to Ayaz, Ayaz) and

/ayãzı/ in the paradigm by means of /a/ and /ı/ one grammatical form differs from the other grammatical form /a/ as well as /ı/ and they (separately) bear no meaning. Through the analysis carried out above, Shcherba comes concludes that all phonemes in a language possess a certain independence. Or at least, they are potentially associated with meaning. Thus, in the 30th year of the XX century Shcherba developed his idea and approached the problem of a main variant. At the same time, Shcherba proved that a phoneme is a unit of understanding. For Shcherba, the most independent unit is one that does not depend upon position. As such, this is the main variant. Undoubtedly, therefore, those pronounced separately are considered as independent variants – since possession has no influence on this variant. For instance, one may see /a/ or /o/. However, /a/ and /o/ in the intercourse are not in an isolated form. Rather, they are used in the texts. That's why they undergoe these influences. In the word /bala/ (shield) the phonation of /a/ at first is labial is observed, but the tongue eventually moves forward, and from the sides rises up to the alveolare of the upper teeth. The result being an influence of the consonants /b/ and /l/.

15) While speaking of the variants, it is necessary to mention one more statement by Shcherba. To his satisfaction, he showed two types of variant in real speech: 1) special; 2) facultative. A special variant in itself is subdivided into two: a) linked with position; b) combinatory.

A facultative variant is called the "realization" of one phoneme in several types. In Azerbaijani, variants of [r] and [r^{o}] are the facultative variants of the same phoneme. Hence, one may easily be used instead of another one. A procedure, which does not complicate any understanding of the word. After all, [r] comes at the end of the word, but [r^{o}] comes before a vowel sound.

In themselves, special variants are established in speech as a result of the mutual influence of the phonemes following one another. The vowel coming after a bilabial consonant – though not being a labial vowel under the influence of a labial consonant at the beginning of pronunciation of the vowel - it is pronounced as if being labialized. For example,

[d° ü z] (straight)
[d°uz] (salt)
[s°u] (water)
[z°ülal] (protain)

16) But not all the linguists accept the conception of a phoneme at it is configured above. Be that as it may, when speaking of the views of I.A. Baudouin de Courtenay, one needs to recall his perspective on the alternation of phonemes. Beyond doubt, this idea alone morally nourished the Moscow Phonological School. Moreover, I.A. Baudouin de Courtenay's and Shcherba's ideas have greatly influenced the establishment of the Prague Functional Linguistic School, as well as American Descriptivism.

17. Modern linguistics on the theory of phoneme.

Across the world, it is difficult to find two linguists who have defined phoneme theory in the same way. Although, this does not mean there is no similarity between their thoughts. In which case, a brief overview on the theory of phonemes is required. For his part, I.A. Baudouin de Courtenay in 1917 wrote, "A constant imagining of sound in our psychology, as well as acoustic impressions created by complicated movements of our speech organs at the same time - we shall call a phoneme" (Избр. труды по общему языкознанию. т. II, M., 1963, p.249).

Additionally, L.V.Shcherba states, "A phoneme is the smallest general sound impression. It has the capability to keep contact with meaningful imaginations and also has a capability to differentiate words…" (Русские гласные в качественном и количественном отношении. С-Петербург, 1912. p.14).

Sagaciously, F. de Saussure contends, "Phoneme is the whole of acoustic impressions and articulary movements. It is the whole of heard and said units: one of them reflecting the other. So, it being a complex unit, a phoneme has support in this and that chain" (Труды по языкознанию. М., 1977. p. 76). Simialry, English scientist D.Jones determined a phoneme like this: "Phoneme is the personifying of the most important sound (namely the family of sounds, the most often used members) together with other sounds - being the most suitable one in a sound systematization in the family of sounds" (D.Jones. English Phonetics. London, 1933.p. 48). On the 49th page of the same work this writer penns, "Phonemes are able to differentiate one word from the other".

Suggestively, in his work: "On the structure of phonemes" R.Jakobson authors, "A phoneme is globally distinguished from all other language signs, and the whole sound value of language. It is purely a distinctive sign, which in itself - being something else - does not say anything positive, whole or constant. Yet, like other sounding means of expression, a phoneme is the sign of signs. It is the sign of grammar and style: a phonostilistic whole of values… Phoneme is a complex unit on the level of movements happening at the same time without a remainder, it is divided into distinctive qualities" (R.Jaлobson. Selected Writings. I. The Hague–Paris, 1971. p.310).

Furthermore, N.S.Trubetzkoy determined the phoneme like this, "We can say that a phoneme is the whole of relevant features from the phonological sound volume… Phoneme belonging to the system of languages, and being a social institute is, at the same time, a value for all other values. It has a form of existence. The price of this value unit (for example dollars) is neither a physical, nor a psychological reality. It is abstract and "fictitious dimention" (N.S.Trubetzkoy. Grundzüge der Phonologie, 1962. 35).

Curiously, French linguist A.Martinet explains phoneme in this way, "As a sign, a phoneme is a bilateral unit. On one side its significant is found in meaning or value, but on the other side is significance is the sounds established by second degree division members. All these are called phonemes" (A.Martinet. Grundzüge der allgemeinen Sprachwissenschaft, Berlin,1963. 36).

True to form, German scientists H.Pilch and H.H.Wängler make suggestive remarks. For instance, Pilch writes, "From the phonematic view, a class of the same segments are called phonemes" (H.Pilch. Phonemtheorie. Basel–New-York, 1965, S. 92). Also, H.H.Wänger determines, "Phoneme is a class of sound abstractions carrying out the function of meaning distinctions" (H.H.Wängler. Grundiss einer deutschen Phonetik, 1967, S. 31).

The famous linguist L.R.Zinder, dealt with phonemes by specifying his view from different perspectives. Hence, it is worthwhile to speak about some of them here. For example, "Phoneme undivided as to time (along a straight line) is the smallest unit, but as to structure it has several features, - though some of them are characterized by common features, whereas others serve to distinguish them… So, phonemes in each phonetic position, along with certain variants (allophones), are represented in various ways - once realized in real speech - in the form of sounds becoming substantiated" (Л.Р.Зиндер. Общая фонетика, 1979, p.42, 48). Moreover, as Y. S. Maslow determines, "The smallest unit of sound is called phoneme, which is only the outer distinguisher of words and morphemes" (Ю.С.Маслов. Введение в языкознание. М., 1975, p. 63). What is more, one of the most prominent representatives of the Moscow School of Linguistics, A.A.Reformatsky, gives the phoneme an unexpected capacity by writing, "Phonemes, being the smallest structure of language, serve to discriminate and establish meaningful units – morphemes and words" (A.A.Reformatsky. Введение в языкознание. M., 1967, p.211).

From the Azerbaijani linguists A.Damirchizadeh and A.Akhundov's one discovers a fascinating determination of phonemes. Indeed, A.Damirchizadeh writes, "Phonemes – establishing the substantial bark of the words in this or that language are the discriminating sounds in a unit of speech. I mean as a unit having social meaning" (A.Damirchizadeh. Modern Azerbaijani language, I. 1972, p. 35).

Tellingly, A.Akhundov too values phonemes like this: "Speech sounds having the duties of a language, namely language units having lexical or grammatic meanings (such language units – are called morphemes), while speech sounds which discriminate one from the other… are called phonemes" (A.Akhundov. Phonetics of the Azerbaijani language. Baku, 1984, p.12).

As for the author of this work, one tends to make the following determination, "Phoneme…is abstract. Phonemes in speech are realized by means of sounds. A phoneme is a unit of understanding. By phonemes, words and word-forms are discriminated from one-another… A phoneme, if separately taken has no other meaning of its own. But in potential, it is associated with meaning… Phoneme is an unshattered unit and that's why it is called a minimal language unit (F.Veysəlov. Alman dilinin fonetikası. Bakı, 1980. 15 (F.Veysalov (Veysalli). Phonetics of the German Language. Baku, 1990, p.15).

18) Only pivotal names are mentioned in this brief summary. Hence, one must also must confirm that these linguists unite around

a certain trend. A trend distinguished from the others by its methods of investigation and principles – as well as by its approach to these investigations. So, as far as attained results are concerned, these are discerned from one other through mere disjunction. For example, the thoughts of representatives in the Prague school, and the "school of Shcherba" on the phoneme system of learned languages, may cause one to protest they simply discriminate from each other. For instance, regarding German, L.R.Zinder marks 40 phonemes (L.R.Zinder, T.N.Stroyeva, 1957), but the Prague School claims there are 39 phonemes (N.S.Trubetzkoy, 1960. 92). The only distinctions is that the Prague Linguistic School doesn't take /ç/ and /x/ as independent phonemes.

19) Here, one would like to deal a little more with the American Descriptive School, because their views are not familiar to the majority of readers. Indeed, the American scientist Twoddel puts forth the idea of macro- and micro-phonemes in order to substantiate them through exemplification. As such, below are some forms, which are often used in speech, or repeated. Let's examine the instace,

/Şirin bulaq kimi süzülür gəlir,
Ömürlər üstünə bir ömür gəlir,
Bakıya Kür gəlir, mavi Kür gəlir//
Like sweet spring comes filtrated,
One more life is added,
For Kur, (river) blue Kur comes to Baku.

In this piece of poetry, 4 times one reads the word /gəlir/, twice /ömür/, whereas twice has /Kür/ been used. So contended, in speech these words differ from one another. Although, truly, with respect to their meanings, they are either the same or similar. Indeed, these are words based on the thoughts of ancient philosophers who argued, "Everything changes, everything is flowing. One can never get twice into running water". Simultaneously, in this piece of poerty there are forms that discriminated between phonetic principles. For example, /bir/ and / pir/ (one, sacred place). For Twoddel, therefore, forms discriminated by minimal phonological distinctions are regulated forms. Obviously, attitudes among class-forms generate phonological confrontations. So, the American scientist calls members of such confrontations "mycrophonemes". Put in other words, features discriminating phonological forms are called mycrophonemes. As such, the word-forms /bir/ and /pir/ (one and sanctury) which one has mentioned above, are discriminated by mycrophoneme /b/ – /p/. Moreover, in this chain each of the phonemes is a called macrophoneme (А.А.Гасанов, Ф.Я.Вейсалов, 1973. 4).

Atop this, American descriptions of these forms take two important principles as their basis. What is more, these principles of distinguished form are elucidated in the works of L. Bloomfield and his followers. This may be why H. Gleason, a scholar influenced by L.Bloomfield, determins each phoneme-composition in every language along the following lines,

1. The principle of acoustic resemblance
2. Additional principles of distribution

So, two sounds like each other in their acoustic features are a phoneme – especially when they act in positions excluding each other. As a case in point, let's consider the following instances in Azerbaijani,

/d¹iz/ – /d°ür/	(knee)- (stand still)
/daɣ/ – /d°uz/	(narrow), (straight)

Of course, in all these word-sounds /d/ acts with different phonetic features. Furthermore, [d′] in the first word is distinguished from the [d°] in other words - nobody denying a certain resemblance among them. On the other hand, these sounds act in positions excepting one-another, i.e. [d_1] can't be used in the position of [d_2] (L.Bloomfield, 1968) etcetera. This is why, according to the conceptions of American Descriptivists, they are considered variants of one phoneme. Indeed, the American linguist, H.Gleason, eventually approaches phonemes as sounds (H.Gleason, 1959).

20) Overall, it is necessary to note that in English and German, the sounds /h/ and /s/ (from an acoustic standpoint) don't have any resemblance and can't act in the same position. Begging the question as to whether one takes them as an individual phoneme at all. Yet, the American school countered this by claiming -though they excude each other there is no resemblance among them. This is why they are dufferent phonemes.

One of the mistakes that the American Descriptivists make is that they do not separate segments from supersegment units. For them, segment units can (partially?) create a morpheme, while supersegment units clearly create a morpheme. All meaning, these scholars naturally try to determine, via intonation, the composition of the phoneme of the morpheme. As we may read, "Tone, stress, pause are considered as phonemes" (K.Pike, 1947).

The fact that segment and supersegment units are not distinguished from each other, whilst accepting intonation as a morpheme, is not reasonable. After all, the concept "morpheme" possesses a certain meaning - as a bilateral unit. Furthermore, intonation as the other phonological unit (even if individually recorded) doesn't possess any meaning - and bears a unilateral character.

This could be why the Prague Functional Linguistic School - by envisaging phonetics as a natural science and phonology as a social science - came to the conclusion that these two sciences of sound compose language study.

21) In some linguistic schools (for no reason whatsoever), they name the prominent author N.S.Trubetzkoy as the father of phonology. A curious notation, since N.S.Trubetzkoy acknowledges the services of I.A. Baudouin de Courtenay and L.V.Shcherba (N.S.Trubetzkoy, 1939. 46). Nonetheless, N.S.Trubetzkoy's works on the conception of the phoneme and their load in language – based on F.de Saussure's principle "there is nothing but contradictions in language" stands alone. Further, N.S.Trubetżkoy models phoneme as the member of phonological opposition. Yet, phonological opposition is the confrontation of sounds able to differentiate the meanings of two words in one language. For instance, /gənt/ (suger) - /kənt/ (village). But if sound opposition is not able to differentiate the meaning of words, then is this opposition non-phonological opposition? For example, /ara/ – /ar/ (look for- search). Herein, he admits, "From phonological features to relevant and non-irelevant features" (N.S.Trubetzkoy, 1963). In the /g/ – /k/ oppositions, backlingual and mediolingual voiceless and voiced sounds are relevant features. This is due to the fact these two phonemes have distinguished features. But other features are considered non-relevant. After some time, therefore, N.S.Trubetzkoy determines phoneme like this, "Those coming one after another within one language, not splintering into small units, are called phonemes", and also, "Phoneme is the whole of relevant features having the character of creating sounds in one language" (N.S.Trubetzkoy, 1963).

22) One of N.S.Trubetzkoy's principle contributions is that he worked out logical characterization principles regarding phonological oppositions. As such, he indicated three types of opposition:

1. From the point of attitude, opposition as a whole belongs to the system of oppositions. Here he discriminates, oppositions with multi-dimentions, oppositions with mono-dimentions, along with isolated and proportional oppositions. Monodimentioned– oppositions –polydimensional

a) The whole of features taken as a basis for comparison is peculiar only to these 2 members. The other members of the system are only repeated. The whole of features taken as a basis for comparison are not

[t]– [d]; —— [f] – [v]
[b] – [p]; —— [s] – [z]
[g] – [k]; —— [s] – [ş]
[b] – [m]; —— [r] – [l]

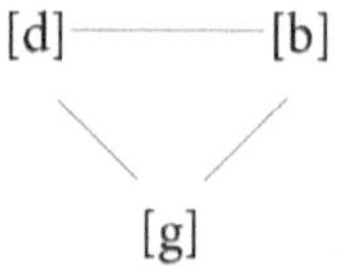

restricted with the members of this restriction, the other members of the system are also observed

b) Oppositions with polydimention in themselves are divided into two: a) homogene, b) heterogene:

[d] – [n]; [t] – [ʃ]
[k] – [n]; [g] – [ħ]
[k] – [x]; [g] – [ʃ]

Homogene oppositions are oppositions with polydimension, so that their members, in the chain of monodimention can't act in side points, compare: (i – e, u – o, o – ø, ø – e).

Different from this, heterogene oppositions are oppositions with polydimention – so none of its members within those criteria can create oppositions with monodimention. Compare: /p/ ≠ /t/.

All phonemes can take part in the oppositions with polydimention. But for phonological weight, and for the general structure of the phonological system, oppositions with monodimentions and oppositions with homogene polydimention are more important.

Oppositions

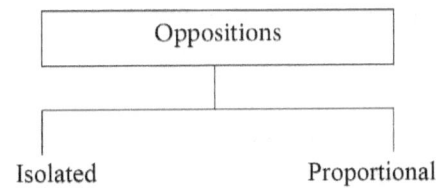

Isolated	Proportional
The attitude among members of this opposition are not repeated in the same form - with none of the other oppositions in a language	The attitude among members of this opposition is absolutely suitable to the attitude of members of other oppositions

Compare:

/p/ # /ş/ with polydimentions	/p/ # /t/ with polydimentions
/r/ # /l/ with monodimentions	/b/ # /p/ with monodimentions
	/d/ # /t/
	/g/ # /k/

2. As to the attitude among the oppositions and characterization of the oppositions. Here N.S.Trubetzkoy discriminates oppositions

Privative	Gradual	Equipolent
One of the members of oppositions has a feature (bearing a feature), but the others don't possess this feature (don't bear a feature): voiced, voiceless	The members of oppositions possess different grades of the same features: as to the revealation of the sentence	Both members of the opposition enjoy the same rights

with privative, gradual, and equipollent oppositions.

Compare:

/b/ + /p/	/u/ + /o/	/p/ + /t/
/d/ + /t/	/y/ + /ø/	/f/ + /k/
/g/ + /k/	/i/ + /e/	

3. Characterization as to the capacity of the power of discriminating the meanings of the members of opposition. Here the constant and neuteralized oppositions are distinguished.

There are such oppositions, the members of which from the view of their usage in the sound bark of the morphemes and words are not restricted. Such oppositions are called constant oppositions.

Compare: /a/ ≠ /æ/, /p/ ≠ /t/

Differing from them /o/ ≠ /ø/ is not used in the absolute endings of words or morphemes. As such, N.S.Trubetzkoy acknowledges neuteralized opposition, even though the situation within which it takes place he calls the "position" of neutralization. Further, the phonemes in these positions he calls archiphonemes (the whole of DF peculiar to 2 phonemes). So, N.S.Trubetzkoy touches on a number of endemic problems and, speaking from the lofty heights of phonological theory, finds their solution (N.S.Trubetzkoy, 1960)[25].

23) While speaking of phoneme theory, one of the Danish structural linguistics, L.Hjelmslev, should be dealt with. Truly, L.Hjelmslev - follows his teacher F. de Saussure in accepting expressers and those being expressed (Ausdruksebene, Inhaltsebene). Moreover, he divides units in a language into two distinct groups. In each, both form and substance are clearly discriminated. According to L.Hjelmslev,

25 A number of theoretical considerations advanced in this work have been specified by numerous investigations, carried out in the field of experimental phonetics, and have been developed in praxis.

therefore, linguists must study pure form, as well as the form of the expresser. For him, any linguist not interested in these substances has missed vital evidences. Thus, L.Hjelmslev designates the pure forms of a language as a "linguistic scheme". In themselves, these linguistic schemes establish the inner prospect of language indepantly of sounds and their meanings. This is why sounds and their meanings can't be considered the real units of a language. After all, real units in language are established by the attitudes of sounds and meanings. Overall then, L.Hjelmslev envisages a phoneme as a unit of expression acting within sounds in the form of an attitude. There is nothing physical in it. Hence, L.Hjelmslev regards phoneme a fiction. Nonetheless, the principle of commutation, which L.Hjelmslev advocates, is the most important of all analytic rules. As L.Hjelmslev wrote: "Commutation between two elements of expression takes place at the time when their substitution with each other should cause the substitution of the expressed elements, or takes place between the two elements of the expressed at the time when their substitution with each other should cause the substitution of the elements of the expresser" (L.Hjelmslev, 1960).

24) At present. the "school" of Shcherba together with the Moscow School of Linguistics, still exert an influence (A.A.Reformatsky, P.S.Kuznetsov) (A.A.Reformatsky, 1970). Furthermore, I.A.Baudoin de Courtenay continues to expound his initial morphological stance. Yet, the Moscow School of Linguistics - acting from the concept of "sameness" between phoneme and morpheme (through phonological analysis), claim phoneme-compositions exist in language largely unchanged. All enunciating their endless puruit of phonemes in strong and weak positions. For example, in German the words /'v⊥nt/(vind) and /'v⊥ndə/ (in the vind) have the same morpheme as /v⊥nt/ is /

v⊥nd/, [d] and [t], while these sounds are considered as variants of one phoneme. Namely, the entire features characterizing the phonemes /t/ and /d/ establish the archiphoneme, or hyperphoneme, of these phonemes. Explaining, possibly, why representatives of the Moscow School state that words alone cannot determine which phoneme exists. As such, it is interesting to mention that while there are /t/ and /d/ phonemes in this language certainly, in the above mentioned word, phoneme, /t/ cannot participate - thereby causing surprise. Now, it's clear in the Shcherba school that /v`⊥nt/ phoneme /t/, although not in the word /v`⊥ndə/ phoneme /d/ occurs. Certainly, the fact there are two different phonemes in one and the same morpheme makes it is possible to understand why, from this viewpoint, the so-called substitution principles of phonemes is debated.

25) Interestingly, R.Jakobson, M.Halle, G.Fant (R.Jakobson, 1962), tried to prove that the phoneme-compositions of all languages (proceeding from acoustic features) are open to characterization. In itself, this characterization is based on the dikhotomic, or binary principle. What is more, they generally defended the existence of 12 distinctive features. Claiming therein, that a language in which not all these features appear is a (theoretical) probability. Certainly, for these authors, a phoneme is the entirety of differential symbols. As may be seen, therefore, this determination reminds one of the rubrics proposed byTrubetskoy. R.Jacobson, M.Halle, G.Fant in the following manner:

I. Vocalic/ non vocalic

II. Consonantic/ non-consonantic. These features serve to differ the approximate and affricate consonants from each other. Vowels, after all, can possess vowels and non-consonants, while consonants may possess consonants and non-vowels. Consider the vocabulary item liquid - /l/ and /r/ possess both the quality of vocality and consonants, yet the affricates /h, j/ possess neither vocality, nor quality in these consonants.

III. Durable – non-durable (with pause, with non-pause). To durable sounds belong all the consonants and /l/. Nonetheless, non-durable sounds are occlusive consonants along with /r/. In any initial establishment, a stream of air rushes out in construction, but in secondary items the stream of air rushes out once, or twice, before a pause takes place.

IV. Abruptive – non-abruptive[26]. In the articulation of abruptive consonants, the stream of air rushes out in small pauses, because in the glottis an occlusion takes place. Hence, mainly occlusive sounds are abruptive. However, in rare cases, constrictive sounds too may become abruptive. Fascinatinly, one may come across abruptive and non-abruptive sounds in the languages of the Caucasus, India, Africa and the Far-East.

V. Sharp – non-sharp (clear – non-clear). One may come across these features in constrictive, occlusive and in affricate phonemes. Sharp consonants differ from the non-sharp consonants by additional obstacles. Besides that, in the initial phases there appears a sharp noise

actue	**non-acute**
/f/,/v/, /č/,/z/	/b/, /p/, /m/, /d/
/s/,/s/,/z/,/x/	/t/, /j/, /n/, /g/
/r/,/h/,/γ/,/z/	/k/, /k`/
	/h/, /l/

VI. Voiceless – voiced. Consonant articulated by the vibration of the vocal cords are voiced consonants, although those which are

---

26 In the articulation of these sounds - together with the creation of occlusion in the mouth cavity in the glotis between the vocal-cords occlusion is created. For example, in Daghestani languages compare: /p$^{c/}$, /k$^{c/}$, /f$^{c/}$.

articulated without the participation of the vocal cords are called voiceless consonants.

Overall, the features indicated above are the characteristics associated with the sources of establishment of the sounds. These features too are divided into two.

1. Basic
2. Non-basic } features

The first one too is divided into 2.

a) tone
b) consonant } features

Obviously, only the second possess consonant features. What is more, the first and the second, basic features, whilst the third, fourth and fifth (features) are called secondary features. The rest of these features are associated with resonance. Lastly, features associated with basic resonance are one.

VII. Compact–duffuse. Compact phonemes are characterized by the relative increase of a central format field. Furthermore, they are opposed to diffusive phonemes. In diffusive consonants, of course, one or several have a diffused format, or field of formats.

From an articulatory viewpoint, compact sounds in any place resonator as louder - either in front of the mouth cavity, or at the back as it narrows.

compact	diffuse
/k`/, /k/, /h/, /g/	/b/, /p/, /t/, /d/
/a/, /o/, /œ/	/i/, /e/, /y/, /ø/, /u/, /ı/

VIII. Low – high. From an acoustic position, the accumulation (concentration) of energy in low frequencies, low voices, - even though high frequencies, loud voices can also be established. From the articulatory viewpoint, these are central and periferic sounds.

low	**high**
/k/, /g/, /x/	/t/, /d/, /s/, /z/, /ş/
/b/, /p/, /v/, /f/	/j/, /c/
/a/, /o/, /u/, / æ/	/i/, /e/, /ø/|, /y/

As may be seen, low sounds belong to labial and backlingual consonants, as well as back vowels. But loud sounds belong to forelingual, mediolingual consonants and front vowels.

IX. Bemol - simple tonal sounds

Bemol sounds are distinguished from tonal sounds acoustically, either by the rise of tone or by the descending of the sound - which causes a sharp descending of the tone in vowels and consonants. That's why this musical term is used. Additionally, the sign "b" as a diacritic sign indicates labialization.

X. Diez – simple. In the articulation of diez sounds, tone rises from an articulatory point of view by adding an extra articulation onto the main articulation palatalization. With the consonants, the rise of tone is associated with palatalization, which is why (in order to show its conditionally), this musical term is used.

XI. Tense – relax. Here phonemes, from an acoustic viewpoint, are distinguished by sharply diminishing the resonance, and the rise of general energy. However, from an articulatory viewpoint, they are distinguished by keeping away from a state of stagnation. When one says "the stagnation state of organs of speech", one means the state in the articulation of /æ/.

Tense	**Relax**
strong consonants	weak vowels
stressed consonants	unstressed vowels

Binarists - it is possible to characterize Azerbaijani phonemes as follows in Table 4

№	Azerbaijani phonemes	a	I	O	i	E	æ	i	ø	U	l	m	n	r	b	v	g	γ	d	ʒ	z	j	K	k	h	p	s	T	f	x	h	vc	vz
	Dist.features																																
1	Voc.-non voc.	+	+	+	+	+	+	+	+	+	0 0	0 0	0 0	0 0	-	-	-	-	-	-	-	-	-	-	-	-	-	-	-	-	-	-	-
2	Cons.-non-cons.	-	-	-	-	-	-	-	-	-	0 0	0 0	0 0	0 0	+	+	+	+	+	+	+	+	+	+	+	+	+	+	+	+	+	+	+
3	Dur.-non-dur.	+	+	+	+	+	+	+	+	+	+	-	-			+ -	-	+	-	+	+	+	-	-	+	+	+	-		+	+	-	-
4	Abrup-non abrup.																																
5	Sharp-non-sharp	+	+	+	+	+	+	+	+	+	-	-	-	+	-	+	-	+	+	+	+	-	-	-	+	-	+	-	-	+	+	+	+
6	Voicel.-voiced	-	-	-	-	-	-	-	-	-	-	-	-	-	-	-	-	-	-	-	-		+	+	+	+	+	+	+	+	+	+	+
7	Compact-diffuse	+	+	+ +	+ +	+ -		+	-	-	0 0	0 0	0 0	0 0	+ =	+	+	+	-	-	-	+	+	+	-	-	-	-	-	+	+	-	-
8	Low-high	+	+	-	-	-	+	+ -	-	-	0	0	0	⊖	+	+	+	-	-	-	-	-	+			-	-			+	+	-	-
9	Bemol-simple	-	+	+	+	-	-	-	+	+	-	+	-	-	+	-	-	-	-	-	-	-	-	-	-	-	-	-	-	-	-	-	-
10	Dies-simple																																
11	Tense-lax	-	-	-	-	-	-	-	-	-	-	-	-	-	-	-	-	-	-	-	-	-	+	+	-	+	+	+	+	+	+	+	-
12	Nasal-non nasal											+	+																				

XII. Signs associated with additional resonators (nasal, non-nasal)

Nasal sounds are characterized by nasal formants. From an articulatory point of view, they are simple and clear. Hence, any dikhotomic characterization of Azerbaijani phonemes can be generalized as follows (see table 4). By this characterization, binarists seem to have solved problems previously seen as unsolvable in classical phonetics - these unsolved problems being issues around sonants. In reality, the principles of classification put forth by classical phonetics made it impossible for sonorous sounds to belong therein.

26) With this classification, however, binarists have encountered a number of deficienies. Although, before going any further, it is necessary to stand by the opinion of the famous French linguist A.Martinet. Tellingly, A.Martinet blamed the binarists for apriorism.

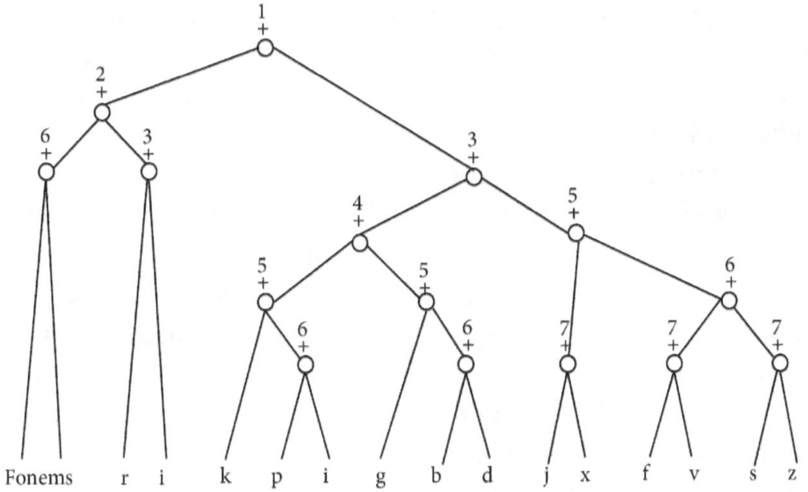

Certainly, he pointed out that in order to check whether the principles put forth by the binarists were universal or not, it would be necessary to examine all the languages of the world. (Theoretically, their number is equal to 6500). But as is known, the results of the binarists are not based on all the languages of our planet.

Conversely, even if these investigations were based on all the languages of the world, it is still impossible to speak about the universal character of any such investigation, because this theory does not involve dead languages, or languages which are becoming established (A.Martinet, 1960).

As such, A.Martinet noted that the theory defended by the binarists looked like the Tower of Babil - and one can only be answered by erecting a new Babil Tower (A.Martinet, 1960). On the other hand, the classification of differential features (as the famous Russian linguist P.S.Kuznetsov pointed out), is only feasible after attaining depth information regarding classifiable language (P.S.Kuznetsov, 1959).

27) Acting according to principles of double-characterization, it is possible to show the phonemes of a language in a tree-like form. Beginning from the first step, one may move step-by-step, up its branches. Each sign etched on the branches of this tree by a positive, or a negative, mark. A positive mark shows those phonemes, which lie under such signs, while a negative mark expresses the rest of the phonemes. One gives 7 of these signs - and together with the branches of the trees - introduces these signs. So, below is the tree whereon proper phonemes are given (see the tree-like description of the phonemes).

28) Each classification of essence is the systematization of differential features. In which case, let's continue by considering the principles of classification within classical phonetics. Including the

articulation of a sound wherein tone is dominant over noise, or noise is dominant over sound. Also, by incorporating the style and place of articulation of a sound etcetera. Yet, aren't all these differential signs (in analysis) a phoneme? Well, the two classifications put forth by binarists - based on these principles - explain why classification principles of differential signs can't be considered as something new. On the contrary, these principles somehow refuse to accept the sound composition of language objectively.

Yet, together with all this (in the conceptions of binarists), there are many valuable things. For instance, these principles make it possible to understand phoneme variations. In Azerbaijani, as a case in point, labialization - being peculiar to the system of vowels (bemol), is not peculiar regarding the system of consonants. That's why in the word /d°ɣz/ (straight) the first sound [d°] - from a phonological viewpoint - in the word /d′⊥z/ (knee) one finds sound [d′] not discriminated. Thus, when one knows that labialization is not a differential feature, one can say beforehand [d′] is the combinatory variant of an Azerbaijani phoneme /d/.

III. 3. Articulation basis of intercourse.

1) Articulation is the second component of intercourse. When one says articulation, of course, one means the entirety of possible movements of pronunciation organs. Usually, this is called the speech apparatus (see picture 2). Now, the creation of sound-speech by the speech apparatus is the achievement of language collectives (albeit later in the history of human society), because the initial function of human organs associated with speech is a physiological function.

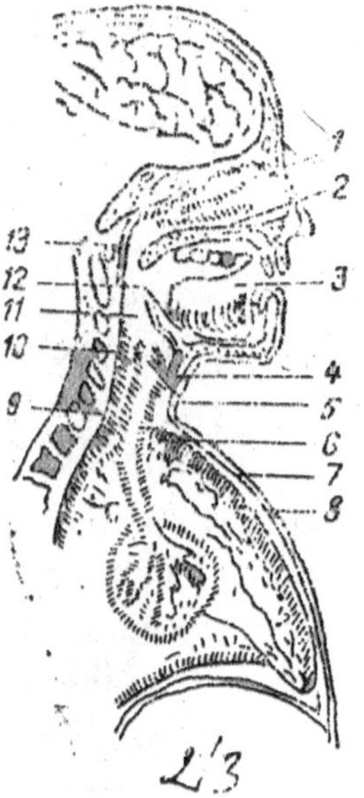

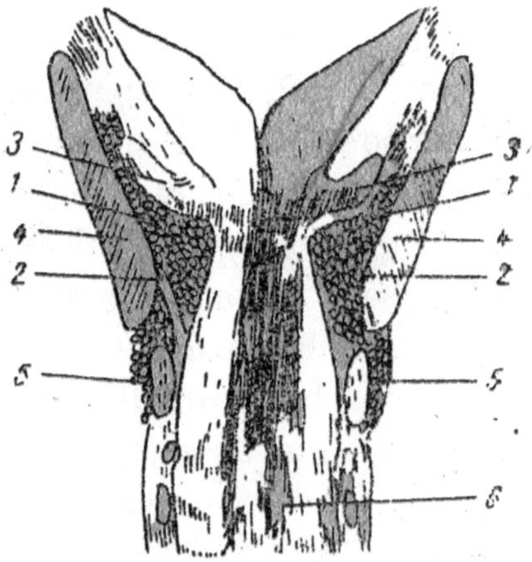

Picture 2.Side view of glottis

1. Nasal cavity Figure
2. Hard palate
3. Tongue
4. Thyroid cartilage
5. Vocal cords
6. Guttural
7. Lungs
8. Chest
9. Gullet
10. Ring-like cartilage
11. Overglottis
12. Under-tongue bone
13. Soft palate (palate pleura)

3. Front view of the glottis

1. Real vocal cords,
2. Vocal cords,
3.False vocal cords4. Thyroid cartilage,
5. Ring-like cartilage,
6. Breath tube,

In themselves, teeth serve to chew food, a tongue serves to turn over this food, while the lungs serve to breathe and give breath. It is not infrequent, that said, when these organs carry out their main functions (when a mouth is full with food it is difficult to speak), a spoken word is not understood by a listener clearly.

So, if a person is busy working with their hands (ploughing, hunting and so on), one can already say that he, or she, does not meet the requirements of intercourse. This is why human beings were obliged to transfer to a sound-based language.

Additionally, the establishment of sounds – from a physiological viewpoint - is associated with a lowering of pressure in the lungs, a widening of the chest, and a releasing of air out from the mouth cavity. Ordinary, taking a breath and giving breath are carried out in this way. Indeed, any transferance of food to the stomach takes place as a result of closing the passage to the vocal cords by means of an on-glotis lead. Hence, the formulation of a sound guttural plays a significant role. As one may see in the picture – speech apparatus (see picture 3).

2) Let's confess, the speech apparatus (including the anatomic structure of gutturals), is not an overarching issue for phonetics. Yet, the pronunciation of individually taken sounds, or learning how this or that organ of speech participates in forming a sound, is pertinent. Certainly, experimental phonetics, from the early days of its establishment, has made attempts to explore such methods and means – thereby making it possible to observe speech and phonation. Before, explaining these things, however, one finds it necessary to discuss the peculiarities of the human speech apparatus.

3) In the guttural, one of the most active cartilages is thyroid cartilage (see picture 4). It consists of 2 square parts differing from each other in their forms. Observed so, they nevertheless join in men at a 90° angle, even though in women at a 100° angle (H.H.Wängler, 1972, S. 71). Moreover, in men, one can see an obvious joining of this division, while in women this division in the thyroid cartilage is flat. This is called the gullet. Now, every movement of the thyroid

cartilage is ensured by outer guttural muscles and constrictors. By the thyroid cartilage, under a tongue, bone muscles ensure both the rise of the glottis and its joining. On the other hand, the thyroid cartilage - together with the muscles of the chest – causes a lowering of the glottis.

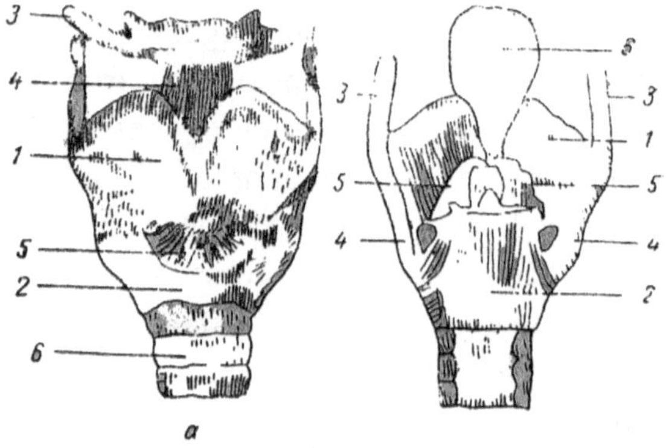

Picture 4. Front and back view of glottis

a : 1. – thyroid cartilage, 2.- ring-like cartilage, 3.- under-tongue bone, 4.- fibres, 5.- fibres uniting the thyroid cartilage and ring-like cartilages, 6.- breath tube; b: 1.- thyroid cartilage, 2. -ring-like cartilage, 3.- the upper horn of the thyroid cartilage, 4.- under horn of the thyroid cartilage, 5.- hollow-like cartilage, 6.- upper part of glottis.

Clearly, the up and down movements of the guttural play a vital role in producing this or that sound. Moreover, when pronouncing vowels, voiced and voiceless consonants (one after another, putting ones hand on the gullet) are easily observed. All meaning, in the pronunciation of closed vowels and voiced consonants, one can identify the rising of the guttural. Within the breath tube, there are 2 thin layers positioned one on the other. Also, between these layers, there is an opening which is called a purse. Oddly, the lower layer is named the real vocal cords, while the upper layer is called the false vocal cords. The purses between them are named the Morgan pockets (see picture 5).

4) The real vocal cords - consisting of two pairs of elastic muscles - tie these cords together with their fibres. Curiously, they differ in length between men and women - in men approximately 1,5., although in women 1,2 sm. That's the reason why the gullet in men is sharp, but in women flat. Indeed, the vocal cords of women are short and thin, making their voices loud and high-pitched. Between the vocal cords is the glottis.

There is no muscle in the false vocal cords. When one catches a cold, these false vocal cords substitute for the real vocal cords. This is why a person's voice becomes thick and weak.

For the establishment of voice, it is important that vocal cords should approach one another. Yet, if they do not achieve closure, the glottis remains open. 5 positions of the glottis are distinguished (see picture 6).

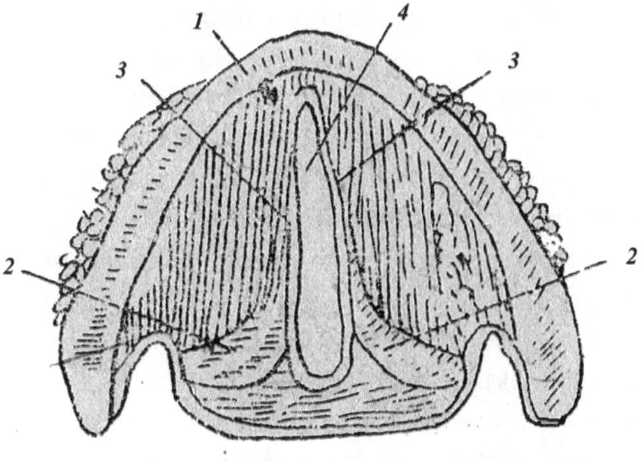

Picture 5. The transverse incision of the glottis

1.- thyroid cartilage, 2.- hollow-like gland, 3.- vocal cords, 4.- glottis

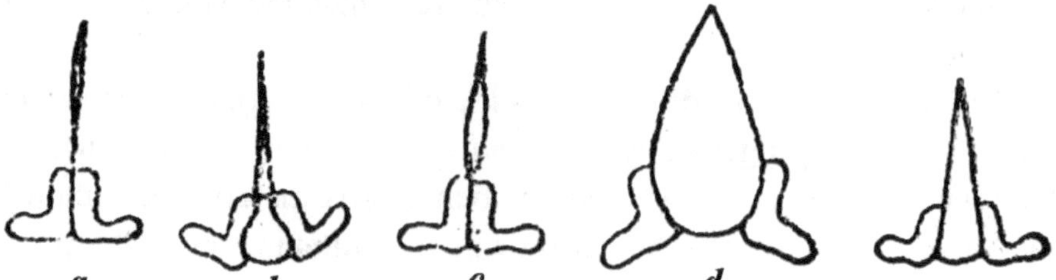

Picture 6. Different position of vocal cords
a-closure, b – whisper, c – sound, d - breath-taking, e –giving breath

Now, the ring-like and thyroid cartilage ensure pressure and an opening of the muscles of the vocal cords – along with their degree of intensity. Moreover, the vibration of the vocal cords depends on the pressure rushing out of the lungs and upon the quality of the sound pronounced.

In themselves, the vocal cords can begin moving in different ways. Giving breath, of course, begins before the vocal cords approach one-another. This is called aspiration. In Azerbaijani, the consonant /h/ is an example to this. If the vibration of the vocal cords take place simultaneously with aspiration, then it has a soft beginning /l/, /n/ and /m/ -can be an example of this. Interestingly, if vocal cords begin any movement towards closure, and again assume their former position, closure takes place. This is called the hard beginning. Yet, in the "absolute beginning" of the lexeme and morpheme (in German), vowels are pronounced in this manner. This is why linguistics named these processes knaklaut even though they have no phonological function. Their only function is a delimitative function, i.e. one that states the boundaries of morphemes and lexemes.

5) In the formulation of sound, a guttural vacancy plays an important role. It begins from the glottis and ends in the lips (in older

people the length of the glottis is 17 sm), consisting, in itself, of three parts: a) mouth cavity; b) nasal cavity; b) glottal vacancy. The pharynx establishes the distance between the glottal lid and the under-tongue bone. In Azerbaijani - out of its innumerable sounds - only /h/ is produced in the glottal vacancy. Differing from this - in Daghestani languages and in Arabic language - there exists the sound /h/ produced in the upper glottal vacancy.

Vocal cords, for their part, can move round 42 times, up to 1708 times, in a second. When singing, this diapason moves from 80 (the lowest tone of bass) up to 1303 hs (the highest tone of a soprano), which is equal to 4 ottava.

The voice diapason of this or that singer is 25–320 hs, while in a tenors voice 128–433 hs. is the lower tone 171–640. However, in a soprano it is 256–853 hs.

In music, male and female voices are divided into three positions:

Male voice	**Female voice**
bass	alt
baritone	metso
tenor	soprano

The volume of register (H.H.Wängler, 1972, S.104) Hz tone. The length of vocal cords

6. Mouth and nasal cavities play the role of resonator in the establishment of sounds. Depending on the quality, as well as the phonological system (and depending on their place in that system), the air-streem resulting from a rising and falling of the palate pleura – and an upwards and downwards movement of the uvula – allow a streem of air to rush out of the mouth and nasal cavities. All formulating the

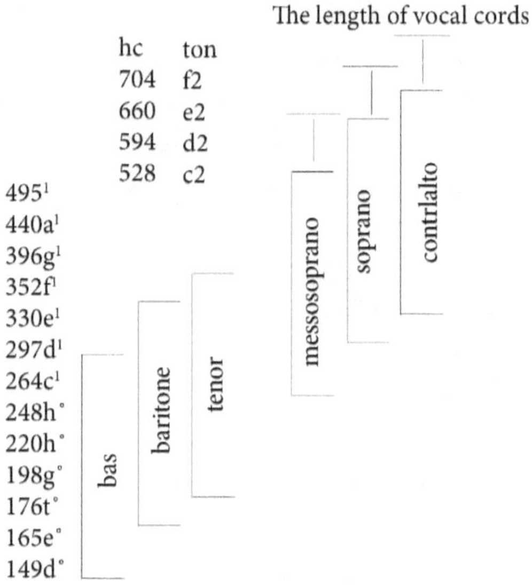

sounds (m), (n), which are nasal sounds, Nonetheless, other vowels and consonants originate from mouth sounds. Speech sounds, for instance, are not always active in the same degree. Indeed, the articulation of some of these sounds, in this or that organ of speech, become active, while others become passive. Overall, the active members are vocal cords, palate pleura, lower jaw, lips and tongue. Yet, teeth, teeth alveoli, hard palate etcetera are not active organs.

One must note that the place of articulation within intercourse - in comparison with other processes - has been deeply studied. That's why, beginning with the first half of the XIX century, physiologists, doctors, and other specialists, took an interest in phonetics. Certainly, any investigation of the physiological sources of speech arose from professional researches on the part of physicians. Relatedly, French Monk J. J. Rousseau in his work "Modification of Speech" opened a new trajectory in this field. However, any investigation of the basis of articulation only gathered momentum in the second half of the XX century. Therein, German scientist H.H. Wängler's book "Atlas of the German language" initiated an unprecedented delving into origination. Regarding Russian, L.G.Skalozub followed suit, while the Azerbaijanians S.B.Sadigov, F.A.Sadigov, F.A.Kazimov and A.A.Akhundov equally performed a great service in learning more about the rudiments of articulation (H.H.Wängler, 1960; Л.Г.Скалозуб, 1963; С.В.Садыгов, 1965; Ф.А.Казымов, 1956; A.A.Axundov, 1973).

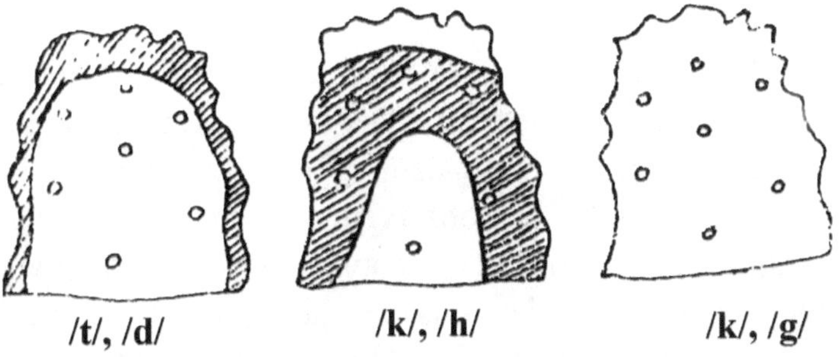

Picture 7. In Azerbaijani, the palatograms of consonants for /t/, /d/, /k`/, /h/, /k/ and /g/.

7) Observations of the organs of speech have existed for a long time. By observing the movement of lips, the position of the jaw, to-and-fro movement of the tongue, as well as the movements of other organs of speech, it is possible to gather detailed information on them. Classical phonetics, by way of this method, achieved much. Indeed, the classification of sounds with articulatory terms (forelingual, mediolingual etcetera) once more proved these techniques. Yet, such observations bore a subjective character - and it is for this reason that involvement with the exact sciences showed a positive influence

on phonetics. On one hand, the movements of members taking part in speech, while on the other hand the exactness of attained results, became apparent. What is more, new methods of investigation pioneered by scholars in other fields of science (when turning their faces to phonetics) revolutionized the topic. In a short period, therefore, pneumatic methods (getting kimograms of sounds), somatic methods (getting palatograms to indicate the movements of speech organs) and roentgenographic methods (by way of roentgenography) began to be widely applied. All of which created ever-favorable conditions for getting objective information. Each technique including additional methods used to explain other acoustic parameters by objective methods.

8) By observing his/her own speech and his/her interlocutors, a researcher could gather a great deal of information on the phonetic structure which he/she studied. Also, depending upon their aim, of course, a phoneticist - having observed segment and supersegment units, among a number of other features – could equally collect data for theoretical generalizations. Furthermore, to attain repeated observation, an investigator would often use a tape-recorder.

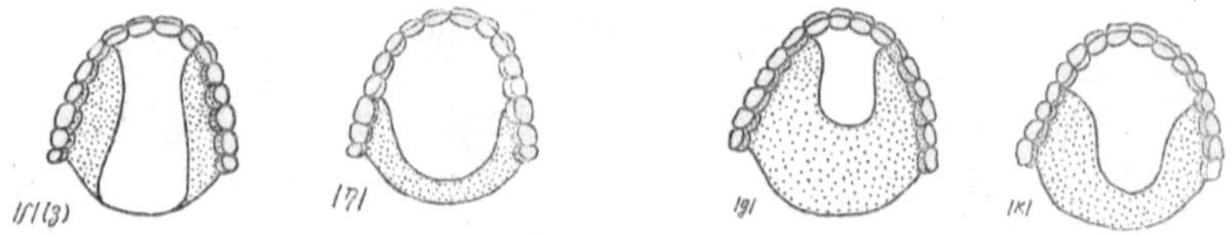

Picture 8. Palatograms of consonants in the German language /s/, /z/, /g/, /k/ etc.

All in all, after getting acquainted with theoretical literature on the phenomenon which investigators observe, a researcher prepared a program in conformity with the object: sounding it, either in his/her studies, or by the performance of another person. Moreover, once tape recorded and following repeated listening (or using other bearers of language), made some tentative conclusions. In fact, by attracting others, an investigator ensured the objectivity of his/her work.

Of late, investigators don't study prepared programs beforehand, but rather they learn about vivid language, generalize, and then offer informed comment on the results attained yo open debate. Indeed, the results, which he/she achieves, are usually reflected in phonetic tables and pictures.

9) Tellingly, the movement of speech organs can be described objectively by somatic methods. What is more, by means of mirroring people's lips or tongue, whole new vistas of inquirey have emeged.

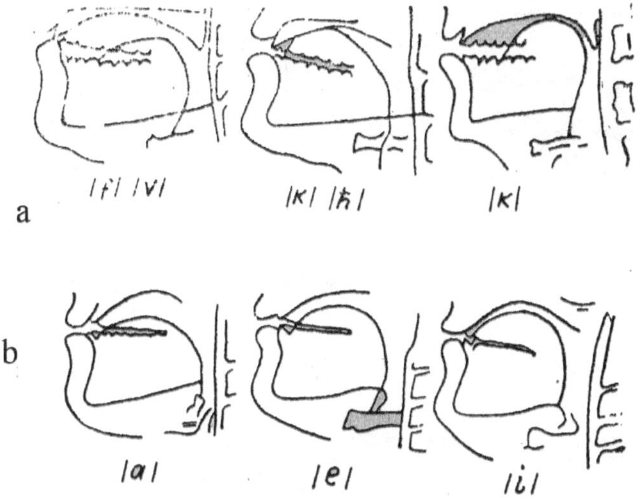

Picture 9. Roentgenorams of Azerbaijani phonemes a: /f/,/v/,/k`/,/gh/,/k/,/u/ b:/a/,/e/,/i/.

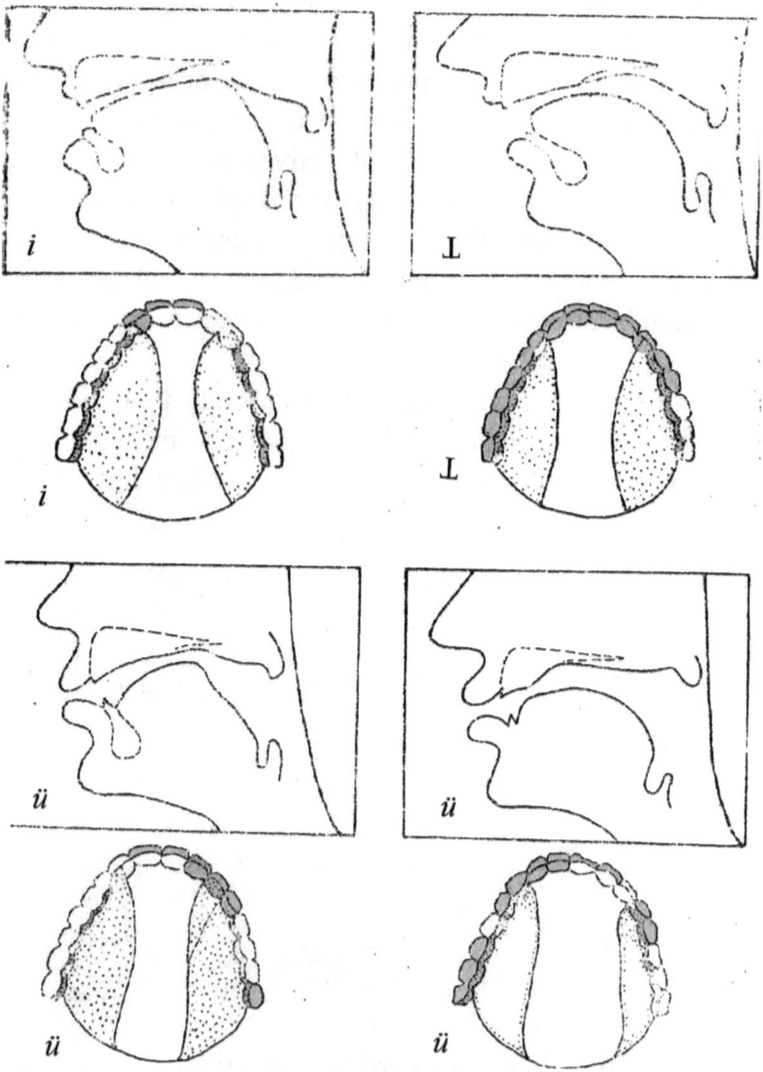

Picture 10. Roentgenograms and palatograms of the vowels of German language sounds:
/i:/:/⊥/, /y:/ /y/.

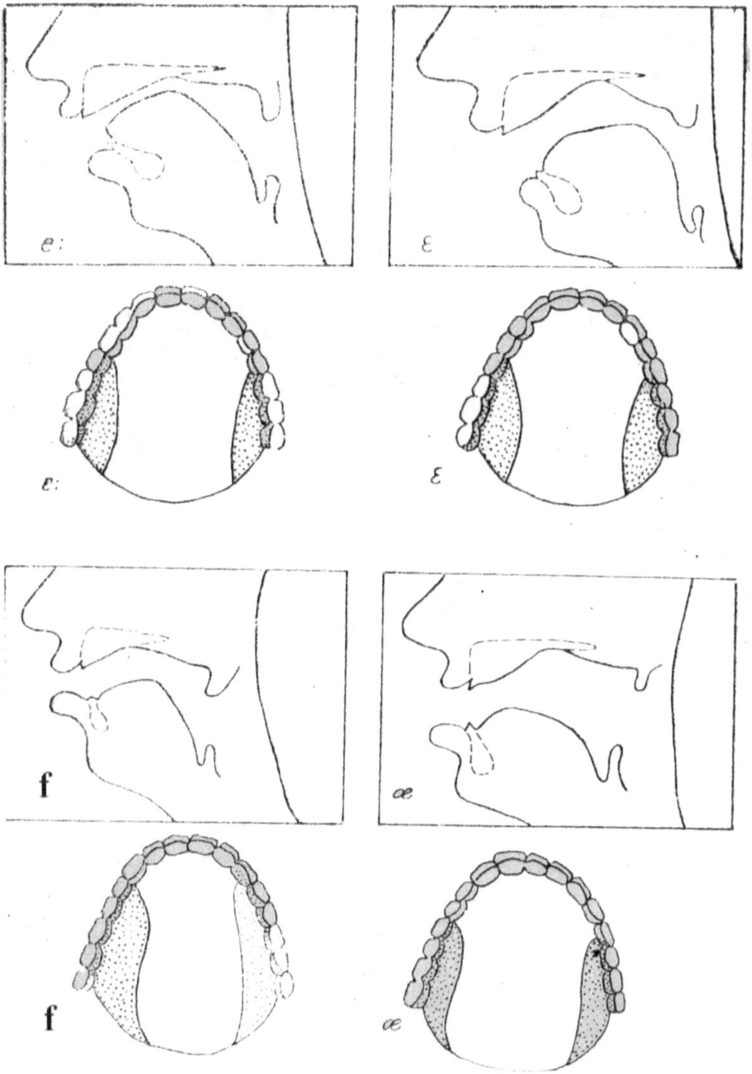

Picture 11. Roentgenograms and palatograms of German language vowels /e:/, /E/, /ø:/, /œ/.

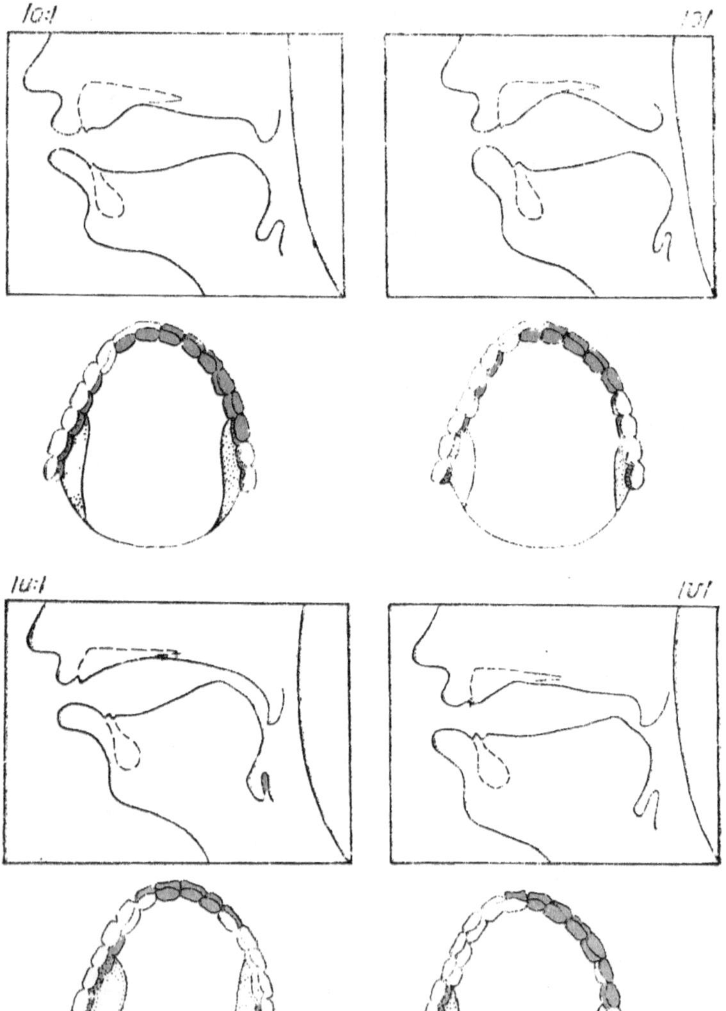

Picture 12. Roentgenograms and palatograms of vowels /o:/, /u:/ and /v/ in the German language.

Even now, in the instruction of a foreign language, mirroring plays a great role. If a teacher uses a mirror during a speech lesson, he/she can visually indicate the position of each organ during the act of pronunciation. Indeed, this or that sound (illustrated through this method), can guide good pronunciation habits in students. But this yechnique may additionally be applied in deep scientific investigation. After all, it seems simple, yet it is the reason why palatography and roentgenography entered phonetics. Now, in order to make a palatogram, an artificial palate is prepared, painted with chemical paints, and then placed in the mouth of the speaker who is going to pronounce an intended sound. By the movement of the tongue, the chemical paint on the palate is rubbed off, while on the palate the track of the tongue touching the artificial palate, leaves its track. In these pictures, roentgenographies and palatograms of vowel and consonant sounds in German and Azerbaijani have been depicted.

In forlingual consonants, the front part of the tongue is used, whilst in backlingual consonants, the back part of the tongue is more active – as can be clearly seen. Moreover, the black shades on the artificially made palates once again prove this. Certainly, though palatagraphic methods, one may envisage the position of the tongue – along with its defective features. Before everything else, it creates obstacles in pronouncing sounds correctly, since it is not a real palate - but an artificial one. The main error, however, is found in the fact palatograms rely upon the pronunciation of a word in an isolated form, not within a sentence or a specific word. A procedure, which is not characteristic for vivid language. This is why investigators (in order to produce natural speech) use roentgenographic methods.

10) In order to dynamically observe the articulation basis, scientists widely used roentgenographic methods. Clearly, this provides possibilities to observe movements not only in the mouth

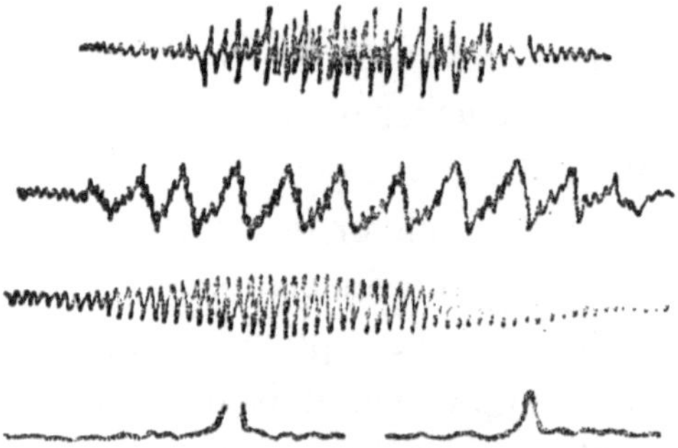

Picture 13. Ossillographic view of the phonemes of the Azerbaijani language

cavity, but also in the gutturals and chest. Yet, it is difficult to look at the sounds in the flow of speech, because a speaker must not be subjected to Roentgen beams. Hence, it is not possible to observe the articulatory position (including the participation of supersegment units), by means of roentgenograms. In the pictures of Azerbaijani and German, however, they have been given. Furthermore, when a reader carefully examines them in the articulation of each vowel and consonant, he or she can easily observe the position of the tongue, as well as the articulatory position created in the mouth cavity. Additionally, regarding the labial phonemes he/she can observe the position of the lips (see pictures 10, 11, 12).

11) As may be seen in the pictures of the articulation of consonants and vowels, the distance between the tongue and palate (depending on the feature of this or that sound) the tip or back of the tongue rises and falls. In a phrase, every sketch of articulation - by this method - can be expounded, Hence, it is possible to give a complete articulatory view of all the phonemes in a language. One more advantage of such picturing is that by comparing similar and different features existing in various language structures, it is possible to achieve invaluable results.

So, in the process of teaching, this method becomes a powerful tool. Now, it is conceivable that studying roentgenograms and palatograms can be done by means of statistic calculation. Although, indicating all the movements of the organs of speech by figures alone is far from desirable. For example, when examining the quality differences of short vowels in German by this method, one may elucidate valuable even though incomplete data. On the other hand, one may still explain the differences and resemblences to other features in the articulation of phonemes by these calculations - albeit somewhat superficially. Nevertheless, once realized, one may create an ideal model of intercourse and take serious steps towards the realization of speaking machines. Indeed, by compiling articulation tables - including the improvement of telephone communication systems - one may play a very positive role overall. Furthermore, in treating persons having defective speech, aphatics or stammerers, it is possible to use the achievements of articulatory phonetics in praxis.

III.4. The Acoustic Basis of Intercourse

1) Any systematization of sounds taking part in intercourse is created through an understanding of language units differing from one another. As such, one of the central issues then becomes the position of the vocal cords in the guttural act. Interestingly, if one pressurizes the chest, a stream of air is pushed out, which causes the vocal cords to vibrate in the guttural. This vibration of airwaves in the guttural vacancy forcing further activity. Following this, a widening occurs that consequently increases, or diminishes, air pressure. Obviously, the unit measuring this sound pressure is a bar. Human ears, of course, can endure from 0,0002 to 250 sound pressure. Even though, in ordinary speech, this is from 0, 02 to 20 bar.

At this point, one must mention that in ones surroundings the airwaves (straight or radial), only allow direct radial diversity by means of megaphones in one direction. Thus, movements continue until these waves weaken and come to an end. The scattering of voice - in the indicated direction - depending on the strength of the airwaves, their pressure, as well as meteorological conditions. For example, in an atmosphere equal to 1 grade, voice (approximately), scatters in one second across 331 metres.

2) So, it is clear from acoustic physics that repeated vibrations - having the same length - are called periodic vibrations. Arising from such vibrations, musical tones (harmony), or simple tones, are created. Thence, language (from this viewpoint) can be divided into 4 groups. Vowels, of course, are completely musical sounds expressing themselves, All meaning, repeated obertones (tones achieved by the vibration of this or that part of the vocal cords) find depiction as rich curvy lines. Indeed, in these ossilograms their presence is pictured as curvy lines distributed one after another (see picture 13).

Non-periodic vibrations produce noise, but in voiced consonants emerging within a neighborhood of vowels, or sonorious sounds (together with a main tone), obertones become weak. What is more, the amplitude of curves (intensivity) is very small (see picture 13),

If vocal cords do not vibrate, the voice created at that time will consist of noise only. In the ossillograms such sounds are reflected as a mixture of lines indistinguishable from one another. Herein belongs constructive noisy sounds (see picture 13).

A process culminating, one must add, by a stream of air coming from the mouth cavity over the non-vibrating vocal cords, which then beat off any closure in either the guttural, or nasal, cavity. Afterwards, there appear sounds, which are called occlusive-plosive sounds. In the ossillogram, such sounds are first indicated with straight lines, then -

by separating from the straight line and by coming back to their former state - are indicated as such in the picture (see picture 13).

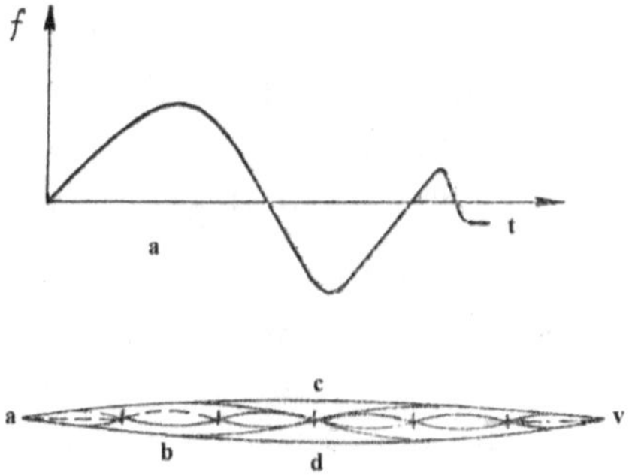

Picture 14.

a- stopping the vibration,

b- stopping the vibrations of the movements and the various parts.

3) Depending on the frequency of the vibration and amplitude of sounds, there is a differing in loudness and power. For instance, in the stringed instrument called "tar" which is widely played in Azerbaijan, one can easily watch how sounds are created. Thusly, by the letter "a" one may see a string tied to a wooden cup, following which the other end of the string is tied to a handle. Moreover, the letter "b" follows suit. So, when one touches the string with a mizrab[27] (according to the power of impact) it begins to vibrate. Indeed, it will move from "a" and "b" to "c" afterwards moving in the direction of "d" - a distance as long as the journey back to "a" and "b". Unsurprisingly, vibration in this direction will continue until it reaches the place wherein it was before the hit – although continuing with a dying away of the sound. If one strikes this string again, a similar situation will arise (see picture 14).

27 Mizrab – a wooden board ised to vibrate strings by touching them.

Now, the strings moving away from "a" and "b" are called a vibration. A measurement named in honour of the German physicist Heinrich Hertz. Technically, of course, any movement of the vibration in one second is equal to one hs. Also, sounds up to 100 hs mean that the number of the sound establishing this vibration is 100 in a second - which is equal to double vibrations.

4) The loudness of the sound depends on the frequency of vibration of the object. But frequency, along with the mass of the object, is in direct proportionate. However, regarding tensity, it is the very opposite proportion. So, the frequency of vibration of the object (the mass of which is small), is powerful, while its loudness is high.

In addition, one must bear in mind that the frequency of objects having thick mass, although weak tensity, produce much weaker voice. Out of two objects, therefore, the one that is subjected to a stronger hit produces a louder sound. All making it clear that a sound equal to 100 hs is louder than a sound with 50 hs. Indeed, the power (intensivity) of a sound is its second most important feature. As such, this process is called "perpendicular transition" - due to the fact the energy in a sound transcends into sound waves in one second 1 sm^2. Nonetheless, the power of a sound depends upon the amplitude of the vibrator separating it from the limitation of stand-still. Yet, one must not forget the surface of the object and the meteorological situation.

Argued so, the unit measuring the intensivity of a sound is a desibel. A measurement nevessary to distinctly hear voice and understand its role. In themselves, of course, the sounds have exactly the same power, even though different frequencies are heard in quite diverse forms.

5. In the example wherein a "tar" was used as a model to explain these topics, one noticed the vibration of a whole string - compared to a part string - produced distinct effects. As a whole, the string (in

speech the vibration of the vocal cords) vibrated in their entirety. This is called the main tone. However, the sound received from vibration in a part string of an instrument is called a partial tone. Certainy, the main tone in comparison with a partial tone, is lower. Thus, the name of obertone[28] - when given to a partial tone becomes clear. What is more, if one divides the object, a main tone which is equal to 100 hs (thereby determining the frequencies of each of them), will increase the frequency of each of them to become twice more – 200 hs. Hence, the frequency $^1/_3$, being three times more and so on. All meaning, 300 hs. is equal to the frequency $^1/_4$ – four times more etcetera. Namely, it will be 400 hs.

The loudness of the compound words is determined with their tones. But obertones give additional colouring or voice. This is called tembre. The speaker or a singer whose tembre is high always is listened with interest. Those whose tembres are weaker their speeches are monotonous and tiresome. In the creation of tembre resonance is of more interest.

As has been said above, vacancies on the guttural play the role of resonator. So, those sounds which are established by the vibration of vocal cords are given to these vacancies - and due to such frequencies become equal to the frequency of these sounds. As a result, the sound strengthens an object, which has no source of sound in itself – making it a resonator. Either way, the height (loudness) of the sound depends upon the mass of the resonator. Indeed, it depends on the largeness or smallness of its mouth. It needs to be said, of course, that sounds spread in resonators (having large mouths) are low, or vise-versa. For example, in the pronunciation of "a" - the way in which a mouth cavity works, in comparison with (i), is expansive. That's why (a) is low pitched, but (i) has a high-pitched voice. Moreover, the resonators having soft walls (in a human being the nasal and mouth cavities)

28 Oberton, being a German word, consists of "ober" meaning high, and "ton" meaning "simple voice".

possess lower selectivities. Hence, they make a frequency unfitted in its tone easily resonant. For their part, vowels are highly distinct. Indeed, each vowel has its own tembre and format. So, it could be claimed resonance creates the spectre of a sound. Although, this spectre shows which the parts the sound consists of (see picture 15).

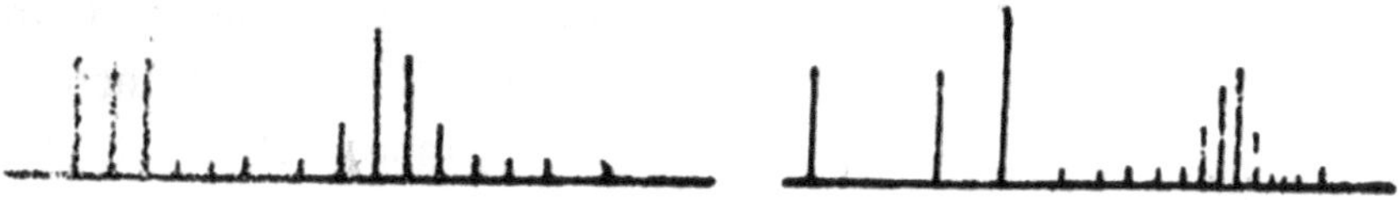

Picture 15. The spectre of the sound

In modern acoustics, the format of two theories complete one another because they both refer to an origination in vacancies of the guttural. So, for Helmholtz, complex vibrations generated in the guttural (as a result of vibration of the vocal cords), depend on the configuration between vacancies (resonators), and the strengthening of tembre in a proper vowel. Fascinatingly, it is claimed an air stream coming from the guttural passes into the mouth cavity and therein establishes a special tone. All being a process vital for each vowel. Now, from a linguistic point of view what is being said acts as little more than a subsidiary. After all, a linguist is not interested in these acoustic features in themselves, but rather in those facets associated with intercourse. Hence, any thesis seeking to establishe the main aim of experimental phonetics by asking what needs to determine acoustic difference is merely begging the question. Consider the following:

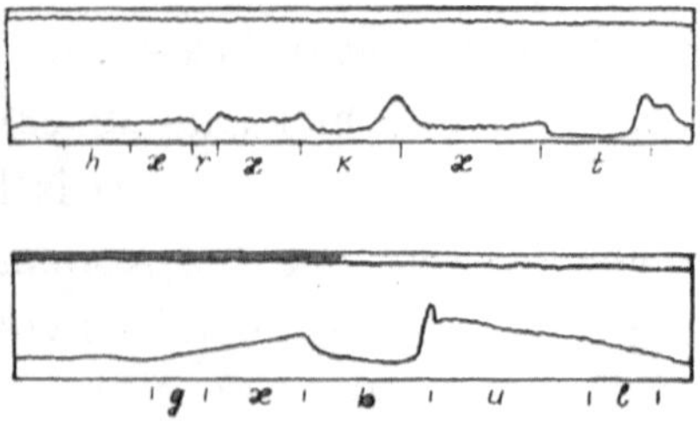

Picture 16.
Kimogramms of /hərəkət/ (movement) and /gəbul/(reception)

6) Therefore, a fascination for phonetic structure within a language (in order to observe all the phonetic phenomena taking place in a language), compelled these scientists to use technical advancements in order to create very notable works. Among them kimograms, ossillography and spectrography must be mentioned. Certainly, in the book entitled "Experimental Phonetics" (which the author has written together with other collectives of authors (the second book, Baku, 1981)), one has already explained the principles behind these mechanisms. Moreover, their technical features - including their rules of usage - has been thoroughly expounded.

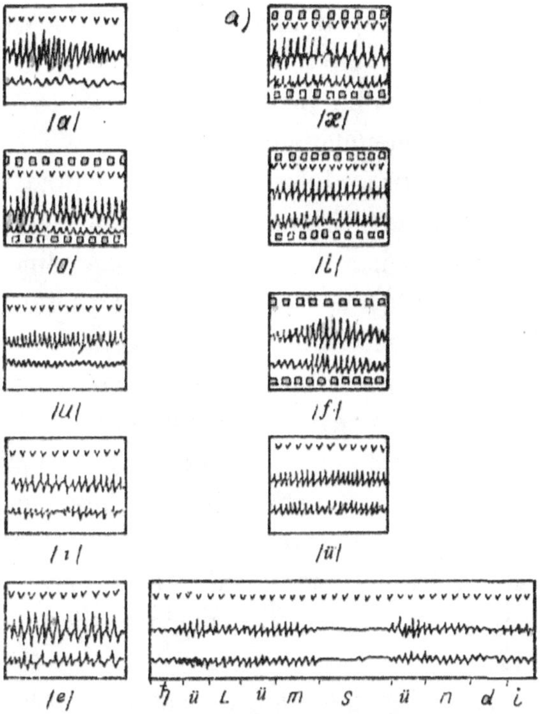

Picture 17. a – ossillograms of vowels; b – the ossillograms of the word / g^{v}lmsyndy`/ (he smiled)

In Europe, of course, long before these investigations were carried out, there was talk of a pneumatic methodology. Indeed, the first kimographic investigation belonging to S.B.Sadigov - and undertaken on materials in Azerbaijani (S.B.Sadigov. XI , 1961). As such, these illustrative materials may be researched in the same article (see picture 16). Nonetheless, as seen from those pictures, the curvy lines of vowel sounds are clearly distinguished. Also, small tooth-like forms are continuously repeated. Besides, their amplitude being greater. Yet, among occlusive-plosive sounds, the curvy lines descend to a low level. All making their character very plain – even though the stage of actual explosion is marked by an increase of amplitude. Moreover, in the kimograms, time spent on the pronunciation of a sound is possible to calculate with the help of boundaries between the sounds indicated by horizontal lines in the picture (see picture 16). However, technical difficulties in the pneumatic method are many.

Firstly, these procedures take too much time. Besides, the process – being cumbersome (beginning with their tape-recording in kimogram until non-exactness is revealed through curvy lines), obviously yields its place to electroacoustic techniques. Despite this, the pneumatic method has been successfully applied for a long, while investigators using these methods doubtless get serious results. Even now, the users of kimography are many. Maybe this is why L.V.Shcherba - when speaking of the importance of technical appliances for phonetics wrote, "Without the participation of vivid language, if it can be written as it is exactly by means of mechanical apparatus (this will be possible soon). Then we might be surprised by how many mistakes we make in phonetics, morphology, syntacsis and in the dictionary" (L.V.Shcherba, 1931, pp.125–126).

7) In revealing the acoustic nature of phonetic structures by electroacoustic apparatuses, ossillography plays an almost unique

role. Improving possibilities, as it does, in the field for writing about acoustic processes on paper, or on tape. Latterly, intonography, (having improved), including techniques centred round spectrography, has allowed the human eye to watch the natural flow of speech. Certainly, through the application of these apparatuses the research materials attained were calculated and then generalized. Nowadays, by their help, one can get enough information on three fundamental parameters of speech signals – intensivity, melody, and tempo. All resulting in a further development in experimental methods. Their advantage over previous techniques being that these mechanisms make the work of investigators much easier, since calculations carried out by hand are performed more or less instantaneously – along with the production of graphics and tables based on ready figures.

Despite ossillographs differentiating from one another in minor ways, their general constructions and functions are just the same. Indeed, they reflect received signals in the form of curves on a screen. Further, within these signal the movement of the main tone, the intensivity, and the time spent measuring it, are clearly expressed (see picture 17–18)[29]. The vibrator of the ossillographs make it finally possible to monitor sound frequencies from 50 – up to 10 000 hs. This is very important, because there are three types of frequencies. One of them is from 50 to 400 hs, being a means by which intonation can be watched in voiced and voiceless consonants. Another calculates the frequency of vowels in a range from 200 – up to 400 hs. Lastly, comes those sounds with the highest frequencies – noisy consonants in which frequency is from 1000 – up to 10 000.

8) When researching into the phonetic substructure of Azerbaijani, ossillographic analysis have been widely used (A.Akhundov, 1973;

29 Those who want to get all-rounded information on the technical characterization of ossillographs and other technical appliances may read the author's book "Experimental linguistics" ("Eksperimental dilçilik") (Baku, BDU, 1980, 1).

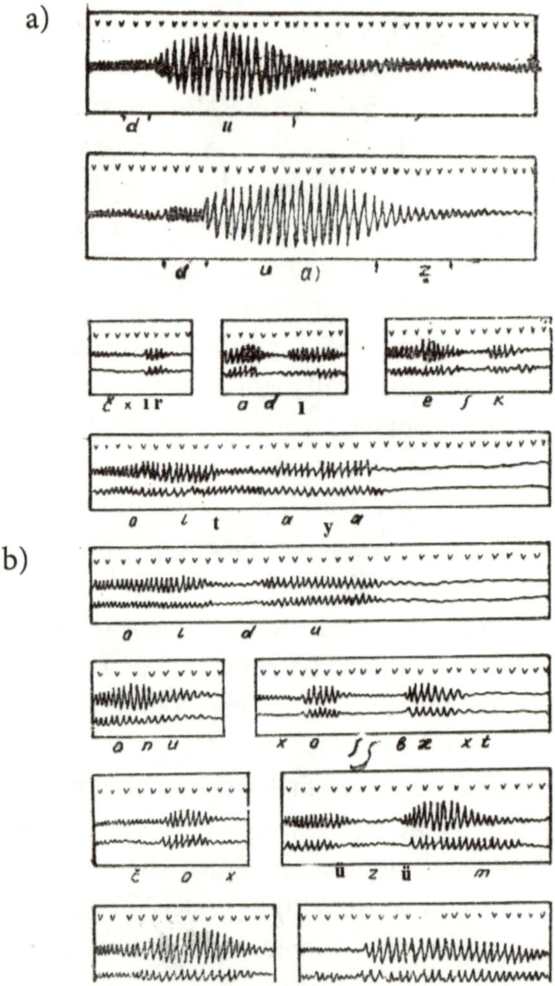

Picture 18. a – ossillograms of the words /duş/(shower) and /duz/ (solt); b – ossillograms from individually taken words and utterances /tş$^{\vee}$xıp/(went out), /adi/(simple), /eşk/(love), /sajı/(numbers), /biy/(interjection), /olm$^{\vee}$ja oldu^{1}/ (it can't be, it become), /onu^{1} / (him), /xoş$^{\vee}$bæxt/(happy), /c$^{\vee}$ox/ (more), /üzüm/(my face).

H.Mehdiyev, 1973; Ə.Cəfərov, 1975; F.Y.Veysəlov, R.İsayeva, 1987. Experimental Phonetics, 1981). The most reliable information and exact calculations being given in the author's own book "Experimental Phonetics" published in (1981, 2). In this book, together with ossillographic pictures, the quantitative and qualified changes inside sounds were fully explained. At the same time, all the parameters reflecting their acoustic nature – the tone of the voice, its intensivity and time, along with position in the intonation centre - and their stresses - are expounded with the aid of concrete language materials. Everything is indicated, of course, depending on the place of phonemes and the condition of their realizations - that their ossillographic pictures change too. This is why the flow of speech often shows the boundaries of phonemes - the most difficult and responsible stage of ossyllographic analysis. Clearly, both from a theoretical and practical viewpoint, the fact that vowels may be pronounced separately and provide ossillographic pictures, may be given in this way. Each new image making still better impressions (see picture 17).

When looking at the picture above, it becomes clear that the curves of the closed vowels differ from open syllables in their qualities. For example, in the vowel /a/ the curves are sparse, but their amplitudes are high, while /i/ is thick and is of a weaker amplitude. Furthermore, the vowel /i/ has a similar quality of curvy lines to the vowels /u/ or /ü/. The distances between the curves being reflective of female speech as shown in ossillograms not largenes. Contrastingly, obertones are very simple, but thick. For their part, the ossillographic curves of a phoneme depend on their places in a word. Be it either before a word, in the middle of a word, or at the end of the word. Moreover, the surrounding of a phoneme (the influence of the phoneme coming at the beginning of the word, or if it is weaker than the phoneme coming after it), is equally necessary to record, due to its attitude towards stressed

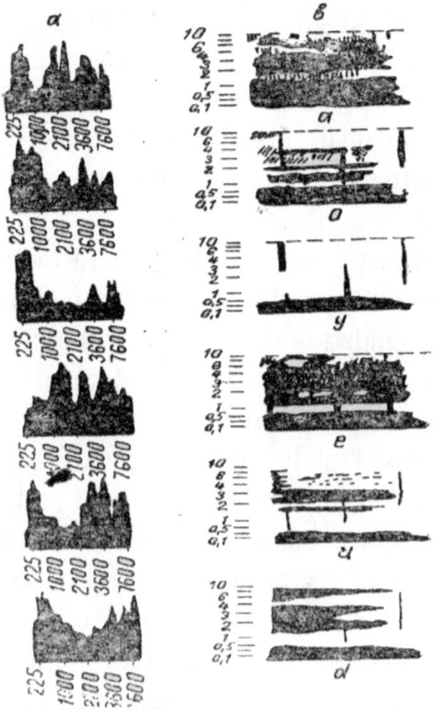

Picture 19. a – momentary spectre of vowels; b – a dynamic spectre of vowels. The spectrograms have been taken from the work of L.V.Bondarko (L.V.Bondarko, 1977. 62)

syllables. As the quality and quantity of the vowels within a sentence become subjected to still more sound influence, their ossillographic picture, (depending on their separation both from and within the word) is differentiated. Curiously, it is extreme weak, whilst the impact of the intonation contre is clearly observable (compare picture 17–18).

9) Generally speaking, vowels are differentiated from consonants by the fact that consonant curves are plain with a weak intensivity. Additionally, sonants - though being more like vowels - have

specific features. Firstly, they show themselves as having uniquely identifiable curves, even though the intensivity of sonants is weaker and also more sparce. Of course, according to phonetic location with voiced consonants, their characteristic curves are weaker, and their obvious amplitudes are very small (see picture 18). However, in voiceless consonants there is no tone. Hence, any observations are far from distinguishable. What is more, with occlusive-plosive consonants, closure is reflected by a straight line, even though an eventual separation from this line is seen: whereas with constrictive consonants mixed lines are observed. Truly, hidden world is revealed by ossillograms. Of a sudden, a sentence may be transcribed on a

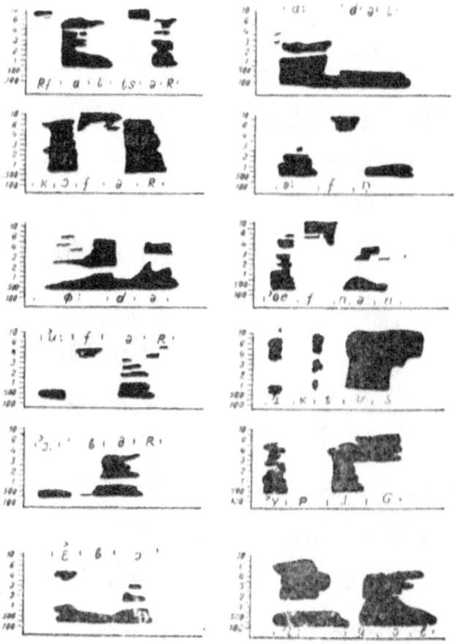

Picture 20. The spectrograms of the Germanic words
/Plaftser, Adel, Koffer, ofen, öde öffnen, ufer, İktus über, üppig, Ebbe, İgel/

tape-recorder. Afterwards, the boundary among necessary phoneme manifestations is determined. At the same time, an investigator having good theoretical preparation easily can distinguish the off stage from a beginning stage. Undoubtedly, one must mention here that these are important conditions for any experiment. Albeit proving impossible, sometimes, to put a boundary between a neighboring vowel and a sonant. In such cases, of course, calculations are carried out together - and by dividing them into two parts, it is possible to get acoustic marks for each of them separately. Every vowel, that said, being away from any stress within the sentence (as well as syllables), is demonstrably unmentionable in the flow of speech (see picture 18b). Especially, with regard to harsh (hissing) consonants, along with the majority of affricates (in their surroundings) - which may be mapped. Certainly, at the end of sentences, the amplitude of curves become weak, while the time spent on the articulation of a syllable – taken as a whole - increases. This is clearly seen in the ossillogram for the utterance of the words /Olmaya oldu/[30].

10) As mentioned above, the start of the 50's in the XX century witnessed the technical investigation of sound composition within language. Following which, spectral examination methods were widely spread. Indeed, to get a view of speech, a determination of sound tembre, or an analysis of the changes taking place in their junctions, it was increasingly felt spectrograms were nearly perfect. Herein, one shall not deal with the technical features of spectrograms, but rather with some of their features. At present, two types of spectrograms are used: a) static; b) dynamic. In the first, a marking of sound frequency strengths occurs. As for the second method, a general impression

30 As we have widely spoken of the vowels and consonants of our language and have given sufficiently more information in the ossillographic analysis, taking vowels and consonants into consideration in our above mentioned book "Eksperimental fonetika" ("Experimental phonetics") we don't think it necessary to deal with them more. Those who are interested in, may get the book and get further information about the issues we are dealing with here.

about the sounds are recorded. This is called a momentary spectre of the sound (see picture 19). It is difficult of course, to learn the cause of changes at the time. Perhaps this is why dynamic spectrograms (sonography) are used (see picture 19).

Yet, in these spectrograms, the frequency of the main tone of a sound is seen as a vertical line, even though its time is given in a horizontal line.

In dynamic spectrograms, the tone spectre of a sound is reflected in the form of layers, which are called formants in the literature. Moreover, the sound spectre may be in different formats. As such, they are marked with F_0, F_I, F_{II}, F_{III}, F_{IV}. Just below the spectrogram, to and above it, FII formants appear. In learning the language sounds, however, F_I and F_{II} are of main importance.

Now, F_{III} and F_{IV} are some of the individual features of a speaker. As such, within these patterns, sonant formats are clearly seen. Interestingly, these sonants too possess a clarifiable format structure. So, in the spectrograms voiced consonants are discriminated. Furthermore, voiceless constrictive sounds in the higher frequencies possess confused spectre, but in the occlusive-plosive consonants there is no F_0. Closure, therefore, is marked with a white field, but plosure is marked in the form of black dots in the spectre (see picture 20).

In order to measure the tone frequency, formant logarithms are used (see picture 21). Also, the intensivity of the voice in this spectrogram is indicated by the grade of its blackening. If blackening in the spectrogram is strong, sound is stronger, although if the grade of blackening is weak, then the intensivity is weaker.

11) **Spectral analysis of the phonemes**. In spectrograms of closed vowels, it is impossible to discriminate F_0 from F_I, because each format concentrates some frequencies in itself (see picture 22). But in the open vowels (as large as the mouth cavity opens), high

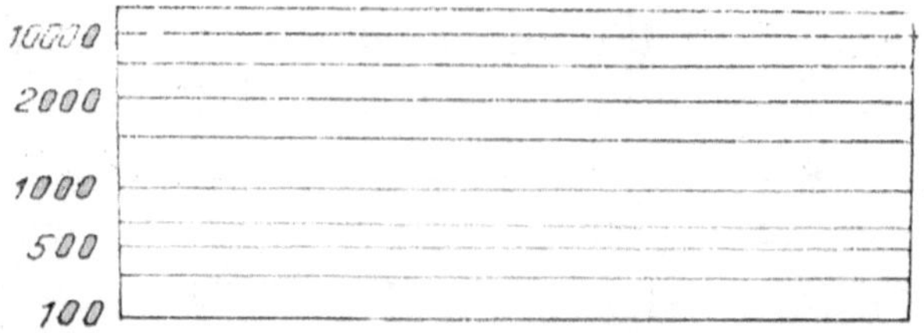

Picture 21.Formant ruler. So, as it is in the ossillogram, it is equally in the spectrogram, too. So commented, each sound has three parameters: the main tone, time, and intensivity. Obviously, it is possible to glean further information about them. Yet differing from an ossillogram, a spectrogram

frequencies are situated (see picture 22). Albeit F_{11} is above /i/, while /u/ is in the lower frequencies.

Different from picture 22, in picture 23 the phonemes of Azerbaijani have been given within the words. That's why, the spectre of the vowels within these words are discriminated from the spectre attained in their separate pronunciations. All caused, of course, by the fact the consonants coming before or after vowels are of different qualities. Indeed, the front of the tongue, the middle of the tongue, or the back of the tongue, strongly influence the beginning and the end of speech – wherein a specific position of transition is created. Now, transition positions show themselves by being high or low positions of format starting as sonors. For instance, if forlingual consonants ensure the higher frequencies of the beginning of backlingual consonants, then the labial consonants - on the contrary - ensure a transition position with the lower frequency.

Generally, in the junction of sounds having different pronouncing places of articulation, impact and contre impact show themselves more clearly. But in the junction of the sounds having the same place of articulation the transition position is not so conspicuous. Depending upon the stressed or unstressed position of the vowel the grade of getting into reduction is clearly seen in the spectrogram (see picture 23).

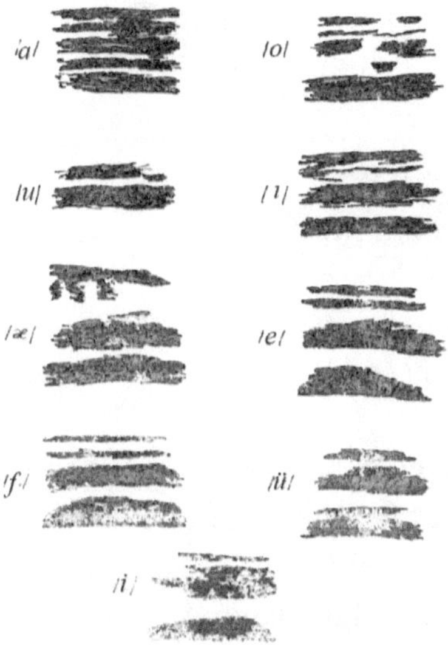

Picture 22. Spectrograms attained from the individual pronunciation of Azerbaijani vowels

Calculating the spectrograms attained from the separately pronounced vowels of Azerbaijani, each vowel was determined as F_1 and F_{II} (see picture 24).

As is seen from the pictures, F_{II} indicates a vertical direction in the pronunciation of the vowel regrding articulatory features, although F_I shows the horizontal direction of the movement. Closed vowels in the performance of both the announcers as to the first format possesses a low frequency, yet as to the second format, possesses a high format.

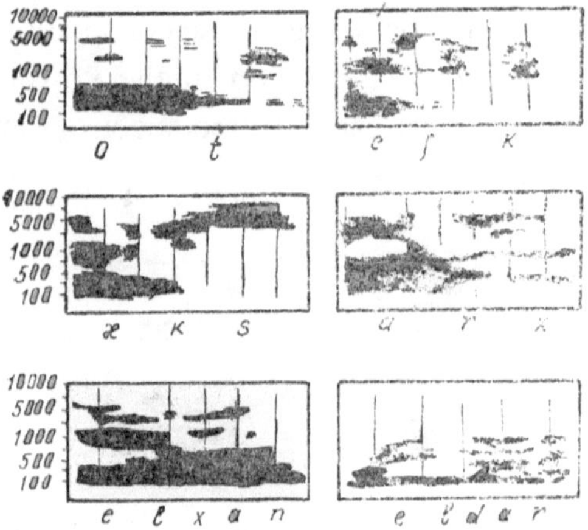

Picture 23. The spectrograms of /ot/ (gras), /eʃk/(love), /iks/ (x), /arx/ (gutter), /elxan/ (Elkhan name) and /Eldar/ (Eldar name)

From the back vowels in /o/ and /u/ f_{II} one sees 800–1000 hs, and in /a/ and /æ/ possesses the highest frequency. In itself, this predicates Azerbaijani vowels as being the most open ones in the system of vowels of the Azerbaijani language. As to F_{II} /æ/ is a great deal higher than /a/. This means that /æ/ and /ı/ as to the spectral characterization can be determined as a mixed vowel. Sonants as to their spectral pictures are more like vowels than consonants. This likeness with sonants - as it is with vowels - show itself by being in format structure. But differing from vowels, intensivity in sonants is weaker. Although, in unstressed syllables, the intensivity of the sonants may be at the same level with vowels - occasionally even higher. (see picture 20, 23). In voiceless occlusive-plosive consonants, closure is marked with a pause, but the explosion is indicated in the form of a small dot in the spectrogram (see picture 23). In the spectre of voiced, occlusive-plosive consonants, vibrations fitting to the field of F_0 and vibrations with weak frequencies are reflected during the explosure.

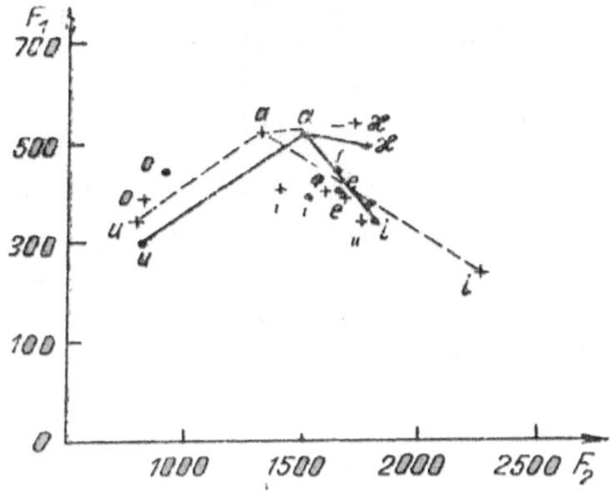

Picture 24.
Frequence of Azerbaijani consonants as to the F_I and F_{II} marks

In the voiceless constrictive sounds, as was said above, the high frequencies are sometimes wide, even though sometimes narrow stripes are created. In the sound /i/ they are narrow, but in /s/ they are wide (see picture 20, 23).

In the spectre of constrictive voiced consonants, voice in the weakest form finds its reflection in higher frequencies (see picture 20, 23).

It is necessary to mention that in order to learn the spectre of individually taken sounds, stationary changes and the first and the second transitional parts are separated. When one says "stationary field" one means the remaining stable part - as a result of isolation of the transitional parts when subjected to the changes of voice beforehand or afterwards. Yet, the first and the second transitions are suitable to the phases of excursion and recursion, within which the voice is subjected to more changes. It's true, nonetheless, that nasal consonants cause a descent into the lower frequencies of the stationary parts of the vowels (see picture 25).

In the spectral analysis of phonemes - in order to find the value of each format logarithm (ruler) - a spectrogram is put on and the format of each frequency is determined (see picture 24). F_0, F_I and F_{II} marks are found. The sound "o" in the word "ot" (grass) is equal to F_I 650 hs, but F_{II} is equal to 160 hs. To attain these marks, of course, the lower and upper limits of every structure are measured and being added are divided into two. The same operation can be done for the transition fields as well.

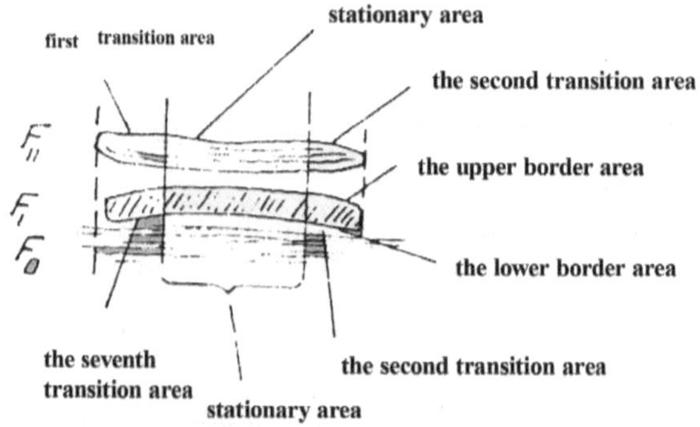

Picture 25. Stationary and transit fields of the spectrogram of the sound

This can be indicated as follows (see picture 25). So, not only the middle part of each word, but also due to the influence of neighboring sounds, the sounds which undergo changes can be easily discerned. As a result of spectral investigation, therefore, it is possible to establish direct connection between the acoustic and articulatory aspects, by which, it is possible to explain the result of articulatory movements in this or that spectre.

III.5. **THE PERSPECTIVE BASIS OF INTERCOURSE**

1) The received information by a listener from a speaker is one of the main conditions of intercourse. In most cases, of course, the speech of a speaker is either directed to himself (inner-speech, monologue), or to his prospective interlocutor (dialogue-partner), or to some other person (reported speech, lecture, etcetera). In all cases, however, it is obligatory that both speaker and listener should be the bearer of one and the same language. On the other hand (differing from the second picture of oral speech), the listener continuously changes his/her functions. Any understanding of sent materials, therefore, or its similarization, requires every significant element to establish the correct perspective-basis of intercourse. That said, hearing and similarization within one language collective tends to be taught from childhood. Only later on in life does this process automatically turns to a norm in human life.

The substantial bark of language, one may say in physical terms, is established by its difference from other signals. Indeed, when hearing and understanding these signals, the ears - being hearing apparatus - play an important role (see picture below).

2) Understanding a sound is a difficult process. Firstly, sounds spreading as waves in the atmosphere reach the outer ear of the hearer. Then, the ear auricle directs these sounds. Indeed, they take passage as a resonator strengthens the pressure of the sound and brings sound anvils into action. Following which, the hearing bones pass this sound onto the oval window. Due to differences between the measure of the window and membrane, a vibration emerges – possessing an extra 50–60 times pressure. Curiously, the thickness of the liquid in the snail membrane excludes the vibration with bigger amplitudes. Yet,

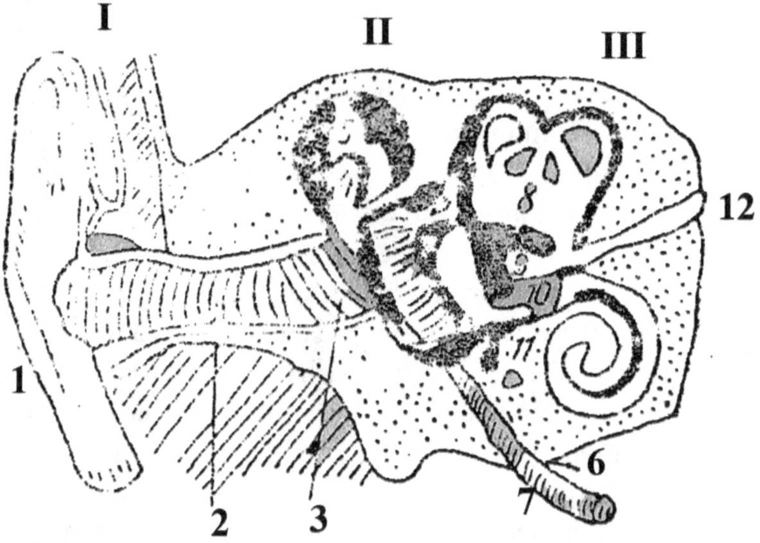

Picture 26. Hearing apparatus:1.–ear auricle, 2.–channel of hearing, 3.–ear pleura, 4.–hammer, 5.–anvil, 6.–stirrup; 7.– Eystax tube, 8.–semicircle channel; 9.–front opening, 10.–snail membrane, 11.–the main membrane, 12.–hearing nerves.

the vibration received from the oval window is transferred to the main membrane. Together both membrane hearing nerves begin to move, stimulating, as this does, the sound within the central nervous system.

3) According to the German scientist H. von Helmholtz, each fibre of the main membrane regulates a tone fixed at a certain loudness. Interestingly then, this membrane reminds one of a resonator reflecting the frequencies available to human ears (frequency from 16 to 22 000 hs).

Furthermore, in a human body, the lower hearing boundary is 16 hs, while the upper hearing boundery depends upon age. For an older person this is equal to 15 000 hs, but in the children it is equal to

22 000 hs. Also, speech sounds are located in this diapasone.

To hear any sound, it must have strength. Hence, the sound diapason of an intelligible noise must begin at 0,000000001 erg sm^2, and must be equal to 10,0000 erg sm^3 in a second. The hearing boundary of intelligible sound depends on the tone having the least strength. Yet, the sensibility of our ear is equal to 1000 hs up to 3000 hs.

In order to hear and understand a sound, its frequency and intensivity play a mojor role. Intensivity, in honour of G.Bell, is measured by decibels:

1:1 db – lower hearing boundary
10:1 from 10 m distance for the whispering of leaves in the wind
100:1 from the distance of 20:1 whispering
1000:1 30 cities having no transport
10 000:1 40 the sound of a vehicle coming from a 10 metre distance
100 000:1 50 sound of radio in a room
1 000 000:1 60 – talk with an interlocutor within a metre distance
10 000 000:1 70 – powerful street traffic
100 000 000:1 80 – very powerful " – "
1 000 000 000:1 90 the sound of an air conditioner put at a distance of 3 metres
10 000 000 000:1 100 – the sound of a hammer from the distance of 10 m
100 000 000 000:1 110 sound of an airplane
1000 000 000 000:1 120 – sounds created by the strike of hammer onto an anvil

130. The last boundary of hearing (pain) (H.H.Wängler, 1972. 168)

4) Any investigation of the perspective basis of intercourse must have recently noticed rapid development. After all, one of the current issues under scrutiny is the way in which a listener understands the information given by a speaker in plain form. Certainly, how a listener (having chosen the substantial bark of the sound), is able to restore the analogue of the same sound in his brain, similarizes different forms of

realization inside the same language units, and finally distinguishes the resemblences other forms, demands the collaboration of other disciplines. Such questions, no doubt, equally reinforcing the main essence of linguistics. However, contemporary investigations show that similarization and discrimination take place by means of zones. In the hearing centre of a person, each language unit has a self-belonging zone. The sounds representing one variant in the zone within the brain are reflected in the form of dots (see picture 27).

On the basis of this picture, one may observe (in the hearing zone), a determining of format fields regarding vowels. As such, one may indicate zones of synthetic vowels as follows (see picture 28):

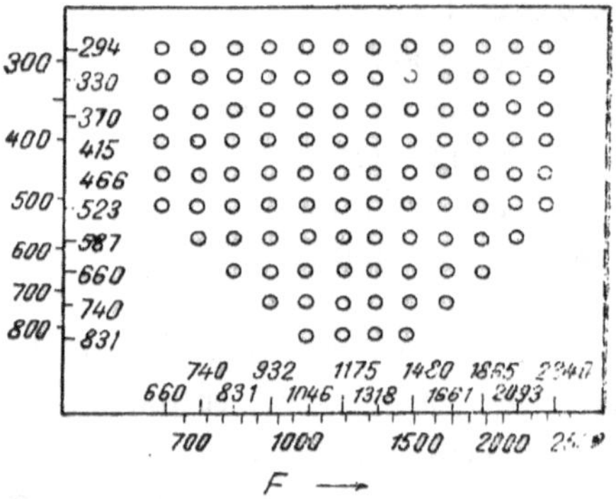

Picture 27. Distribution of the language sounds in the human brain

5) Hearing zones, as to their features, are divided into two parts: 1. the zone of similarity; 2. the zone of resemblance (Z.N.Japaridze, 1974). So, when learning a foreign language, sounds that are not recognizable either fall into the zone of similarity, i.e. the sounds which we hear in this foreign language are assimilated by our mother tongue and understood, or as having no equivalent. In which case, these sounds fall into the zone of resemblance, i.e. are sent to a zone of hearing wherein

sounds resemble each other. In both cases, serious pronunciation mistakes occur. Yet, when understanding diverse language units, one or two related insights must never be separated. Primarily, these ideas focusing on "understanding bases" by distinguishing features. However, investigations of the latest period do not accept this assertion and point out distinguishing features do not ensure comprehension ….. even the entire gamut of distinguishing features (DF) are not enough to understand itmes outside a speech chain. Stated so, information on phonemes is concentrated more in the phonemes themselves. This is why investigators come to such conclusions – claiming that the initial "understandable unit" is a syllable (L.V.Bondarko, 1977).

CHAPTER IV

EXPERIMENTAL INVESTIGATION OF THE PHONETIC STRUCTURE OF THE AZERBAIJANI LANGUAGE

IV.1. FROM THE HISTORY OF EXPERIMENTAL PHONETICS

1) When speaking about learning the phonetic structure of Azerbaijani by experimental methods, and by viewing the history of this type of methodology, one uncovers the possibility of getting close to the history of this technique.

Now, in the science of world linguistics (without depending on the experience of learning national languages), the method of experimental investigation into these languages obviously bears an international flavor - and may be applied in the same degree when learning phonological systems of sound in all languages. That's why it is worth discussing such an approach to learning languages a little more. Indeed, it is necessary to mention that at present - despite the fact attained sources give some information on the history of this method - they can't discover an engaging means of approach to this problem. In fact, excluding some exceptions, one must say that the science of world phonetics, pays little attention to writing its own history. Rather, it continues searching for methods and means of uncovering new knowledge in phonetics. As such, an electroacoustic apparatus recently appeared in the USA, Germany and France almost affirming this stance. As a case in point, a famous firm KEJ has created a speech laboratory to investigate communication by the application of computers within which it is possible to configure communicative models of speech (see picture 29).

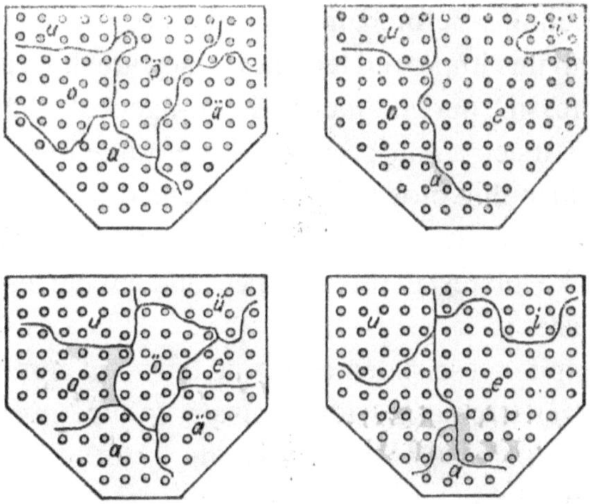

Picture 28. A picture showing the format zones of vowels

Picture 29. Investigation of speech and hearing.

Picrure 29. Apparatuses used in the investigation of speech and hearing by the firm KEJ.

In this picture, principles of working with the apparatus (along with the curves of diverse characters received from it), show that this method is highly advantageous compared to previous techniques, After all, work involving a number of disciplines have been concentrated within one machine. Beforehand, calculations were carried out by hand, while with this improved technique they are done automatically. Clearly, by expressing our gratitude to the co-agent of KEJ (in Gettingen city), Brigitta Karsten - and because of the guidelines sent by him - one may introduce this progressive mechanism to you, dear readers, picture 29. Confessedly, one supposes those who are enthusiastic in this field will take interest in this advance, and having learned this new technology, master it.

2) But despite these statements, one may still come across some invaluable sources associated with the history of experimental phonetics (G.Panconcelli-Calzia, 1942; M.V.Panov, 1973; M.I.Matusevich, 1976). Tellingly, the creation of a scientific view took well over 2 centuries to achieve Moreover, its foundation required the writing of significant works in the evolution of this topic. Hence, A.von Hellwag's contribution can be considered as the first historical step ever made in the extablishment of this discipline (A.von Hellwag, 1786). Herein, one may read observations on the articulation of vowels, while the author - for the first time - constituted a triangle of German vowels. A triangle, which has not lost its value with the passing decades. Atop of this, his groundbreaking work shows, visually, the melodic structure of the language (only approximately published by this time) - nowadays considered the first step in studying speech (R.Martens, 1952, p. 32).

3) In 1881, following the initiative of the French Academy of Sciences, the Russian Empire Academy announced a competition to create an artificial language. As such, the Russian scholar Kratsenstayn won this competition with an apparatus that was able to pronounce

individually taken sounds (Академические известия, 1781). After a while, W.von Kempelen - from Vienna - repeating the work of Kratsenstayn - built another speaking apparatus. His machine, however, could pronounce individually taken sounds as well as words and small sentences (W. von Kempelen, 1791). Since that time, any tendency to explore the features of sound-creation, by means of an instrument has only strengthened phonetics. What is more, this functional aspect of linguistics determined the future orientation of phonetics as a science of linguistics.

4) Inerestingly, the European scholars R.Rask, Y.Grimm and F.Bopp's enriched thoughts on linguistics by gradually aiding the foundation of a strong background for phonetic experimentation. On one hand, therefore, linguists like Y.Grimm proved unable to part company with "dead languages" (Y.Grimm, 1822), whilst, on the other hand, physiologists, naturalists, psychologists etcetera, approached sound study from their own circle of interests. Undoubtedly, they couldn't resist experiments on a linguistic table of contents.

5) By 1876, in Germany, E.Sievers, is noteworthy after a year in England. Additionally, A.Sweet's books of phonetics makes these two pathfinders (first books) significant in Europe (E.Sievers, 1876; A.Sweet, 1871). It is fascinating, of course, to read that E.Sievers acts as an opponent of experiment, even though his work is fundamental in defending personal observations by a writer. For their parts, O.A.Sweet, P.Passi, D.Jones, in Russia I.A.Baudouin de Courtenay, A.Thomson etcetera albeit not using the objective results gained through experiment, make observations considered as the most elegant illustrations of subjective method.

In Germany E.Sievers, J.Winteler, M.Trautmann, F.Techmer, O.Bremer (J. Winteler, 1876, M.Trautmann, 1884-1886, F.Techmer, 1880, O.Bremer, 1893) and other famous scientists slowly matured.

Certainly, F.Techmer was the first scientist to use a "science of phonetics" in the sense this phrase is applied now. Oddly enough, experimental phonetics did not develop either in England, or in Germany. Instead, it began to flourish in France - under the supervision of Monck J.J.Roussleau. Indeed, his legendary work – wherein he adapted methods employed by the natural sciences - directed the results of experiments to centre on language phenomenon (J.J.Roussleau, 1894, 1924. 25).

6) J.J.Roussleau, along with L.Roudet, and side-by-side with M.Grammont, led their Germany disciples. Of J.J.Roussleau - G.Panconcelli-Calzia, M.Menzerath, later E.V.Skripchur and O.von Essen (L.Roudet, 1910; M.Grammont, 1933; Panconcelli-Calzia, 1924; P.Menzerath und A. de Lacerda, 1934; O.von Essen, 1966). Meanwhile in Russia, V.A.Bogoroditsky and L.V.Shcherba played great role in the development of experimental phonetics (Л.В.Щерба, 1911; А.Богородицкий, 1930). In Europe, by the end of the XIX century and at the beginning of the XX century, I.A. Baudouin de Courtenay and F. de Saussure couldn't help spreading their positive influence over the realization of ideas in experimental linguistics.

Thusly, the development of phonetics (especially the emergence of experimental phonetics in the field of ideas), sought to find out which one - of so many valuable ideas - was most accurate. Really, looking back, it is impossible to show any field of linguistics (wherein the colourfulness of concepts and the differentiations of thoughts are as rich) as energized as phonetics. Instructively, those sides - getting into heated arguments over phonemes - (trying to show her/ his insight) had to appeal to the methods of objective investigation as their Crown Court. Indeed, each was nourished by other sciences, especially philosophy, psychology, physics and so on – all of which undoubtedly influenced the development of phonetics. On the other hand, getting gradually away from "dead languages" as a litmus test of investigation, and learning the mechanisms of language as a means of intercourse, were the causes of experiment. Ordinary tape recording started this enterprize. Clearly, listening to a speech, and stopping it to relisten in any point, attracted the attention of the linguistics.

7) I.A. Baudouin de Courtenay's disciples B.A.Bogoroditsky and L.V.Shcherba were the first ones to establish an experimental laboratory in Russia. Indeed, at the beginning of the century, L.V.Shcherba carried out experiments in P.J.Rousselot's laboratory, afterwards returning to his native country to wrote his famous work "Quantitative and Qualitative Features of Russian vowels" (1912). Different from other cities in Europe - especially differing from Germany - L.V.Shcherba did not make experiments for the sake of experimentation, but rather made those investigations to scrutinize certain language phenomenon. For example, in his article "Quelques mot sur les phonemes consonnes conposes" (1908, XV. 1–5), L.V.Shcherba pointed out that the length of sound combination - not being longer than the length of other phonemes in language - had the same sound combination, and could be considered as one phoneme.

At the end of the XIX century, in Europe, some journals and collections were published. In France "Maitre de phonetique"[31], in Holland "Archives Neerlandises de phonetique experimentalle" can be considered examples to this. Furthermore, in this period the International Phonetics Society began its activities.

As a result of the intensive labour of this society, in the field of learning phonetic structure, a number of suggestions were made to advance research – eventually being approved. So, tables were worked out through transcription signs, reflecting vowels and consonants in the languages of the world. All of which can be seen as an instance

31 One must note that our native M.Shakhtakhtly took an active part in the work of this journal and did his best to help the transcription established in Latin graphics.

of projects fulfilled by the International Phonetic Association, 1904).

8) Beginning, moreover, in the XX century - the circle of interest widened to involve issues surrounding the practical learning of languages. O. Jespersen.

Originally from Danmark (O.Jespersen, 1808) and L.Hjelmslev (L.Hjelmslev, 1938), from Germanany W.Vietor (W.Vietor, 1931) as well as T.Siebs (T.Siebs, 1901, 1969) and from Russian V.Bogoroditsky (В.А.Богородицкий, 1930), and L.V.Shcherba (Л.В.Щерба, 1977) - alongside the theoretical issues of phonetics - kept practical topics in their focus of attention. What is more, in the 20's of the XX century "TCLP" created, in Prague city, a way to learn such systems synchronically. So, they accepted as a dominant orientation (Travaux de Cercle Linguistique de Prague, 1929–1939. T. I–IX). Now, the 9th volume of the collection - published by this society - consists of N.S.Trubetzkoy's work "The Principies of Phonology". As is known, of course, N.S.Trubetzkoy and his supporters when considering phonetics - especially experimental phonetics - were largely correct. By contrast, E.Zwirner was busy working out theoretical principles of his own, in order to develop phonometrics in Germany (E.Zwirner und K.Zwirner, 1936). Overall, he thought it possible to determine the coefficient of sound variations by statistical methods - and in this way find mathematical solutions to speech norms. He acted, therefore, from real existence, making observations, writing notes (by means of apparatuses), and measured speech events so as to find a medium mark for sound classes - along with sound norms. Through this, he aimed to determine the marks of variation zones therein related.

On the basis of E.Zwirner's work, many of the German dialects were recorded. The biggest defficiency of E.Zwirner's conceptions, however, was that he separated phonetics and phonetic phenomena from its linguistic background.

9) Recently, experimental phonetics - developing still wider - caused the creation of this, or that, field of science. Certanly, B.Malmberg (B.Malmberg, 1960), A.Martinet (A.Martine, 1954), L.R.Zinder (L.R.Zinder, 1960), K.Pike (K.Pike, 1945) and other scientists worked out methodological and theoretical principles of phonetics - especially experimental phonetics. Indeed, L.R.Zinder wrote: "Experiment is distinguished from the observation by the fact that, an investigator in different conditions does not take into consideration the activity of the object as passive, in order to learn the connection between the condition and interesting him the phenomenon, he puts the object which he wants to learn under condition" (L.R.Zinder, 1979, p. 20).

10) At the start of the 50's in the XX century, P. Jacobson, G. Fant and M. Halle (R.Jacobson etcetera, 1955), investigated the spectre of acoustic structure within language sounds - trying to solve the problem of "Visible speech". Fascinatingly, by getting format characteristics of sounds from spectres, they made out 12 differential features - and put a forth possibility of learning languages based on these features (G.Fant, 1964). Since that time, the perspective aspect - being brought-up by experimental phonetics, and experimental psychology, began to be established (Дж.Фланаган, 1968).

Beginning with the 20's of the XX century, 17 international congresses of phonetics (exploring the science of phonetics, experimental phonetics, and other issues), have been held:

1.Congress: the Hague, 1933
2."–" : Cambridge, 1936
3. "–" : Gnet, 1938
4. "–" : Helsinki, 1961
5. "–" : Muntser, 1964
6. "–" : Prague, 1967
7. "–" : Montreal, 1971

8. "–" : Luds[32], 1974
9. "–" : Copenhagen, 1974
10. "–": Monreal, 1980
11. "–": Tallinn[33], 1987
12. "–": Aixon province, 1991
13."-" : Stockholm, 1995
14."- ": San Fracisco 1999
15 " –": Barcelona 2003
16 "- ": Saarbrucken 2007
17. "- ": Hong Kong 2011.

At present, the works of world phoneticians and phonologists are published in the International Journal (Phonetica, Zeitschrift für Phonetik, Sprachwissenschaft und Kommunikationsforschung)[34].

In Azerbaijan, experimental phonetics is approached as part of a methodology serving to learn language phenomena. Indeed, world linguistics from the very beginning of this enterprize - in order to carry out concrete duties – required a large amount of money as a means of widening the activity of the Experimental Phonetic Laboratory (EFL). Nowadays, in different countries of the world, the EFL-s are operating.

11) Azerbaijan, as in all fields of science, began its activities at the start of the XX century. In 1926, during the First Turkological Congress in Baku - together with other aspects of the language - its phonetic aspect was also dealt with. Moreover, changes in the Azerbaijani alphabet became possible as a result of a number of observations carried out in the field of native phonetics. Increasingly, interest in phonetics has shown itself more clearly by investigations

32 In the materials of this Congress, from the Azerbaijani scientist Z.X.Taghizadeh, a theses on syllables was published.

33 In the XII International Congress held in Tallinn, the author delivered a report in German - and the text of the report was published in the materials of the Congress.

34 In the editorial board of this journal (from our Republic) A.Akhundov also took a part.

of materials in this field. Furthermore, after the 40's, any thoughts on learning the sound side of language by these means found more supporters. Meanwhile, in this present period, a number of works on the phonetics of Azerbaijani have appeared.

12) F.Kazimov (1925-1989) during the 50's - for the first time in history - learned the phonemes of Azerbaijani by experimental method - afterwards contributing a number of articles to the central newspapers (F.Kazimov, 1952. I–XI. 1958). Clearly, Azerbaijan, in the history of developmental thoughts on phonetics, in the 60's of the XX century, assumed a special importance. Indeed, 1960, witnessed the first book on "Phonetics of the Azerbaijani language" - using the results of experiments previously published, (Ə.Dəmirçizadə 1960). Moreover, within this book palatograms, roentgenograms and photo pictures were widely presented. Simultaneously, S. B. Sadigov using experiments published in a number of books, equally investigated these problems (S.Sadıqov, I–XIII, I–XIX, 1961).

For his part, T.Hidayetzadeh in the comparative investigation of Azerbaijani and English consonants (for the first time), utilized electroacoustic apparatuses (T.Hidayətzadə, 1961, 1962). Thereby, he studied supersegment units from an acoustic viewpoint Z.Taghizade (Z.X.Tağızadə, № 1, 1971), Sh.Abdullayev (Ş.T.Abdullayev, 1964), J.Akhundov (C.M.Akhundov, 1968), S.Babayev (S.Babayev, 1960), M.Garayeva (M.Garayeva, 1976), A.Jafarov (Ə.Cəfərov, 1975) and N.Mehdiyev's (N.Mehdiyev, 1973). Additional works can be shown as examples. Significantly, A.Akhundov's work, "System of Phonemes in the Azerbaijani Language" continues to occupy a special place in Azerbaijani linguistics as a fundamental work. Yet, beginning in the 60's within Azerbaijan the creation of EFL was realized as an equal contribution. Thus, in 1970, a laboratory attached to the Azerbaijan Pedagogical Institute of Languages (APIL) – nowadays the Azerbaijan University of Languages (AUL) was founded. During a short period of time, therefore, inspired by laboratory projects, the book, "Introduction to Experimental Phonetics" was both prepared and published (Z.X.Tağızadə, 1970).

13) Associated with the development of scientific-technical progress, the methods used in phonetic investigations, and apparatuses, are being constantly improved. Ossillograph and ossillographic techniques are seen as something unsubstitutable in learning about the acoustic structure of sounds. Although, they are gradually yielding to spectrography. After all, with spectrography it is possible to learn all the changes in a sound spectre. Hence, Z.Taghizade's 2 articles with co-authorship by R.K.Potapova "Experimental Phonetics" were in the book published under our supervision (Р.К.Потапова, З.Х.Тагизаде, № 1, 2, 1971. Баку. I, 1980; II, 1981), including other booklets, articles, and dissertations (F.Veysalov, R.Isayeva, 1987. 3), wherein serious steps were taken in the spectral field of the Azerbaijani language[35].

Undoubtedly, these notes cannot throw light on the whole history of experimental phonetics. Intellectal history, this recalled, inside experimental phonetics should be carefully studied, while the future development of this science should be outlined.

IV.2. THE PLACE, AIMS AND OBJECTIVES OF EXPERIMENT

1) Any advance within experimental phonetics increases confidence in the investigations carried out in phonetics. What is more, they cause an increase in the authority of phonetics as an exact science.

35 In explanation of the further sections of the book, one has used the work "Experimental phonetics" published in 1981. In writing these chapters the associate professors Y.Kerimov and F.Aslanov have directly taken parts.

Seeing the advantage of experimental phonetics, therefore, a number of known phonetists have began to carry out their own investigations on the basis of this method. For instance, L.V.Shcherba - regarding the explanation of language facts and the experimental method wrote: "I have definitely know for a long time that, by way of personal observation, for example, in the Russian language it is impossible to reveal the meanings of conditional mood" (Л.В.Щерба, 1974). Now, L.V.Shcherba, continuing his thoughts, he then wrote - by using experiment - the meaning of a verb, if dealt with convincingly, may be explained. Thenceforth, he contended that in linguistics based on this method, tendencies towards subjectivism lose their importance. So, academician L.V.Shcherba, debating experimental phonetics resolutely said: "On the basis of my linguistic thoughts, stand language materials attained from experiments, language facts" (Л.Щерба, 1974).

2) At this modern stage, wherein languages are widely investigated, the necessity of experimental phonetics increases more and more. Currently, linguistics has the richest collected materials. Tested, as they are, by experiment - and on the basis of facts. All causing trust in the objective results received. Generally, in modern linguistics the majority of attained results are based upon experimental phonetics. This realization finds its justification in the increase (in number), of research works carried out by the method of experimental phonetics in the day-to-day world. However, new global laboratories still need opening to meet modern demands. Of course, if these were the initial stages of experimental phonetics, one could name the laboratories established by V.A.Bogoroditsky, L.V.Shcherba. Presently, this recalled, experimental phonetic laboratories operate in Moscow, Minsk, Kiev, Baku, Tbilisi, Alma-Ata, and Tallinn, along with other cities. Moreover, these laboratories do not replicate research (F.Veysalov, 1978). So, the working plans of these laboratories is

to study different languages and involve the study of segment and supersegment units and phenomena[36].

Undoubtedly, the method of experimental phonetics has specific requirements. As such, each experiment requires special theoretical preparation and exact information on the phonological system and phoneme repertour. Otherwise, an investigator may fall into confusion before the numerous sound varieties.

3) Existing literature on the phonetic problem is intended to explanation (after being studied) the state of materials previously investigated. So, at this time it is necessary to pay special interest to the usage of studied sound in possible combinations. For example, it is necessary to regard any vowel belonging to the Azerbaijani language, whether it comes before, or after, the consonants. In addition, whether it is under stress, used before or after the stressed syllable, whether it is used in a position before or after a stressed syllable, or whether it is used in further positions at the beginning, or in the middle or ending, of morphemes, words, or sentences.

Unarguably, it is known that an entire language cannot be studied. That's why only a portion of language materials subjected to investigation are asked to represent the whole language. As such, this grounded portion offers a working perspective on the entirety of materials. Different experiments, however, have show that increased freedom in theoretical choices allow an investigator to approach "absolute" truth. So, the exactness of measurements is determined in relation to the greatness number of relative mistakes. Hence, experimenters invite the bearers of native language to their sessions, since, presumuably, they know the norms of literary language. Accordingly, the number of informants is also determined by these

---

36 Until the end of this section, explanations of some materials are based on J.S.Ahmadov and F.Y.Veysalov's article called "Experiments in Phonetics and on some Issues of Experimental Phonetics" (Дж.С.Ахмедов, Ф.Я.Вейсалов, 1975. № 2).

statistic means.

IV.3. THE STYLE OF SPEECH AND RECORDING OF THE MATERIAL

1) The style of utterance is not only associated with profession, but equally with individual psychology and the social level of a person. Depending upon intellectual ability and the speech object (which a speaker chooses), the speaker may use different forms of pronunciation. These forms in linguistics are called “prouunciation style”. In which case, L.V.Shcherba, when dealing with different speech styles writes, “Learning different speech forms, fitting to different conditions and aims, is called speech style” (Л.В.Щерба, 1963. 20).

Dependent on the aim and the condition in which communication takes place, therefore, the speech style changes too. Indeed, these styles differ as to both lexic-syntactic and phonetic features. For instance, the speech of oil workers and cotton workers are distinguished not only by lexical composition, but also regarding phonetic features. Comparing any person’s speech in a meeting with his speech in a family, one witness the connection existing between different “objective realities”, along with the intellectual level of the speaker - and the life experience attached to his/her social position. Together with the features mentioned, moreover, in pronunciation style, the general level of the interviewer must be taken into consideration. At this juncture, the object of speech is additionally one of the factors establishing the formulation of stylistic features. Obviously, there exist styles linked with different fields. For example, newspaper, journalist, office, scientific speaker’s styles. As such, style-linguistics is busy learning all these variations. That’s why sometimes these styles are said to be phonetic styles (М.И.Матусевич, 1976. 10).

2) A.Damirchizadeh, admitted two meanings (in a wide and narrow sense), discriminated these forms of style by penning, "That's why pronunciation styles in the wide sense of meaning mean the system of purposeful colourings of phonetic means and possibilities of the language, namely they mean the system of phonetic possibilities in the oral literary language styles. Pronunciation style in the narrow meaning, means pronunciation variants formulated by the manifestation of phonetic possibilities only on the frame of orphoepic norms, on the basis of purposefullness" (Ə.Dəmirçizadə, 1969. 7). Speaking on pronunciation styles L.V.Shcherba also indicated two types: 1. free style; 2. complete (absolute) style (Л.В.Щерба, 1957. 154). Thus, A.Damirchizadeh in his book "The Principles of the Orphoepics of the Azerbaijani language" talks about orphoepics as necessary to give

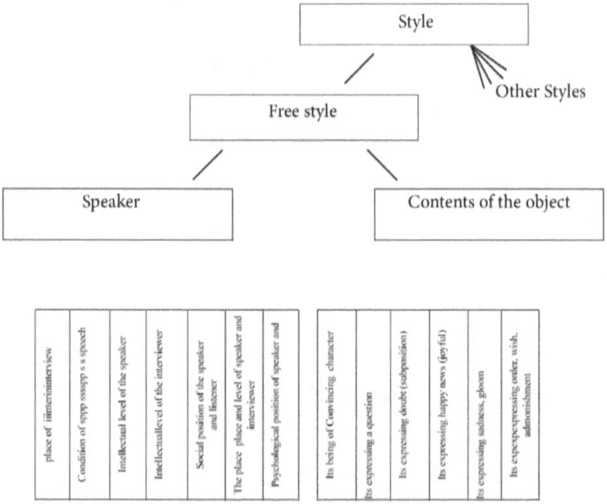

Scheme 2. As it is impossible to show the factors influencing free style this graphic, it bears a relative character.

information on two styles, while speaking of the different types of style – complete or free style (Ə.Dəmirçizadə, 1969. 10). The first one is often encountered in daily speech. Herein, the norms of complete style are not observed. The main distinguishing feature of this style is that in the process of communication, some sounds and syllables are abridged.

3. Azerbaijani words, such as "/pişık (a cat), bıçag (a knife), oxuyur (he reads)" etcetera, in speech style are pronounced as /p'ˇşık/, /bᵘˇçax/, /oxᵘjur/. But, they are not necessary sharply distinguished as in free style. Additionally, free style is based on certain objective laws. Depending on whom the intercourse takes place with (between people of the same age, family, among fellow workers), wherein free style shows itself in different forms. Hence, free style is more often met as fluent speech. For instance, in Azerbaijani, ossillographic analysis of sentences like "Başa düşdüm", "İşimizdə nöqsan axtarsan, taparsan", "Kitab maraqlıdır", "Mən çay içirəm" ("I understood", "You are looking for an error in our work", "The book is interesting", "I am having tea"), allow both of the speakers to pronounce sentences in the following way /baş¯a dγ¯şdγm// (I understand), /iş¯imızdəe nøksan axtarsa'n ta'parsan// (If you search for mistake in our work, you can find it), /k'tap maraqlıdır// (the book is interesting), /mæn čaj ıçˈræm// (I am drinking tea), and so on.

In given examples, the speech style of the announcers has been clearly pointed out. Yet, one shouldn't forget that in free style changes take place, which must not go beyond the norms of literary language. Those factors influencing free style being generalized in this way (see scheme 1).

4) A complete style is distinguished from free style by a number of features. So, A.Damirchizadeh, dealing with some specific features of complete style characterizes it like this: "The words establishing the

phonetic bark of the words as to the place of articulation are very clear, but the syllables formulated from these sounds, usually in the divided case are pronounced as the clearly distinguished rings in the speech chain. The stresses being considered as obligatory in the formulation of a word are put exactly on their places. Using individually taken words, word combinations and expressions calmly by separating them with punctuations and stress we achieve pronunciation with satisfactory quality and quantity. The pauses among the words are more than the pauses among the members of the sentences".

Generally, orphoepic norms are completely observed (Ə.Dəmirçizadə, 1969, p. 9). This style is used to deliver thought clearly and exactly to a listener.

5) Literary style norms are mainly used on radio and TV broadcasting, in reports, and in official talks. Words and sentences written in complete style - regarding their phonetic composition must be said in the complete form - and clearly. However, in ordinary speech, complete style is not obeyed as a whole. From this perspective (speaking of literary norms in German), H.Pilch's views attract ones attention. He notes this is such a style that no bearer of language obeys this rule in his/her daily speech (H.Pilch, 1967). So, complete style shows itself when one wants to dispatch this, or that, information to a listener in an understandable form. During this time, a speaker pronounces the word in the complete style – with a full reflection of the phonetic components. While pronouncing the sentence "Şagird kitab oxuyur" (a pupil reads a book) in vivid speech, exactly speaking, in free style, the first syllable of the word "kitab" (a book), and the first vowel not being pronounced, /şagırd k'tab ox"jur// a listener can't understand the speaker - and replies to the speaker with this question: "Şagird nə oxuyur?"(What does the pupil read?). Yet, the speaker at

this time pronounces this word according to the complete style norm / şagird kitab oxujur//. Both free style and complete style are based on the real conditions of objective reality.

6) Any investigation of phonetic material may be empowered by basing itself on experiment, more than the observation alone. The correct implementation of experiment, of course, is associated with different conditions. One of the conditions is the principle of choosing the material for experiment, and the announcer recorded in this material. Now, recording highly experimantal materials is made possible by using the bearers of language as announcers. In themelves, announcers may be men or women. But if the material for experiment is recorded by two persons, then it is purposeful for them to both be men, or women. Otherwise, generalizations and "quirky" results may follow. When selecting announcers, therefore, it is necessary to pay attention to the norms of literary language - in speech there shouldn't be artificiality. Furthermore, the announcers (in order to get acquainted with the materials), may read them beforehand. Indeed, the text must be read distinctly and fluently. Sometimes, as the announcers begin reading the material in a high tone, one finds in the second half of the process (as they get tired), their tones become weaker - creating obstacles for obtaining real results. That's why the material for the experiment must be recorded in parts, along with pauses. In order to learn the phonetic changes of speeches between people of other nationalities (speaking in Azerbaijani), the material for the experiment must be in the Azerbaijani language. As such, announcers must be invited from among those who know Azerbaijani well. During the analysis of the material, the choice of informants must be scrutinized. Hence, in any investigation of those who (usually) speak Russian, the material compiled in Russian must be tape recorded by the performing

Azerbaijanians. During the analysis, an auditor aids understanding - depending on the aim of the work carried out. Ceratianly, both bearers of language must be used as informants.

7) The choice of the material and its recording

For this experiment to succeed, special attention should be paid to the choice of proper material under investigation. Indeed, materials must be selected in such a way that the language units presented for analysis are appropriate to the speakers. After all, it is important that each language unit is associated with real conditions. In Azerbaijani, any experimental investigation of word stress (as a case in point), needs to follow such guiding principles for conclusive results. Certainly, with words of one, two, three and more syllables, each must be presented in the same phonetic surrounding. Compare:

1. a) /vəl/	b) /əl/	2. a) /dələ/	b) /vələ/	3. /bəxt/	4. / sər`in/	
/nəl/	/əs/	/dədə/	/zədə/	/sənət/	/s`ərin/	
/ sən/	/ək/	b) /tələ/	d) /hələ/	/sənətə/	/gəl`in/	
/gəl/	/ət/	c) /kələ/	/sələ/	/tər/	/g`əlin/	
/kəs/	/hə/	/lələ/	/òələ/	/Tərtər/	/süzm`ə/	
/tək/	/nə/	/nənə/		/Tərtərin/	/s`üzmə/	etc.

1.a) threshing board b) a hand 2. a) squirrel 3.fortune 4.cool
horse shoe blow daddy a trade cool you plant b) a trap to trade a bride
come meat c) an ox sweat of the bufallo cut yes father Tartar (a region)
filtrated sour milk alone what granny of Tartar filtrated sour milk

These words - including the first group – are stressed monosyllabic words. Moreover, such indicated examples as /əl/ along with vowels in monosyllabic words, take differing positions. What is more, within these words, obligatory principles have been upheld at the beginning and at the end of the word, although the second group of words (being of two syllables (in both the syllables), equally have vowels of the same quality as /æ/. By this, one takes the stress, as well as the influence, of different surrounding vowels into full account and uncovers the physical changes a vowel undergoes. However, in the third group of words (in different word positions), it is possible to determine chances - from an acoustic point of view - undergone by a stressed syllable. Interestingly, the same situation shows itself in the fourth group of words too. Namely, the unstressed syllables used in the first row, (and in the second), are syllables used by stress. But it should not be forgotten that words included into the fourth group involve different language branches (morphology, syntax).

8) Associated with solutions regarding the division of a sentence (in terms of intonation), the materials chosen must be selected for both the syntagmatic composition of a sentence, along with the syntactic structure of a sentence. Furthermore, only appropriate sentences will do, which depending on their syntagm division, should be chosen to express different meanings. Simultaneously, the place of syntagm-stress plays a crucial role in member-division - and must be carefully taken into consideration. So, in the choice of the sentences, one must try the same word in different meanings and different phonetic loads. For example,

1. */səhər // (morning)*
2. */səhər gələrsən // (you'll come in the morning).*
3. */bizə səhər gələrsən // (you'll come to us in the morning).*
4. */Günai əsəri nəʃr etdirdi // (Günay had the work published)/*
5. */Qanun amansızdır//, /qanun amansızdır, lakin qanundur // (law is merciless, law is merciless, but it is a law).*

6. */hava garalır// /hava qaralr, jağış jağır // (İt gets darker// it gets darker, it rains).*

7. */O,/ gözəl müğənnidir // O gözəl müğənnidir // (She is a beautiful singer. That beautiful girl is a singer).*

8. */Kim olsa / Atabəj kimi. oğlana dʒansağlığı istər // (Whoever he may be, he will wish good health to a boy like Atabay)*

9. */Kim olsa Atabəj kimi / oğlana dʒansağlığı istər // (Who ever may be as Atabay will wish good health to the boy*

10. */Kim olsa /Atabœəi kimi / oğlana dʒansağlığı istər // Who ever he may be as Atabay will wish good health to the boy).*

9) Now, in the first three syntagms - the same word /səhər/ (morning) being used in different positions - caries out different phonetic functions. In the fourth sentence consisting of one syntagm, its centre is in the word /nəşr/. This same word, bearing the syntagm-stress, can be compared with the word "günəş" which is used in the same phonetic surrounding to bear the word stress. In the fifth and the sixth sentences, the same syntagm (in one case), has been used as a terminal, but in the other as a progredient. Conversely, in the seventh and eighth sentences (depending on syntagm bounderies), the sentences express different meanings. Thusly, sentences of such a type - included into experiment material – make it possible to determine the structural role of the signs of a syntagm. Atop of which, distinctive features of word and sentence stresses, the role of syntagm-stress in division of a sentence into syntagms, become observable. Undoubtedly, depending on the aims and objectives of investigation, the experimeter may include systemized language materials into the experiment. On the basis of such, language material carrying out generalizations and analyses, enables the work of an investigator to become easier, while also createing the possibility of highly fruitful results. Recording

experimental material is, of course, the most important stage. Certainly, depending on the aim of the experiment, research materials can be given to announcers either before, or on the time, as the experiment is being recorded.

10) Any division of sentences into syntagms and their consequent function in syntagm-stress (within the material compiled on stress-intonation and stress), requires that every type of sentence must find its reflection. Besides this, the inner structure of a sentence, and its lexical composition - must be taken into consideration. That's why all material is taken within a context. Obviously, announcers must read the material clearly, without giving way to any artificiality - as it is in ordinary speech. Moreover, this research work (if devoted to learning dialects), demands that reading these sentences must be representative of the dialect subjected to investigation.

11) It must additionally be mentioned, which tape recorders was used, if the material was successfully recorded, and at what speed it was recorded. Under laboratory conditions, usually, tape – recorders with the epithet "Tembre" are employed. Also, the speed of recording is sometimes associated with technical conditions, and sometimes with the objectives put forth before investigators. Aiming to check on the quality of recorded materials (and how well the material has been read by the announcers), investigators may then carry out an analysis of hearing and listening. After an investigator specifies that the recording is at the proper level, the investigator may continue the experiment. Thence, the investigator - depending on the material put forth - may get the ossillogram, intonogram or spectrogram, from this material. In the study of segment and supersegment units of a language. it is equally possible to use all three of them. Yet, it is necessary to take into account that the results attained by such calculation (in an ossillogram the frequency of the main tone, the line of intensivity) is

given in a ready-made form by the intonogram. All making the work of an investigator easier (see picture 29, 30).

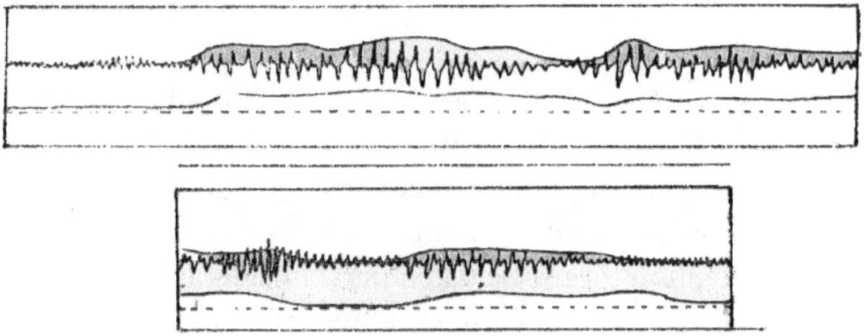

Picture 30. The ossillogram of the sentence /Mənim xoşbəxtliyim sənsən//
(You are my hapiness)

12) At present ossillographs marked with "H-102", although shleyfs 2-8 are more popular. By this apparatus, sounds with 1200–10 000 frequencies (the movement speed of the tape is from 50 till 10 000 mm) are registered. But experiments show that for the investigation of language sounds the movement speed of the tape 250 mm per second is more favorable.

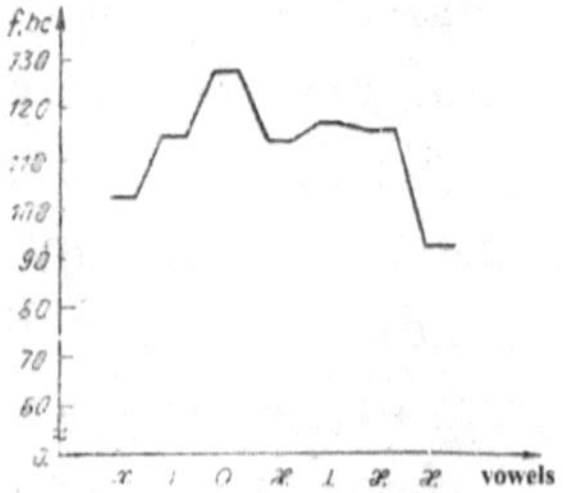

Picture 31.
Intonogram of the sentence /Səhər gələrsən//
(You'll come in the morning)

If working with ossillograms, the main difficulty is in the correct divisions of the segments, and in the determination of their boundaries (L.V.Bondarko, 1965, B.A.Artyomov , 1965, Z.X.Taghizade, 1970; F.Veysalov & other. 1981, II).

IV.4. CALCULATION OF ACOUSTIC PARAMETRES

1) **The Frequency of Sound Tone**. In the process of speech, depending on the tone-height of the pronounced sounds, the types of sentences (declarative, imperative, interrogative, exclamatory), the attitude of a speaker to the object of speech and on its emotionality change seems continual. The rise and fall of tone in the flow of speech establishes the melody of speech. At the end of a research project, therefore, the attained results (depending on calculations of the tone of voice), insist on special attention. Certainly, those curves marked on the type of an ossillogram make it possible to determine the number of the circumference emerging from the movement of vocal cords, as well as the frequency of the voice. Thus, it is necessary to estimate the relativity of a complete circumference, taking place in the pronunciation of a concrete sound on the ossillogram, along with the time taken. This can be indicated as follows:

$$f = \frac{1}{T}$$

f – indicates the frequency of concrete circumference in the articulation of a sound;

T – indicates the time spent on the creation of one complete circumference during the articulation of the sound.

If one also takes into consideration the type of recording of the material with 1000 m/sec. speed, the given formula can be generalized in the following form:

$$f = \frac{1}{T} 1000$$

2) Let's suppose that in the pronunciation of the sound /a/ the time spent on one circumference is T = 8 m/sec. Then, the frequency of that circumference shall be calculated like this:

$$f = \frac{1}{T} \cdot 1000 = \frac{1}{8} \cdot 1000 = 125 \text{ hs}$$

Perhaps, it is necessary to mention that the calculation of a whole experiment in this way, and its analysis, requires extra time. That's why it is necessary to calculate the frequency of the main tone. For this one should use the formula f=I·n/T

n – indicates the number of the repeated circumference in the pronunciation of a certain sound;

T – indicates the time spent on all the circumferences, taking place in the pronunciation of a certain sound. For example, the sound tone of the vowels in the sentence /Mənim xoşbəxtliyim sənsən// (You are my happiness) have been calculated on the indicated formula and have been introduced in picture 31.

If one pays attention to the calculation of the first vowel sound in the given sentence, one will see the time spent on the pronunciation of the sound T = 70 m/sec., although the number of complete circumferences is 7,2. So, if one puts figures as to the formula in their place, one can determine the frequency of the sound (æ) as follows:

$$f = \frac{7{,}2}{70} \cdot 1000 = 102 \text{ hs}$$

Accordingly, one can say that in the pronunciation of the announcer who is reading the sentence, the frequency of the sound is /æ/ is 102 hs.

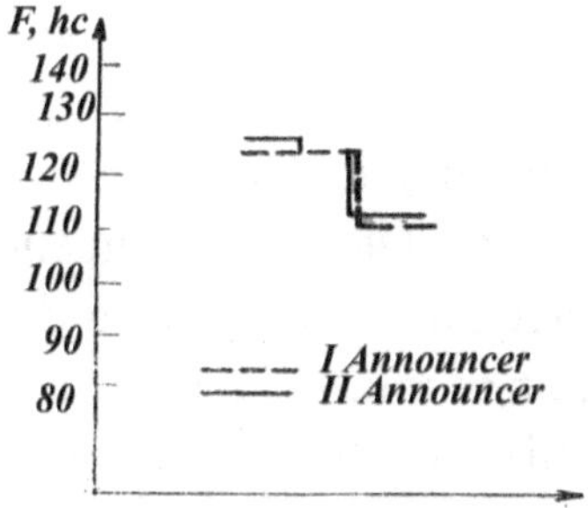

Picture 32. The graphic illustrating the frequency of the main tone of the vowels in the sentence /Mənim xoşbəxtliyim sənsən// ("You are my happiness")

Any calculation of the tone of other vowels in the same sentence is grounded on this principle.

3) Depending on the character feature and purpose of the experiment, the frequency of sound tone may be calculated in different forms. Thusly, if one divides the ossillogram of a certain sound into two, ot three pieces, these separately taken items can be calculated individually. Undoubtedly, here too the explanation indicated before is taken as a basis. So, in the graphic below, the tone of the sound /i/ has been divided into three parts and then has been calculated

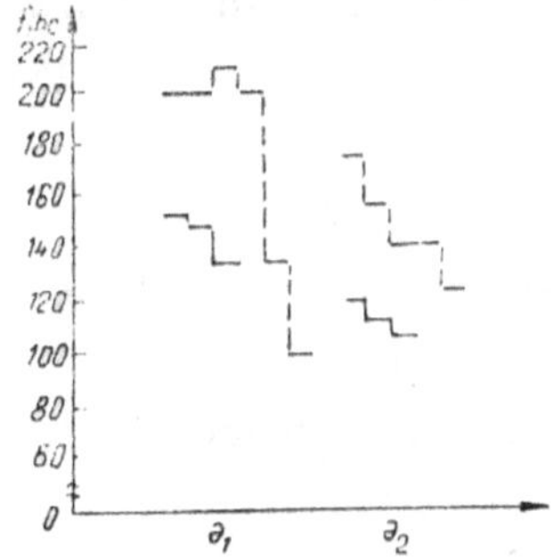

Picture 33. The frequency of the sound /i/ (as to three pieces)

As is seen from the graphics, during the pronunciation of this sound, tone does not always and everywhere have the same frequency (at the beginning, in the middle, at the end).

4) Regarding some completed works on experimental phonetics, one more manner of calculation emerges - a determination of sound frequency by the alteration of tone-frequency on three circumferences. As a result of this calculation, the change of tone within the sound becomes imaginable. For instance, in the sentence /Vəzifə istəyən o adam vəzifə görmədi// (The person desiring a post didn't have any) in the word "vəzifə" (post), in the last stressed syllable, the sound (æ) reflects the acoustic feature. Now, in order to determine different recirpical features, the main sound frequency tone of the same sound has been determined respecting the three circumferences (see picture 33).

5) Alongside calculating the separately taken sounds, it is possible to calculate the medium frequency of the sound within a word, syntagm, or sentence within a text. Latterly, it is also possible to calculate relative frequencies of separately taken sounds. For example, in the sentence /mænim xoşbæxtlijim sænsæn// (you are my happiness).

The medium mathematical pronunciation frequency of the vowel sounds can be expressed by the formula x = s fxin

Here x – indicates the medium mark,

ε – indicates the whole of our observations,

f – frequency of the observations,

x_1 – individually taken observation,

n – amount of observations

Frequencies	Sounds						
Absolute frequency	10 2	11 4	12 7	11 3	11 6	11 5	91
Medium mathematical frequency	11 1	11 1	11 1	11 1	11 1	11 1	11 1
Medium relative frequency	0.9	1.0 3	1.1	0.0 1	1.0 5	0.0 4	0.8

("The person desiring a post didn't have any"), in the word "vəzifə" (post), an alternation of the main tone of the last vowel of the sound /æ/ as to the three circumferences have been indicated.

I announcer – – –

II announcer –

As a result $\Sigma fx^i = 778$ hs has been determined, but any conclusions regarding this sentence are equal to 7, in which case, in the given sentence the medium pronunciation frequency of the vowel sound shall be calculated by mathematical means as follows:

$$x = \frac{\Sigma fxi}{n} = \frac{778\text{ hs}}{7} = 111\text{HZ}$$

6) Consequently, through calculations for individually taken sounds within that sentence, it is impossible to determine the medium relative pronunciation frequency. To achieve this, however it is necessary to divide the absolute frequency of the sounds into the medium frequency calculated for the vowels in the material. For instance, in the word [sænsæn] (you are), the absolute frequency of the first sound /æ/ is 115 hs, but the medium mathematical frequency

is 111 hs. So, the vowel medium relative pronouncing frequency shall be like this:

$$x \text{ medium relative } \frac{f+}{x \text{ medium mathematical}} = \frac{115 \text{ hs}}{112 \text{ hs}} = 1{,}04 \text{ hs}$$

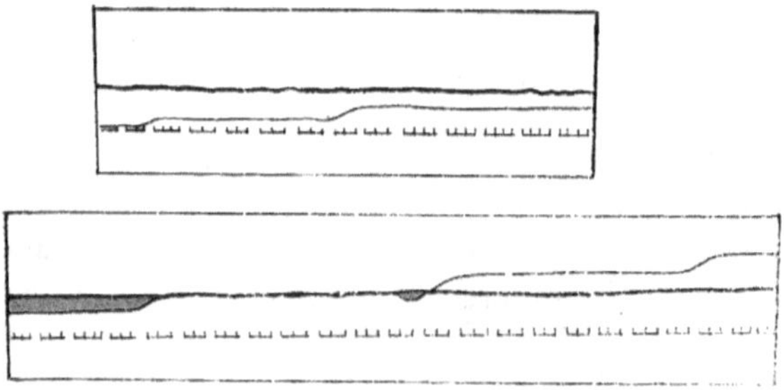

Picture 35. Electro-acoustic measure used to determine the frequency of the main tone in the intonogram

The medium relative frequency of the sounds in the given sentence can be generalized as in the table given below.

7) Certainly, the frequency of the main tone can be determined on the basis of the intonogram. In comparison, therefore, with an ossillogram the calculation of the sound tone is a little easier.Also, there is a line determining the frequency of the main tone on the intonogram tone. The line below is for this (see picture 35).

Of course, in order to measure the frequency of a certain sound, this measurement must ne put on the tape of the intonogram. The subsequent line indicates the frequency of the main tone as it departs from a position of standstill – all specified by this measurement[37].

In the intonogram, the frequency of the main tone in comparison with an ossillogram is marked by slowness - which is connected with the fact that signals enter an ossillogram relatively late. This differentiation may be determined through calculating how late the intonogram is in comparison with the ossillogram at the beginning. Moreover, the completed calculations once more prove that in research work associated with experiment, (undertaken statistically), how close the attained results are to the objective mathematical laws required in the projects of linguistic scientists. So, having a general notion on the laws of statistics and probability theory is vital (Б.Н.Головин, 1971. 19).

8) **The intensivity of sounds**. The power of sound depends on the widening degree of the vibration, namely on its amplitude. With an increase in amplitude, the intensivity of the sound increases. In order to calculate the intensivity of the sound in the ossillogram therefore - by taking the zero line passing from the centre of the ossillogram tape

37 Shows the absolute frequency of the sound.

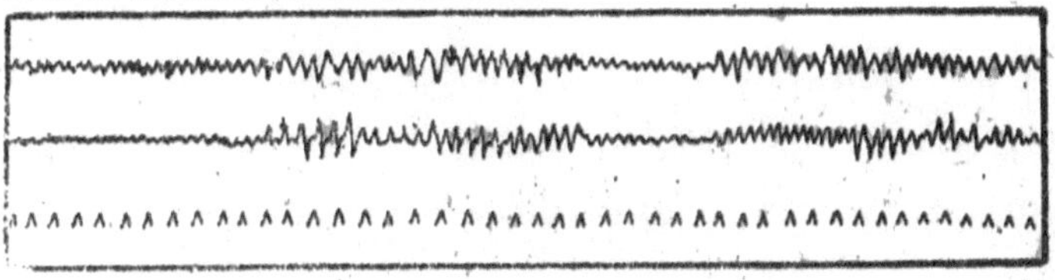

as a basis - it is necessary to determine the results of this widening: of the vibrations on both sides (up and down) from the zero line during pronunciation. Afterwards, putting them on a paper marked with mm, it is possible to measure the intensivity of the sound.

Picture 36. The ossillogram of the word /gülümsündü/ (smiled) taken from the sentence /Səməd acı-acı gülümsündü// (Samad smiled bitterly).

Intensivity of sounds depends, of course, on their pronunciation strength - and the quality of this pronunciation. That means closed sounds, when compared with open ones, are less intensive (Л.Р.Зиндер, 1960. 185), namely the sound /æ/ which is pronounced in the same position - and out of the sounds /i/, /æl/, /il/ - is more intensive than the second one. In the ossillogram, the intensivity of vowels and voiced consonants have been registered (marked) (see picture 36).

/Sæmæd acı-acı gülümsündü// (Samad smiled bitterly). In this sentence the fact that the sounds change as to intensivity has been

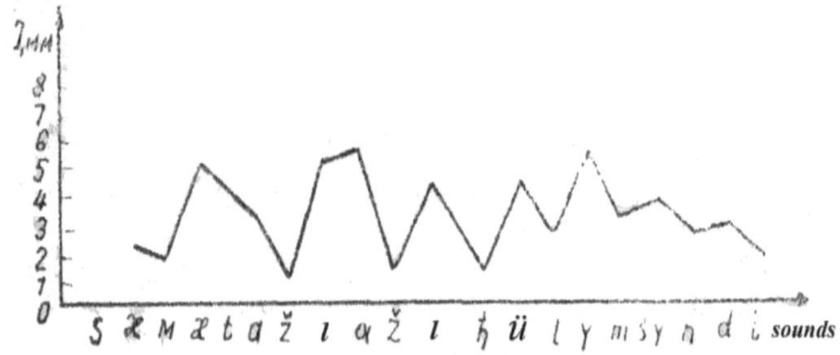

indicated in the following picture (see picture 37). Hence, by the analysis of ossillograms, the intensivity of the sounds are investigated both separately (within the syllablic word), and by syntagm within the sentence.

Picture 37. In the sentence /Səməd acı-acı gülümsündü// (Samad smiled bitterly) the intensivity of phonems.

9) As with calculations of the sound tone, any calculation of the intensivity of a sound may be done in two different forms. In which case, depending on purpose, the intensivity of a sound can be calculated in general, or as parts (the beginning, the central part, or the end). In the

process of investigating sentences, therefore, the absolute intensivity of separately taken sounds does not play a major role (Л.Р.Зиндер, 1960. 186). So, in order to calculate a relatively medium mark of intensivity, it is necessary to find the mathematical medium mark of a certain sound, and then divide it by the absolute mark of intensivity for the same sound – then into the medium mathematical intensivity mark, The attained mark shall be a relative medium mark of intensivity for

Marks	Sounds								
	g	ü	l	ü	m	ü	n	d	i
Absolute mark	1	4	2	5	2,5	3	2	2	8

that sound. Assuredly, in the sentence /Səməd acı-acı gülümsündü// (Samad smiled bitterly) the absolute, medium, and relatively medium, marks change in all the sounds of the word "gülümsündü" (smiled) - you can see in the following table:

As may be seen, regarding vowels and consonants taken together, a general mathematical mark has been calculated. A mark, moreover, which can be assessed for specific consonants as well. As such, it becomes clear from the table that the vowel /ü/ - which is repeated in the same word – possesses a variety of intensivity. Herein, undoubtedly, the intensivity of the same sound influences the position of the sound in the word. Furthermore, within the syntagm and in the sentence, one can observe whether it is used in stressed or unstressed positions (see picture 35). So, concluded investigations have already proved that the sound used at the absolute end has an intensivity (when compared with another sound having the same quality), even though it is less intensive if used at the beginning of the sentence (F.Y.Veysalov,

1970; Л.В.Бондарко, 1965). For this, it is enough to see the picture illustrating the intensivity of the sentence indicated above.

10. Sometimes, in the ossillograms, within the pronunciation of sounds, a separation of dimentions in the vibrations (from the zero line) are different. At this juncture, it is necessary to make a calculation on the direction in which intensivity is greater (F.Veysalov, 1970). Any such calculation must be carried out either in the direction above the zero line, or below the zero line from the beginning till the end. It is not correct to carry out these calculations from above the zero line, or below the zero line. Additionally, the intensivity of the sounds are calculated by the intonogram. This is done with respect to the electrographic line: which indicates the intensivity given on the tape. Here too, paper divided into mm (or special scale divided into mm) is used. Also, separating the distance from the zero line - which indicates the electrographic line of the intensivity of the sound, shows the difference in the intensivity of the same sound. All without having phonematic meaning in the sounds not establishing oppositions as to the features associated with positions of the sounds in the words. In Azerbaijani, there are not even two phonemes, which are discriminated from each other as an aspect of their features. However, in Azerbaijani, any distinction of sounds respecting intensivity reveals itself through acoustic features as relevant signs of syntagm and sentence stress. This can equally be important in determining the communicative type of the sentence.

11) Time of the sound. Now, speech sounds, like other sounds, may be of different lengths. In the articulation of some sounds more time is required, while in the articulation of other sounds less time is demanded. Depending on the object of the research work, sound, syllable, word, syntagm, sentence, and the bounderies of concrete

speech units, are determined by an ossillogram. Indeed, the time spent on the pronounciation of any unit in the ossillogram is determined by the sign "vvvv" indicated above (see picture 35). The distance among these signs being of the same dimentions: each dimention being equal to 10 m/sec. While determining the pronunciation speed of a sound, therefore, the amount of ridges among the boundaries are vital. For instance, in the sentence "Mənim xoşbəxtliyim sənsən" (You are my

Sounds	s	æ	n	s	æ	n
Time Amount of the ridges	9	8	5	8,2	6,7	5,2
The speed time	90	80	50	82	67	52

happiness), the speed of pronunciation in separately taken sounds have been calculated by the ossillogram (see picture 31). In this sentence, each sound of the last word (sənsən) is examined according to its pronunciation speed in the following table:

12. The attained results once more prove that not always (and not all) of the speech sounds - having the same speed of pronunciation - are in different lengths. Although, the speed of the same sounds in a word such as [$æ_1$] and [$æ_2$] differ from each other. For the pronunciation of [$æ_1$] 80 m/sec. is recorded, but for the second 67 m/sec. of time have been spent.

In written works on experimental phonetics, length is determined by the amount of language units pronounced within a one second (time) unit. The length of language units being measured by milliseconds. If one marks the length of a speech unit within one millisecond by the sign t, one can express the whole pronunciation time of a syntagm, or a sentence by the following formula:

$$T = \frac{L}{\Delta t} \cdot 1000$$

13) Those figures, which one gets in connection with tempo, are the obligatory marks for these sounds. What is more, this initial calculation (not being satisfactory for linguistic generalization), is necessary to calculate the medium, and relatively medium, marks. This calculation can be made for a word, syntagm, sentence, and text.

In the given word /sænsæn/ (you are) in order to find the marks of the medium length of the sound, it is necessary to divide the whole of the pronunciation time (of 6 sounds) into the amount of sounds taking place in this word. For example,

s æ n s æ n
90 + 80 + 50 + 82 + 67 + 52 = 421 m/sec.: 6–70 m/sec.

So, in the given word, the medium length of the sound is 70 m/sec. In this manner, one can also find the medium mark for vowels in this word.

LITERATURE

Ağayeva F. Azərbaycan dilinin intonasiyası. Bakı, 1978.
Axundov A. Müasir Azərbaycan dilinin fonetikasından mühazirələr. Bakı, 1969.
Axundov A. Azərbaycan dilinin fonemlər sistemi. Bakı, 1973.
Axundov A. Azərbaycan dilinin fonetikası. Bakı, 1984.
Axundov C. Müasir Azərbaycan ədəbi dilində sual cümlələri. Nam.dissert. Bakı,1968.
Babayev S. Müasir Azərbaycan dilində feili bağlama tərkibli sadə nəqli cümlələrin intonasiya xüsusiyyətləri. Bakı, 1966.
Veysəlov F. Alman dilinin fonetikası. Bakı, 1980.
Qarayeva M. Müxtəlif sistemli dillərdə sadə - ara cümlələrin intonasiya – qrammatik xüsusiyyətləri. Bakı, 1976.
Dəmirçizadə Ə. Azərbaycan dili orfoepiyasının əsasları. Bakı, 1969.
Dəmirçizadə Ə. Müasir Azərbaycan dili (fonetika, orfoepiya, orfoqrafiya). Bakı, 1972.
Eksperimental fonetika (müəlliflər kollektivi). Bakı, I, 1980, II, 1981.
Mehdiyev N. Müasir Azərbaycan dilində əmr cümlələri və onların eksperimental tədqiqi. Namizədlik dissertasiyası. Bakı, 1973.
Müasir Azərbaycan dili. I cild (Azərb. EA Nəsimi adına Dilçilik İnstitutu; Məsul redaktorları M.A.Şirəliyev, Z.İ.Budaqova). Bakı, 1978.
Tağızadə Z. Eksperimental fonetikaya giriş. Bakı, 1970.
Hidayətzadə T. Azərbaycan və ingilis samit fonemlərinin müqayisəli surətdə öyrənilməsi. Bakı, № 2, 1961, № 3, 1962.
Cəfərov Ə. İngilis və Azərbaycan dilində qarşılaşdırma – zidiyyət əlaqəli tabesiz mürəkkəb cümlələrin intonasiya quruluşu. Bakı, 1975.
Абдуллаев Ш. Место и природа словесного ударения в современном азербайджанском языке. АКД. Баку, 1964.
Алекперова А. Фонематическая система современного азербайджанского языка. Баку,1964.

Артемов. В.А. Экспериментальная фонетика. М.,1956.
Богородицкий В.А. Фонетика русского языка в свете экспериментальных данных. Казан, 1930.
Бодуен де Куртене И.А. Избранные труды по общему языкознанию. М., 1963, т. 1-2.
Бондарко Л.В. Осциллографический анализ речи. Л.,1965.
Бондарко Л.В. Звуковой строй современного русского языка. М., 1977.
Вейсалов Ф.Я. Еще раз о минимальной единице членения речевого потоко. «Ученые записки» АПИРЯЛ им. М.Ф.Ахундова, 1973. №4 (в соавторстве с А.А. Гасановым).
Вейсалов Ф.Я. О дифференциальных и интегральных признаках фонемы. «Ученые записки» АПИРЯЛ им. М.Ф.Ахундова, Баку, 1975. № 2.
Вейсалов Ф.Я. Об эксперименте в фонетике и о некоторых вопросах экспериментальной фонетики. «Ученые записки» АПИРЯЛ им. М.Ф.Ахундова, Баку, 1975. № 2. (в соавторстве с Ахмедовым).
Вейсалов Ф.Я. Проблема варьирования фонем в современной фонологии. «Вопросы языкознания». 1990, 3.
Глиссон Г. Введение в дескриптивную лингвистику. М.1959.
Головин Б.Н. Язык и статистика. М. 1971
Грамматика азербайджанского языка. Баку, 1971.
Ельмслев. Пролегомены к теории языка. « Новое в лингивистике». М., 1960, III.
Зиндер Л.В. Общая фонетика. Л, 1960, 1979 (2).
Зиндер Л.Р., Строева Т.В. Современный немецкий язык. М., 1957.
Звегинцев А. История языкознания XIX и XX веков в очерках и извлечениях. II часть. М., 1960.
Матусевич М.И. Современный русский язык, (фонетика). М., 1976.
Кузнецов П.С. Об основных положениях фонологии. «Вопросы языкознания». 1959. № 2.
Кязымов Ф.А. Классификация азербайджанских согласных. Тезиси докладов научной конференции. Баку, 1968.
Кязымов Ф.А. Система гласных фонем азербайджанского языка. «Изв. АНСССР», ОЛЯ, 1952, вып. 4.
Кязымов Ф.А. Английские согласные в сравнение с азербайджанскими. «Иностранные языке в школе». 1952, № 1.
Мартине А. Принципы экономии в фонетических изменениях. М., 1960.
Маслов Ю. С. Об основных и промежуточных ярусах структуры языка.

«Вопросы языкознания». 1967, № 2.
Реформатский А.А. Введение в языковедение. М. 1967
Реформатский А.А. Из истории отечественной фонологии. М., 1970.
Садыхов С.Б. Согласные фонемы в потоке речи. «Труды» АГПИ им. В.И.Ленина, XI, 1961.
Садыхов С.Б. Харастеристика согласных фонем азербайджанского литературного языка с экспериментальными данными. «Труды» АГПИ им. В.И.Ленина, XIII, 1960.
Скалозуб Л.Г. Палатограммы и рентгенограммы согласных фонем русского языка.Киев, 1962.
Томсон А.И. Общее языкознание. Одесса, 1910.
Тагизаде З.Х., Потапова Р.К. Акустический анализ гласных современного азербайджанского литературного языка. « Советская тюркология», Баку, 1971,№ 1, 2.
Трубецкой Н.С. Основы фонологии. М., 1960.
Фердинанд де Соссюр. Курс общей лингвистики. Труды по общему яз-н. М., 1977.
Фердинанд де Соссюр. Заметки по общей лингвистики. М., 1990.
Фант Г. Акустическая теория речеобразования. М., 1964.
Шеннон К. Э. Работы по теории информации и кибернетики. М., 1956.
Щерба Л.В. Языковая система и речевая деятельность. Л.М.,Наука, 1974.
Щерба Л.В. Фонетика французского языка. М., 1963.
Якобсон Р. и др. Введение в анализ речи. « Новое в лингвистике», II, М., 1962.
Яглом А.М., Яглом И. М. Вероятность и информация. М., 1973.

J.A. Baudouin de Courtenaye. Versuch einer Theorie der phonetischen Alternation. Strassburburg, 1895.
Bremer O. Deutsche Phonetik. Leipzig, 1893.
Bloomfield L. Language. New York, 1933/
Bergsveinsson S. Wie alt ist die phonologische. Opposition in sprachwissenchaftlicher
Anwendung "Archiv für vergleichende Phonetik", 2, 1942.
Brücke E. Grundzüge der Physiologie und Systematik der Spachlaute. Wien, 1876.
O. von Essen. Allgmeine und angeüandte Phonetik. Berlin, 1964.
Ernst O. İndogermainsche Forschungen, 1937.
E. Fischer Jörgensen. The phonetic basis for identification of phonetic elements. In: "JASA", 1962, №6.

Forchhammer G. Grundlagen der Sprechkunde. Halle, 1924.
Greenberg J.H. Some methods of dynamic comparaison in Lingustics. Berkeley, Los Angeles, 1969.
Grimm J. Deutsche Grammatik. 1.Buch, 2. Aufl, 1822.
Grammont G. Traite de phonetique. Paris, 1933.
Hjelmslev L. Über die Beziehungen der Phonetik zur Sprachwissenchaft. "Archiv für vergleichende Phonetik". 1938.
Helvag H. von. Dissertation de formation logulate, 1781.
IPA. International Phonetic Association. Aim and Principles of the IPA. Bourgla-reine, 1904.
Jespersen O. Phonetische Grundfragen. Berlin, 1925.
Jakobson R. und Halle M. Grundlagen der Sprache. Berlin, 1960.
Jakobson. R. Halle M., Fant. G. Preliminaries to Speech Analysis. Mass. TU, 1955.
Jones D. An Englisch Pronuncing Dictionary. Cambridge, 1909.
Kuhlman W. Lautwissenchaftliche Fragestellungen. "Archives Neerlandaises de phonetique Experimentall". 1937.
W. Kempelen W. von Mexanismus der menschichen Sprache. Wien, 1791.
MSL. Memoires de la Lingui tique de Paris, 1908, t.XV.
Malmberg B. Instrumentale und struckturelle Analyse der Sprachlaute. "Kongres-berichte der germ. Tagung für allgem und angew. Phonetik", Hamburg, 1960.
Merkel C.L. Physiologie der menschlichen Sprache (Phyiologie der Laletik). Leipzig, 1866.
Marten P. "Uber Joshua Steds abhandlung melody and meosure of spreech", London, 1775.
Menzerath P. und A. de Lacerda. Koartikulation, Steuerungen und Lautabgrenzung. Bonn-Berlin, 1934.
Menzerath P. In Hamburg "Phonetische Beitrëge", 1956.
Martinet A. Accent ethoues Vischellanal phonetica, 1954.
Pike K. Phonetica. Ann-Arbor, 1943.
Pike K. Intonation of American Englisch. Ann-Arbor, 1917.
Panconceelli-Calzia. Geschichtszahlen der Phonetik. Hamburg, 1941.
Panconceelli-Calzia. Die experimentale Phonetik und ihre Anwendung auf die Sprachwissenchaft. Berlin, 1934.
Rousselot P. J. Les modifications phonetiques de language. Paris, 1891; Principes de phoneticques experimentalies, Paris 1924-25.
Roudett L. Elements phonetique generale Paris. 1910.
Saussure F. de Grundlagen der allgemeinen Sprachwissenchaft. Berlin, 1967.

Sapir E. Language. An Introduction to the Study of speech, 1921.
Siebs T. Bühnendeutch, 1901.
Sievers E. Grundzüge der Lautphysiologie. Leipzig, 1876.
Scripture E.W. Die Anwendung der graphischengen Methode auf Sprache und Gesang, Leipzig, 1927.
Sweet H. A Primer of Phonetics, Oxford, 1906.
Sweet H. Handbook of Phonetics, Oxford, 1877.
Trubetzkoy N.S. Grundzüge der Phonologie. Praque,1939.
Techmer F. Phonetik. Leipzig 1880.
TCLP. Travaux de cercle linguistique de Prague 1929-39, t 1-9.
Trautman U. Die Sprachlaute im allglmelnen und die Laute des Englischen, Französischen und Dt-en im besonderen. Leipzig, 1884-86.
Veysalov F. J. Die phonetische Wissenschaft in der UdSSR und einige Problems der Phonologie. Wissenschaftliche Zeitshrift der Humboldt-Universitët. Ges-sprwft Reihe, №3, 1978.
Veysalov F. J. Probleme der Phonemvariierung im Deutschen. The XI the JC PHS, Tallinn, 1967,11.
Veysalov F. J. Lehrbuch der deutschen Phonetik. Baku, 1989.
Vietor W. Elemente der Phonetik der Deutschen, Engilschen und Französischen, Leipzig, 1918.
Wängler H. H. Physiologische Phonetik. Marburg, 1972.
Winteler J. Die Kerenzer Mundart des Cantons Glarus. Leipzig, 1876.
Zinder L.R. Zur phonologischen Bewertung der deutschen Diphthonge. Kiev, 1975.
Lindner G. Hören und Verstehen. Berlin, 1977.
Zemanek H. Elementare İnformationstheorie. München, 1959.
Zwirner E. und Zwirner K. Grundfragen der Phonomesrie, Berlin, 1936.

INDEX

NAMES

www.ingramcontent.com/pod-product-compliance
Lightning Source LLC
Chambersburg PA
CBHW032021230426
43671CB00005B/163
* 9 7 8 1 9 1 0 8 8 6 1 8 2 *